MILLENNIALS KILLED THE VIDEO STAR

MTV'S TRANSITION TO REALITY PROGRAMMING

Cover designed by Aimee C. Harrison and Drew Sisk
Text designed by Aimee C. Harrison
Typeset in Minion Pro and Univers LT Std by Copperline Book Services

Library of Congress Cataloging-in-Publication Data
Names: Klein, Amanda Ann, [date] author.
Title: Millennials killed the video star : MTV's transition to reality programming / Amanda Ann Klein.
Description: Durham : Duke University Press, 2021. | Includes bibliographical references and index.
Identifiers: LCCN 2020024439 (print)
LCCN 2020024440 (ebook)
ISBN 9781478010265 (hardcover)
ISBN 9781478011309 (paperback)
ISBN 9781478012870 (ebook)
Subjects: LCSH: MTV Networks. | MTV Networks—History. | Music videos. | Generation Y. | Popular culture—United States.
Classification: LCC PN1992.8.M87 K545 2021 (print) | LCC PN1992.8.M87 (ebook) | DDC 791.450973—dc23
LC record available at https://lccn.loc.gov/2020024439
LC ebook record available at https://lccn.loc.gov/2020024440

Cover art: Stills from *Laguna Beach*, "A Black & White Affair," season 1, episode 1 (MTV, September 28, 2004); *The Real World: San Francisco*, season 3 (MTV, 1994); *The Real World: Seattle*, season 7 (MTV, 1998); and "Video Killed the Radio Star," the Buggles, music video (first aired on MTV, August 21, 1981).

CONTENTS

ACKNOWLEDGMENTS

The process of getting this book from inside my head and onto the page was a long one. It started in 2009, when I first published on this topic in an issue of *Jump Cut*, and was completed in 2019, when I hit send on the final manuscript. I want to offer my gratitude and appreciation to Duke University Press for believing in this project, and especially to my editor, Sandra Korn, who was with me every step of the way. I could not ask for a better or more reliable editor to shepherd me through peer review. Along the same lines, I am grateful to the peer reviewers for their time and helpful feedback. My work is better because of the time and thought they put into their reviews.

I owe much thanks to the English department at East Carolina University, specifically to my writing group at ECU, the "Femidemics," who have been going strong since 2008. Marianne Montgomery, Anna Froula, Marame Gueye, and Su-ching Huang, you are wonderful readers and wonderful colleagues, and you have all made me a stronger writer and a more empathetic editor.

This book would have never come together if not for the formation of the Lazy Bottom Writing Retreat in 2015 with my ECU colleagues, including Anna Froula, Jennifer McKinnon, Anne Ticknor, Stacy Weiss, Amber Wigent, Cindy Grace-McCasky, Allison Crowe, Beth Thompson, and Paige Averett. This retreat offered me the much-needed time and space to, as Virginia Woolf once put it, "dream over books and loiter at street corners and let the line of thought dip deep into the stream." These women have taught me that it really does take a village to write a book.

I am also grateful to the amazing scholars, in the field of media studies and beyond, who offered invaluable feedback on chapters or pieces of this project over the years, including Jason Mittell, Brenda Weber, Chuck Kleinhans, Erin Meyers, Faye Woods, Jon Kraszewski, Caetlin Benson-Allott, Ethan Thompson, Amy Borden, Anne Ticknor, Nicole Sidhu, the editors at *Flow* and *Antenna*, and my virtual coven of scholars, the "Back Channel."

The scope and tone of this book shifted the day that Max Joseph of *Catfish* agreed to grant me an interview for this project. His generosity opened the door for me to interview *Teen Mom*'s Dia Sokol Savage, who, in turn, introduced me to *The Real World*'s Jonathan Murray. The information revealed in these interviews proved integral to the trajectory of my arguments. I also want to thank Irene McGee, Paula Beckert, and Bret Oliverio for taking the time to speak with me, and for their candor.

Last but not least, I want to thank my husband, Zach, and our children, Maisy and Jude, who learned to back away from my office door when I was writing. You are my biggest cheerleaders and I could not have completed this book without your support.

What Killed
the Video Star?

T his book's title, *Millennials Killed the Video
Star: MTV's Transition to Reality Programming*,
is a play on two significant moments in the cultural
representation of American youth, albeit from two
different moments in time. One alludes to the first
music video to air on MTV on August 21, 1981, the
Buggles' "Video Killed the Radio Star." The song was
most likely selected as the inaugural video for the channel due less to its popularity and more to its timely lyrics, which are ambivalent about advances
in technology and culture. The chorus includes the refrain "Video killed
the radio star / Video killed the radio star / In my mind and in my car /
We can't rewind we've gone too far." These lyrics imply that contemporary
technology is committing violence against the technology of the past. But
whether these developments are positive or negative, it doesn't really matter:
we can't rewind, we've gone too far.[1] The video features a young girl, part of
MTV's target youth demographic eventually labeled Generation X (American children born between roughly 1965 and 1982).[2] Over the course of the
video, the girl literally and symbolically turns away from her radio and toward her television, which is playing MTV's videos. "Video Killed the Radio
Star" proved prescient; by 1983, just two years after the launch of the world's

I.1 The Buggles' "Video Killed the Radio Star" was the first music video to air when MTV launched on August 21, 1981.

first twenty-four-hour video-music channel, music videos, rather than radio programming, became the standard way for record companies to promote artists and their new singles (Ed Levine 1983).

Video might have killed the radio star in 1981, but between 1995 and 2000, the number of music videos airing on MTV dropped by 36 percent. By the early 2000s, it was difficult to locate *any* music videos on the cable channel (Hay 2001). So who killed the video star? This question leads me to the second important cultural moment referenced in this book's title: Millennials, their presumed consumer tastes, and their (assumed) economic power.[3] Throughout the 2010s a series of articles was published across the media spectrum, blaming the demographic known as Millennials, American children born between 1981 and 1996, for the financial woes of several once-thriving industries, including fast food, paper napkins, and the entire film industry (Dimock 2019). For example, a 2013 *Wall Street Journal* article, entitled "McDonald's Faces 'Millennial' Challenge," found (based on data compiled from a "restaurant consultancy" firm) that the fast-food giant's economic slump at the time was based primarily on generational shifts, such as Millennials' desire for "fresher, healthier food" and "customizable menu options." The article includes an interview with McDonald's global chief brand officer, Steve Easterbrook, who describes picky Millennial consumers as "promiscuous in their brand loyalty" (Jargon 2014). This representation of Millennials, as obsessed with the concept of choice and, consequently, unable to commit, was published so frequently, in fact, that it became its own meme ("Millennials Killed *X*"). Most iconically, the May 20, 2013, issue of *Time*, with the headline "The Me Me Me Generation: Millennials Are Lazy, Entitled Narcissists Who Still Live with Their Parents. Why

They'll Save Us All," featured the image of a white, cisgendered teenage girl splayed on her tummy, her smartphone raised at an angle above her face (Stein 2013). This image of Millennials—as narcissistic, addicted to screens, and white—did not originate in 2013 but can be traced to the early 2000s, when Millennials were old enough to become a demographic with purchasing power. Publications from *Time* magazine to *Business Insider* painted a fairly homogeneous, and mostly unflattering, image of Millennials at this time. This was also the moment that Millennials first entered the workforce. Older coworkers had to contend with this generation as adults, rather than as children, further highlighting the gaps between generations. Consequently, Millennials also took the hit for the decline of major industries and cultural norms because, historically, young people are often seen as the locus of social change, whether or not that change is seen as positive. They are the cause of contemporary social ills but are also repeatedly invoked as the only possible cure.[4]

These narratives—of the ratings-starved MTV and the industry-destroying Millennials—converge in the late 1990s, when the channel's target audience of Gen Xers slowly aged out of the way, allowing Millennials to become MTV's youth audience du jour. In the late 1990s, MTV's overall ratings were also dropping. This was precipitated by a number of cultural, economic, and industrial factors, including a loss of interest in the "faddishness" of music videos and the escalating costs of producing music videos. MTV knew it needed to change the content it produced for this new youth audience, the Millennials, and so the channel invested in extensive audience research to figure out what this demographic might desire. A key finding was that Millennials wanted to be a part of the media they consumed. As Jonathon I. Oake writes, "Thus, the deviance of Xer subcultural subjectivity lies in its perverse privileging of 'watching' over 'doing.' While baby boomers are mythologized as those who made history, Xer identity is presided over by the trope of the 'slacker': the indolent, apathetic, couch-dwelling TV addict" (2004, 86–87). In contrast to the stereotypes of passivity, voyeurism, and cynicism that were ascribed to Generation X, Millennials were imagined as being quite the opposite; they were described as "earnest" and engaged, with a belief that their actions and words matter and make a difference (Arango 2009). Popular culture represented Millennials as active "makers" who exude optimism about the possibilities generated by the rise and prevalence of information and communication technologies (ICTs). In response to these findings, MTV created a live countdown show hosted by Carson Daly, *Total Request Live* (TRL), in 1998. TRL offered one possible stopgap to MTV's plummeting viewership and was one of the channel's highest-rated programs. But in the years that followed, with the rise and prevalence of digital music platforms like Vevo, YouTube, and others, which allowed youth consumers to watch a video at any time of day, even TRL could not convince Millennials to watch music videos on their televisions. The series was canceled in 2008.

But MTV did not die with the video star. Commensurate with the final years of TRL, MTV created an original cycle of scripted, identity-focused reality shows that began with *Laguna Beach* and continued with series like *Catfish* and *Jersey Shore: Family Vacation*. This programming engaged, either implicitly or explicitly, in debates about what identity means; what it entitles the individual to say, do, and have; who has the right to claim an identity for themselves; and who has the right to be labeled with a particular identity by someone else. These series made evident multiple identity norms (like the Guido, the Redneck, or the Teen Mom) as well as presuppositions that MTV had about its own target youth audiences in the 2000s (that they were primarily white and primarily interested in establishing an identity *other* than "white" for themselves). Therefore, MTV's reality programming from approximately 2004 until the present served as an identity workbook for its primarily white audience and is partially responsible for producing Millennials' sense of whiteness and white identity. Laura Grindstaff describes this approach to production as "self-serve" reality television (2011a, 206). As I discuss in chapters 2, 4, and 5, MTV also created reality series featuring nonwhite cast members, like *Washington Heights* and *The Real World*. These series also served as identity workbooks for MTV audiences, but the representation of identities in these series were received and deployed differently. This cycle of reality programming is a prime case study for understanding the ways in which Millennials, the target twelve- to thirty-four-year-old audience in the early 2000s, were instructed to govern the self and to self-brand. Alice Marwick defines self-branding in the age of social media as "a series of marketing strategies applied to the individual. It is a set of practices and a mindset, a way of thinking about the self as a salable commodity that can tempt a potential employer" (2013, 15). There are many reasons why American Millennials were so identity-focused at this moment in history: the rise and spread of social media; the election of America's first nonwhite president, Barack Obama, in 2008; and the oft-discussed, unprecedented "diversity" of this new generation. But this book is invested in delineating and analyzing a single discourse: MTV's reality identity television programming in the 2000s.

Millennials Killed the Video Star examines the major historical, cultural, and industrial factors that led to MTV's historic shift in programming away from music videos and into the realm of reality television. I outline the launch of MTV in 1981 and the trajectory of its programming decisions toward the channel's original cycle of scripted, identity-focused reality shows in the early 2000s and 2010s. *Millennials Killed the Video Star* offers a major intervention into discussions of MTV's prolific output of reality programming created for Millennial youth audiences in that it is the first book to examine this successful group of reality TV series as a coherent production cycle. Cycles are series of texts (in film, television, and other media platforms) associated with each other due to shared images, characters, settings, plots, or themes (see Klein 2011a). While genres are conventionally defined by the repetition of key images (or semantics) as they relate to a set of repeated themes (or their syntax), cycles are primarily defined by how they are used (their pragmatics) (Klein 2018, 200). Studying these MTV series together, as a production cycle, makes plain some of the discourses surrounding reality TV, celebrity, and identity in the 2000s, as well as the way this programming was used by Millennial audiences.[5] These series have only ever been examined in isolation, but, as I will argue over the next five chapters, discussing them as a production cycle, with a shared producer, audience, aesthetic approaches, subjects, and ideological underpinnings, illuminates how MTV's reality programming generates a coherent discourse on youth and identity, offering a macro view of the channel's approach to studying, and then creating content for, youth audiences in the first two decades of the new millennium.[6]

Since the early 2000s, with the release of reality TV series like *Extreme Makeover* and *The Biggest Loser*, media scholars have been studying the role that reality TV plays in discourses of self-governance.[7] At this time, reality TV shifted from simply documenting people to actively regulating their behaviors (Kavka 2012, ch. 4). In an increasingly privatized government, reality TV shows like *The Swan* and *Honey, We're Killing the Kids* demonstrated how entertainment can double as self-management and betterment. However, this is true even of series that do not advertise themselves as self-improvement programs as self-consciously as do series like *The Biggest Loser*. A series like MTV's *The Hills*, to name one example, tells young women how to manage their social lives and dress for a big date (Taylor 2011, 120). In this way, the series making up MTV's reality identity cycle are a prominent example of what Aniko Imre and Annabel Tremlett have called a "technology of citizenship in a neoliberal moral economy" (2011, 89) because they instruct youth audiences on "how to be" in the twenty-first century's iteration of free-market capitalism. It is also important to remember that the cast members on these series are not simply participants in a reality show—they are also its progeny. Years of watching reality TV, particularly on MTV, has taught viewers how to think and act in order to clearly portray an identity, to produce what Allison Hearn (2014) has called the "branded self," a self that audiences can select and develop for themselves based on the identities presented in each series. "The labour of watching television is intensified as audiences watch in order *to learn how to be seen by television cameras*" (2010, 66; emphasis mine).[8]

The specific, highly circumscribed stereotypes, like the Guido of *Jersey Shore*, the Redneck of *Buckwild*, and the Teen Mom in *16 and Pregnant*, can be made intelligible by analyzing a variety of texts: MTV's casting calls and promotional materials, the performances of cast members on the reality series themselves, and how these identities are referenced and discussed in public discourses (reviews, think pieces, social media, fan sites, etc.). MTV's reality identity series from the early 2000s highlighted some of America's key vulnerabilities in terms of racial equity, gender parity, and class divisions. These series underscore what American audiences had the ability to discuss, as well as their desires to efface race and class through proper consumption (*The Hills*, *The City*), concerns over the role and place of whiteness and white bodies (*Jersey Shore*, *Buckwild*), and the impossibility of truly knowing who someone is online (*Catfish*). This book argues that MTV's reality programming is part of the dominant discourse on the subject of identity and youth in the twenty-first century, and this programming has contributed to the contemporary, sometimes liberating, sometimes contentious, conversations that Americans, and American youth in particular, are having about who and what they are. So, no, Millennials did not, in fact, "kill" the video star, or the music video for that matter. As is so often the case in coverage of Millennials, the answer is far muddier and more complicated. This book is an attempt to answer one part of this question.

What Is Identity on MTV?

In order to understand how MTV presented itself as an identity workbook for Millennials throughout the first decades of the 2000s, it is necessary to define how the term "identity" is deployed in this specific context and the way MTV reality programming represented different youth identities and identity norms. First, although "identity" is incredibly slippery and difficult to define in real life, MTV's reality series constitute one of the few places where it is relatively clear-cut. As Grace Wang has argued, in reality TV, "individuals are chosen to represent certain types and then slotted (self-consciously or not) into a limited array of available characters: the angry black woman, the conservative Christian, the fabulous gay (usually white) man, the non-white immigrant grateful for the opportunities afforded to him or her in the United States, and so forth" (2010, 405–406). These types on MTV might be manifested as a set of behaviors, languages and dialects, body adornment, or expressed belief systems. A *Jersey Shore* Guido, for example, is more defined by physique, clothing, and grooming (aka his "GTL"), while a Redneck who is cast for *Buckwild* is defined more by where they live ("the holler") and what they do for fun ("muddin'" in a 4 × 4 truck).[9] Here it is useful to call on the work of Stuart Hall and the nuanced way he defines the concept of identity as well as the process of identification. He writes, "I use identity to refer to the meeting point . . . between on the one hand the discourses and practices which attempt to 'interpellate,' speak to us or hail us into place as the social subjects of particular discourses, and on the other hand, processes which produce subjectivities, which construct us as subjects which can be 'spoken'" (1996, 5–6). In the case of the TV series analyzed in this book, MTV hails youth audiences into place as particular identities that can be articulated via the reality TV text. This meeting point of identity on MTV is never a single location, since it can stem from both internal and external forces, and can change depending on the context of the series. For example, as I argue in chapter 5, in *Washington Heights*, which focuses on the lives of Dominican American youth, the sole white cast member, Taylor, is considered to be more a part of her Dominican peer group than Eliza, who is Dominican but was born in New Jersey. Tyler's identity as part of this community is tied to her geographic location, rather than her ethnicity or race.

Concepts like identity, subjectivity, and the self/selfhood are notoriously difficult to define, and they have long, complicated histories of debate in the fields of sociology, philosophy, psychology, and education, to name just a few. In the simplest of terms, and for the purposes of this book, the word "identity" is a placeholder word, a way to refer to a collection of gender, racial, ethnic, sexual, and regional identities that are represented in MTV's reality programming. I use identity to reference the representation that is negotiated between the audience, MTV's framing of the series, and the performances of identity, or self-branding (as the Guido, the Redneck, the Virgin, etc.), in the series themselves. MTV reality series hopefuls self-brand themselves as a salable commodity according to a particular, codified identity, expressed through clothing or grammar or perhaps a moment of *iden-tity confession*, the moment when a reality-show cast member declares allegiance with a particular identity in front of MTV's cameras (Marwick 2013, 193–194). In the context of a reality series like *The Real World*, a roommate might announce, "I am gay," "I am Mormon," or "I am Southern" in front of fellow cast members (or sometimes just the cameras). This moment of identity confession produces what Herbert Gans has called a "symbolic ethnicity," specifically, "a nostalgic allegiance to the culture of the immigrant generation, or that of the old country; a love for and a pride in a tradition that can be felt without having to be incorporated in everyday behavior" (1979, 9). Moments of identity confession demonstrate how the identities represented and performed on MTV function as a "pull" rather than as a "push" because audiences and series participants can adopt them or remove them as needed.

Even in this imaginary context of MTV's reality programming, however, where identity appears fluid and "up for grabs," the opportunity to choose just any identity is not available to all who seek it, and it is not distributed evenly among those who can. As Mary C. Waters points out, "Black and Hispanic Americans, Asian Americans, and American Indians do not have the option of a symbolic ethnicity at present in the United States" because the material existence of members of racial minorities is always already influenced by their race or national origin (1996, 449). For many racial, sexual, and ethnic groups, no amount of self-narrative about one's symbolic identity will ever change the material realities of the individuals' lived experiences. Furthermore, Catherine Squires argues that in the context of reality television, "'being ethnic' is framed as an option that is equally open to all but that some [women of color] must be vigilant to control" (2014, 275). This is why MTV's successful cycle of identity programming focused almost exclusively on white, straight, cisgendered youth (*Laguna Beach, The Hills, The City, Teen Mom*) or on marginalized youth who can "choose" to be white (the Guidos of *Jersey Shore* or the Rednecks of *Buckwild*). These programs provided viewers, particularly white viewers *without* a clear sense of self, with convenient ways to self-identify. Cast members who might otherwise be labeled as "white" are able to self-script more specific micro slices of that white identity for themselves (Hirschorn 2007). For example, *Buckwild* cast members are not simply "white": they are Rednecks or West Virginians, identities that provide a sense of community, history, and specificity. Similarly, the cast members of *Jersey Shore* are not simply assimilated Italian Americans; they are Guidos with their own rituals of dress and grooming.

Whereas the seeking out, understanding, and embracing of one's race or gender or sexual orientation was once a project mostly for those with minority identities, MTV extended this project of identity formation and acceptance to everyone, even those whose identities *have not* been systematically marginalized and/or oppressed.

When I interviewed Jonathan Murray, a cocreator of *The Real World*, for this book, he explained that casting a "diversity" of identities was central to the series. I asked him to define what a diversity of identities might look like and he told me, "Diversity for me is people from different backgrounds, it can be socioeconomic, it can be regional, it can be racial, it can be gender orientation, it can be disability, it can be outlook on the world—whether you're a pessimist or an optimist—it is the full rainbow of types of people." As I will discuss at length in chapter 2, by arguing that identity could also extend beyond race and ethnicity to something like whether someone lives in the country or the city, *The Real World* opened up a range of possible identities for MTV's largely white, suburban youth audience, who may not have thought of themselves as even *having* an identity. Indeed, while Generation X was encouraged to be colorblind and ignore race (an ultimately harmful construct), Millennials are more defined by their interest and investment in the *differentiation of identity*. It is important for Millennials to know who they are and where they came from, but just as important is the desire to make those identities clear and visible to those around them in a moment of identity confession, whether through social media or perhaps by appearing on an MTV reality series.

Beginning with *The Real World* in 1992, but not picking up steam until the 2000s, MTV generated a possible worldview in which even white, suburban, primarily heterosexual and cisgendered youth were able to "find themselves." Laura Grindstaff argues that reality programming is a kind of "self-service television" because it "affords the opportunity for acquiring celebrity cafeteria-style; it enables ordinary people to walk in and serve themselves to celebrity status without the bother of extensive training, scripts, rehearsals or even talent" (2011b, 46). *Millennials Killed the Video Star* analyzes how and why only a few of these series—*The Real World, Virgin Territory, Catfish*—regularly cast nonwhite, gay, or transgendered youth; the absence of such youth in other series highlights an important aspect of the way identity was deployed in American discourse throughout the 2000s (namely, which of them matter on MTV). Ultimately, MTV programming offers Millennials the *fantasy* of identity construction by creating pathways for understanding what it means to self-define or be defined, and what this process looks like on TV. These MTV series highlight the ways in which identities are commodities to be built, distributed, sold, copyrighted, and plagiarized. MTV is wisely tapping into the conditions of modern life, and the way the living labor of its audience fuels the industry (Horning 2012a).

The identities featured in MTV's series are already determined before a single frame is shot because it is always already constructed in relation to the particular needs of the reality TV production. When individuals audition for an MTV series, they audition for a particular identity (a Virgin, a Teen Mom, a Redneck) and whether they can fit into the larger narrative for the series, which is determined by the series' producers. For example, a casting call for *Teen Mom 4* is phrased this way: "MTV is looking for mothers from varying backgrounds who had children in their late teens and those children are now between the ages of 4 and 7; who would like to share their dramatic personal stories about their complicated journeys" (qtd. in Lynne 2016). The ad assumes that any teenaged mother who answers this casting call will have had "drama" and "complications" stemming from their status as teenaged mothers. Self-selecting *Teen Mom 4* hopefuls will still further have to fit the criteria that the series producers already have in mind. For example, when I asked *Teen Mom*'s executive producer and co-creator Dia Sokol Savage to explain how cast members were selected for the first season of her landmark series, she listed a series of traits, which I will summarize here. Sokol Savage told me they were looking for young women who were open and willing to speak frankly on camera; women who have enough intrigue in their lives to provide an interesting story arc that viewers want to follow; and women who were "TV friendly."[10] To be on *Teen Mom*, a cast member must be more than simply a teenage mother: she must be an extrovert who is comfortable speaking on camera, is surrounded by family and friends who are willing to speak on camera as well, and who has an appearance that is pleasing to MTV's producers.

As Sarah Banet-Weiser (2012) argues, creating and maintaining an identity is central to the postcapitalist neoliberal economy. Thus, the success of MTV's reality programming in the 2000s is tied to its ability to instruct youth audiences in the important work of finding an identity. The structures of reality TV make it easy for MTV to deploy the class, race, ethnic, and gender identities of the subjects profiled in their reality series as a kind of shorthand. Indeed, reality television demands a public performance of the private, of making what appears on the inside visible on the outside (see Grindstaff 2014, 330). I am less interested in either defining how cast members perform on camera, or the authenticity of these performances, topics well covered by Misha Kavka's (2014) notion of flaunting, Therí A. Pickens's (2015) term "ratchet imaginary," and Jon Kraszewski's (2017) concept of "amplifying."[11] Instead, this book examines the factors that shape the ways in which these identity performances are framed and understood by MTV. This book analyzes the visibility of these identities that shaped discourses about youth and selfhood at this time. How, and what, did this programming contribute to prevalent discourses about youth and identity in the new millennium?

Defining Millennials

The Millennial generation, like all generations, is a concept rooted both in the real and in the imaginary, in physical bodies as well as in the data collected by marketers *about* those physical bodies.[12] When invoking the concept of the Millennial generation in this book, I am referencing the way a generation of viewers is imagined both by public discourses (film, TV, music, the media, and scholarly work) and, most centrally, by MTV. Public discourses centering on Millennials throughout the 2000s portrayed the entire swath of youth culture as relatively homogeneous, as promiscuous and inscrutable consumers who feel entitled to all the world has to offer. This representation of Millennials was created by marketing executives, film and television studio heads, magazine publishers, anxious parents, and well-meaning sociologists. This book examines closely these representations, these collective imaginings of youth, tracked through the products created for them, including MTV's programming. The latter, the focus of this book, can usefully be subjected to generational thinking. This book rests on the understanding that identity factors like class position, gender, and race, among other factors, impact an individual's experience of the world, and *also* that generational factors play a role in constructing the self. I rely on Karl Mannheim's belief that being born at roughly the same time in history means sharing a "common location in the historical dimension of the social process" (1972, 290). Mannheim sees "generational thinking" as a "negative delimitation," in that it *restricts* the range of possible experiences. All members of the same generation share a similar "restriction of possible experience," regardless of the other identities impacting the lives of individual members of the generation (which create their own restrictions differentially as well). Mannheim points to "a tendency 'inherent in' every social location," arguing that individuals who experience the same social, historical, and cultural events have a shared social location, even if their experiences

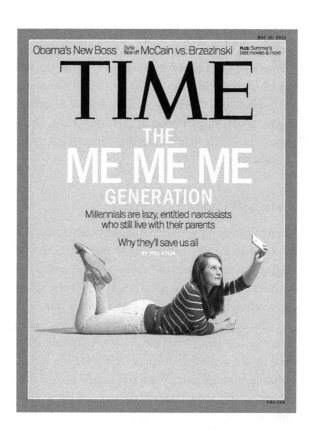

I.2 The May 20, 2013, cover of *Time* is representative of the popular discourses surrounding Millennial youth.

of and reactions to these major events are very different (291). It is this "tendency," however imprecise, that I am tracking in this book.

For the purposes of my study of MTV, I adopted the Pew Research Center's definition of Millennials ("Generation Y," the "Net Generation," and the "Look at Me Generation" were also circulated as possible names for this group) as American children born between 1981 and 1996. Of course, these parameters shift depending on the text being consulted. In their 2000 book *Millennials Rising: The Next Great Generation*, Neil Howe and William Strauss argue that Millennials include anyone born in or after 1982, as does a March 2008 *Newsweek* article, entitled "Here's Looking at You, Kids," by Jennie Yabroff. However, an article in the *Journal of Business and Psychology* (Ng, Schweitzer, and Lyons 2010) claimed that Millennials included anyone born after 1980. In her 2006 book *Generation Me*, Jean Twenge described Millennials as anyone "under 35" (i.e., anyone born after 1970). The Pew Research Center decided on the parameters of 1981–1996 for a few key reasons. Americans born in this window of time were old enough to remember the terrorist attacks on September 11, 2001; were the youngest generation to vote for Barack Obama; were the first generation to grow up with smartphones and social media; and were the youngest group to enter the workforce just as the Great Recession was starting (Ciampaglia 2018).

As mentioned above, throughout the early 2000s, MTV conducted hundreds of focus groups (nearly two hundred per year) with youth audiences. MTV executives also turned to the research of William Strauss, a "generational expert," in order to figure out what the new youth generation—the Millennials—wanted to watch. Todd Cunningham (who was then senior vice president of strategy and planning for MTV) explained the process to *Frontline* back in 2001 for their special *Merchants of Cool*: "We go out and we rifle through their closets. We go through their music collections. We go to nightclubs with them. We shut the door in their bedrooms and talk to them about issues that they feel are really important to them." MTV researchers filmed these fact-finding missions from the homes of American teens and then edited them into slick video packages that were later screened for MTV's executives to examine. The executives, in turn, used this intel to create new programming. In 2009, Stephen Friedman, then MTV's general manager, reflected on this moment in MTV's history: "It was very clear we were at one of those transformational moments, when this new generation of Millennials were demanding a new MTV" (qtd. in Arango 2009). As these studies would make clear, in the late 1990s and early 2000s MTV needed to alter its approach to programming from studying and marketing what youth audiences like and consume (i.e., contemporary music and fashion) to studying and marketing youth audiences *themselves* (*Frontline* 2001).

So how were Millennials understood around the time that MTV began to make content tailored for them? In the mid- to late 2000s a variety of public discourses, both academic and mainstream, argued that Millennials were insulated from criticism and disappointment at an early age by anxious parents who wanted their children's academic and extracurricular experiences to be collaborative rather than exclusionary, positive rather than ego-bruising. A 2008 issue of *Young Lawyer* in which Lauren Stiller Rikleen described the new generation in her workplace is typical of these discourses: "From their early days of shared rewards, constant media stimulation, and technology savvy, they have become a generation accustomed to quick answers, a constant flow of information and new ideas and immediate gratification." These discourses implied that Millennials were raised in the so-called culture of praise, in which every milestone was documented on video and every accomplishment, big or small, was commemorated with an award. An article in *Business Week* argued that a prevailing belief among employers who worked with Millennials is that they had been imbued with a "false self-confidence" (Erickson 2008; see also Yeaton 2008). And, according to a 2007 CNN article, 87 percent of hiring managers and human resources professionals said that Millennials, who were just beginning to enter the workforce, exhibited a sense of entitlement that older generations did not have (Balderrama 2007). These beliefs about this generation are also found in academic studies. For example, in her aforementioned book-length study of generational differences based on data culled from 1.3 million Americans over the course of fourteen years, psychologist Jean Twenge found that the gap between expectation and reality was far greater for Millennials than it had been for previous generations.

While these discourses were exaggerations, and standard examples of "kids these days" op-eds, at their heart they come at the precise moment when expectations and reality were at odds. Between 2007 and 2009, just as Millennials were increasingly the subject of studies on "today's youth," the US economy experienced the Great Recession. In this two-year period the American unemployment rate rose from 5 percent in December 2007 to 10 percent in October 2009. Businesses closed, the value of homes across the country dropped, and families lost their savings in a volatile stock market (Rich 2013). Millennials, who were just graduating from college as the Recession hit America, faced reduced salaries and benefits, degree inflation, and rising unemployment and underemployment (Conlin 2008). The American Dream—the idea that hard work and a college degree will lead to a lucrative and satisfying job—ceased to be a structuring myth for this youth generation, as it had been for previous generations. Most of the reporting on Millennials in its early days of definition (2008) was critical and dismissive.[13] As I argue in chapter 3, there is a link between the success of reality series like *The Hills* and its reliance on narratives that appear to imply that an exciting, lucrative career in the field of one's choice is attained not so much through hard work and perseverance but because one is wealthy and white. At this moment, living a documented, commodified life, whether as a brand or a reality TV star, is palatable for Millennials in a material way because the odds of becoming a successful reality star appear just as likely as getting a job that will pay off their college loans, which are higher than for any other generation in history. The success of MTV's reality series among its target audience of twelve- to thirty-four-year-olds is tied to viewers' ability to imagine themselves as future workers in the reality TV economy.

While professional actors are, in general, unionized and paid living wages in exchange for the labor of being watched, reality TV labor is labor that is given freely (Andrejevic 2004, 24). Anita Harris notes that this is a feature of contemporary society and that "the devolution of economic and personal security onto the individual is a way of articulating a new conception of the citizen as self-actualizing and responsible in a world that appears unpredictable" (2004a, 66). Self-promotion through the establishment and commodification of a specific and clearly defined identity is one way for (some) Millennials to achieve the economic security no longer guaranteed by state, local, and federal governments in the aftermath of the Great Recession.[14] This recession marks a moment when, according to Alice Marwick, "personal branding transcended white-collar consulting and technology, and became a popular career strategy for people in all industries" (2002, 15). The transition from Web 1.0 to Web 2.0, when more and more internet users became content creators, nurtured this sense of self as product (18). Furthermore, successful and long-running reality TV series like *Big Brother, Survivor*, and *American Idol* set a precedent for self-disclosure, self-definition, and self-branding, teaching viewers how to turn themselves into monetizable commodities (Andrejevic 2014, 46).

In his study of the relationship between Millennials and the internet, Louis Leung (2003) describes the generation as "bombarded with information and [more] media savvy" than older individuals. They have "grown up understanding the electronic economy" (see also Neuborne and Kerwin 1999). And as a result, "Net-geners find it easier to expose their inner thoughts online and the anonymity of the Internet allows them to reveal their feelings as much as they like" (Leung 2003, 108). It is beyond the scope of this book to offer a history of the internet in general, or social media in particular, but it is necessary to explain how the relationship between Millennials and social media was understood at the time that MTV was producing its reality identity cycle. One reason why this reality identity cycle was so appealing to Millennial audiences is because of the way that social media, a central part of their adolescent experience, has shaped their approach to intimacy and public performance. Social media encourages the drive to locate, define, and embody a specific image. As Rob Horning argues, social media platforms like Twitter, Facebook, and Instagram demand that users construct a coherent, defined identity, and that they broadcast it to an audience of observers, turning subjectivity into a form of capital (2012b). Participation in social media demands the revelation of personal details. *Buzzfeed*'s now iconic personality tests—endlessly replicated across the internet—

offer a crystallization of this process, the way the internet can offer us a chance not simply to pretend to be someone else, but to truly *become* ourselves by discovering ourselves. Horning calls this phenomenon the "productivity of subjectivity," explaining that "social media compel labor not through wages but through the promise of apparent self-actualization" (2012a). This focus on the role of ICTs in the lives of Millennials has led to dozens of studies about the impact of these developments on a generation of Americans; conceptually there is a strong link in contemporary thought between the rise of ICTs and the implied personalities of Millennial youth.[15]

The self-surveillance engendered by the structures of social media has become a fundamental characteristic of contemporary life. MTV's reality identity programs similarly allow cast members to live their lives as guided by the "Facebook eye," constantly aware of how actions and words and dress and demeanors fit or don't fit with the image each cast member is tasked with curating onscreen (Jurgenson 2012). Social media enables those with shared racial, ethnic, and/or sexual identities to come together for friendship, support, resource sharing, and, as the recent high visibility of the Black Lives Matter coalition demonstrates, activism and collective organizing. But social media also leads to divisions among identities, as can be witnessed by the rise of the alt-right, and even violence, as I will discuss in chapter 4. Knowing which identities to claim, reclaim, or reject has become increasingly fraught, and so the imbricated spaces of reality television and social media highlight both the potential opening of expressions of identity as well as a simultaneous, rigorous policing of what sorts of identities matter in public life.

One final way that media discourses frame the Millennial generation is through the lens of their presumed diversity. This belief is partially rooted in fact, since Millennials were, at the time, "the most [racially and ethnically] diverse generation in U.S. history" as well as the largest generation since the Baby Boomers (Rikleen 2008). As Reniqua Allen (2019) argues, "Obama looms large over this generation, a symbol less of progress than of the fundamental ambivalence of being a black millennial," and, indeed, the 2008 election of Barack Obama seemed to cement this vision of the future's racial harmony. However, a 2014 Applied Research Center survey of Millennials revealed that white participants were more likely to see the world as "postracial," or beyond race, than nonwhite participants. Even when white participants did mention racial injustice, they "tended to focus their comments on racial profiling and speak about things that they'd heard about, [while] people of color, particularly African Americans, often spoke in starkly personal terms" (Apollon 2011). A *Washington Post* study based on five measures of racial prejudice from the General Social Survey conducted by the National Opinion Research Center concluded that "when it comes to explicit prejudice against blacks, non-Hispanic white millennials [born after 1980] are not much different than whites belonging to Generation X (born 1965–1980) or Baby Boomers (born 1946–1964)" (Clement 2015). In other words, being more diverse does not necessarily lead to a tolerance of diversity.

Millennials are one of the most analyzed and documented generations of all time, but race, specifically Blackness, is frequently absent from these discourses (Allen 2019). According to 2016 numbers, African Americans make up 14 percent of all US children born between 1982 and 2000, or about 11.5 million (Nielsen 2016). The incorrect assumption that an increase in youth diversity correlates with more racial acceptance and harmony may explain why so much research on and representations of Millennials aim to erase the specificity of nonwhite experiences. In her study of "colorblind casting" in contemporary television, Kristen Warner calls it "a utopian social construct" that "aims to create a model of fairness by which all individuals can be judged fairly and without bias or regard to skin color" (2015, 8). Colorblindness as a policy continually fails in its aim to generate "fairness" because "the non-recognition of difference ensures many systemic inequalities go unchallenged and enables the maintenance of white supremacy as the status quo" (8). It has led to the unrealistic and therefore unfulfilled expectations that are placed on this generation.

Consequently, Millennials were faced with a difficult position vis-à-vis racial identity; they grew up in an America structured according to the ideologies of colorblind liberalism, and yet they cannot help but see how strongly racial difference (and other markers of difference) have profound, differential, material impacts on American bodies (Apollon 2011). MTV's colorblind approach to its youth audiences, a myopia that has plagued the channel since its 1981 inception, also haunts its reality programming, which is populated by, and seemingly made for, a white, middle-class viewership. MTV extended the project of identify formation and acceptance to everyone, even those whose identities *have not* been systematically marginalized and/or oppressed. MTV's lasting impact on discourses about identity and youth is that it made whiteness visible to white people, and then provided them with ways to differentiate and specify their own whiteness.

Methodology

The aim of this book is to demonstrate the value, scope, and stakes of studying MTV's wholesale shift away from music videos and into identity-focused reality programming, circa 2004. These programming shifts on MTV mark a moment when the channel rebranded its content to appeal to an audience that was defined for them by marketing companies and public discourses and, to a lesser extent, by ethnographic research conducted with samples of its youth audience. Because this book is not intended as a comprehensive history of MTV, its launch in 1981, or the production models the channel followed when it was still a twenty-four-hour video-music jukebox, I allot just a single chapter to the history of MTV prior to this crucial historical shift (1981–2003). There are many detailed histories devoted to this period in MTV's history, and I do not wish to replicate the achievements of these works.[16] These texts will inform the history I recount in chapter 1, but their focus on MTV during its video-centered days (1981–1992) will become less illuminating as this book shifts into its main focus: MTV's reality identity cycle (2004–2018).

The work that follows is indebted to the scholars who first began analyzing the presence and success of reality television, including Mark Andrejevic (2004), Susan Murray (2009), and Anna McCarthy (2009), and also to those who first began linking reality TV to cultures of confession and self-disclosure, particularly the work of Jon Dovey, who argues that reality TV programming impacts the way we understand the very concept of truth or authenticity, by demanding "a grounding in the personal, the subjective and the particular" (2000, 22). I also rely heavily on Misha Kavka's *Reality TV*, and the book's clear delineation of modern reality TV's history into distinct periods, including the "camcorder era" of the first generation (1989–1999), the "surveillance and competition" formats of the second generation (1999–2005), and the "economies of celebrity" found in the third generation (2002–). Finally, Laurie Ouellette's recent scholarship (2018) on the "prosocial" function of MTV programming and its related campaigns, like their 2009 partnership with the National Campaign to Prevent Teen and Unplanned Pregnancy and 2014's Be Different campaign, has helped me to better articulate my own observations about the relationship between MTV's reality series and contemporary understandings of youth identity formations. Much of the work in chapter 3 is also built on the fine scholarship of feminist theorists Rosalind Gill, Sarah Banet-Weiser, and, of course,

Anita Harris, whose concepts of the At-Risk Girl and the Can-Do Girl structure that chapter's claims. Although Harris's book (2004a) is broadly about young women in the Western world, the conclusions she draws about the relationship between girls, capitalism, consumption, and neoliberalism offer a way to understand MTV's representation of white girlhood in the 2000s. *Millennials Killed the Video Star* is also rooted in contemporary scholarship, like the work of Rob Horning and Nathan Jurgenson, that links up reality TV, social media, and identity.

This project relies on textual and discursive analyses of MTV reality series released between 1992 and 2016. I perform close readings of the series themselves, understanding them to be pragmatic objects used by youth audiences as models of behavior, as instructional texts, and, of course, as entertainment. I argue that these series appealed to youth audiences at this moment in time due to the rise of confessional reality television and the centrality of social media in the lives of American Millennial youth. If history is, as Michel Foucault argues in *The Archaeology of Knowledge* (1969), the study of discursive practices, then an important component of understanding the image of Millennials in popular culture is to read the discourses that circulate in and around MTV. Therefore, I also analyze the contemporary reviews, print and video advertising, tabloid coverage (specifically in the early 2000s), spin-off series, the side projects of cast members who appear in these series (including clothing lines and speaking tours), as well as other paratexts and markers of public discourse.

This book also relies on a series of first-person interviews I conducted over the last few years with the producers and stars of some of the most prominent reality series airing on MTV, including Jonathan Murray, producer and cocreator of *The Real World*; Max Joseph, cohost of *Catfish*; and Dia Sokol Savage, executive producer of *16 and Pregnant* as well as the *Teen Mom* franchise. I was also fortunate enough to speak with Irene McGee a former *Real World* cast member, and Paula Maronek Beckert, an alum of *The Real World: Key West*. These interviews offer detailed and candid insights into casting, filming, and editing MTV reality series over the last twenty-five years, as well as the changes to format and content that have occurred in long-running series like *The Real World* and *Teen Mom*. My experiences speaking with reality TV participants and creators both confirm and complicate the arguments of this manuscript, and, whenever possible, I include corrections and feedback from my interview subjects on my interpretation and use of their words.

Chapter 1, "'It's Videos, Fool': A Targeted History of MTV (1981–2004)," opens with a brief history of youth-targeted television in America, from *Bandstand* in the 1950s to the *Afterschool Specials* that aired on ABC in the 1980s. Although TV networks did not begin to explicitly target youth audiences until the late 1970s, teenagers were still watching TV and finding programming that resonated with them *as* teenagers. I then discuss the industrial context for the launch of MTV in 1981, as well as MTV's decision to target suburban, white youth audiences. I outline how MTV's shift from music videos to reality programming was precipitated by a number of cultural, economic, and industrial factors, including a loss of interest in the "faddishness" of music videos; the escalating costs of producing music videos; the rise of digital music platforms like Vevo, YouTube, and others, which allowed youth consumers to watch a video at any time of day; and, perhaps most importantly, the application of data gathered from years of careful focus group studies that revealed that MTV's target audience was interested in and shaped by ICTs. This research led MTV network executives to produce reality TV focusing on "ordinary" teenagers and young adults in series like *Made, Rich Girls*, and *Sorority Life*, to name just a few precursors to MTV's reality identity cycle.

In chapter 2, "'This Is the True Story . . .': *The Real World* and MTV's Turn to Identity (1992–)," I argue that the very concept of identifying documentary subjects as specific identities that can then be inserted into a narrative framework that looks like "the real world," but is highly controlled behind the scenes, begins with the landmark series *The Real World* in 1992. This chapter is therefore devoted exclusively to the history, origins, and influences of *The Real World* on MTV's later reality programming. This chapter also charts how the series changed and adapted as other networks began to focus on reality TV, and how MTV perfected the art of learning about identity through a form of social experimentation. Unlike early social and televisual experiments, such as *Candid Camera* (1948) or Stanley Milgram's obedience experiments from 1962, the subjects who volunteer to be cast on MTV's series do so with the hopes that they will emerge from the experience transformed. They are not just there to be studied; they are there to "grow," leading to other MTV series like *From Gs to Gents* and *The Girls of Hedsor Hall*. I argue that *The Real World* has been successful because it uses identity and the conflicts generated by bringing together diverse individuals as a

I.3 MTV's first commercial featured archival footage of Neil Armstrong planting a CGI-ed MTV flag into the moon's surface.

pedagogical moment for the audience. This chapter is supplemented by interviews I conducted with Jonathan Murray, producer and cocreator of *The Real World*; Irene McGee, a former *Real World: Seattle* cast member; and Paula Beckert, who was in *Real World: Key West*.

In chapter 3, "'She's Gonna Always Be Known as the Girl Who Didn't Go to Paris': Can-Do and At-Risk White Girls on MTV (2004–2013)," I situate the beginning of MTV's reality production cycle in 2004 with the premiere of *Laguna Beach: The Real Orange County*. Released during the peak of reality TV production, experimentation, and prestige in America, *Laguna Beach* provided MTV with the impetus to create more and more reality series showcasing youth identities. The series' success led to *The Hills, The City, 16 and Pregnant*, and *Teen Mom*. These series share the same structure: featuring the same characters all season, and across multiple seasons, creating a serialized narrative, which builds bonds between the audience and characters (Mittell 2015). Upper-class white women, like *The Hills'* Lauren Conrad and *The City's* Whitney Port, are characterized by the control they have over the stories told about them. As a result, their stories are aspirational—audiences are encouraged to dress, consume, and behave like them. They are, by Harris's definition, high-achieving Can-Do Girls, who can use their celebrity status to build successful careers. By contrast, working-class white women, like *Teen Mom's* Amber Portwood and Farrah Abraham, or Harris's At-Risk Girls, are unable to build careers based on their celebrity since they are associated with negative representations of delinquent motherhood and their overall failure to live up to gendered expectations. These series were successful because they were aspirational, but they also showed what behaviors and choices to avoid. This chapter is supplemented by interviews I conducted with Dia Sokol Savage, creator and producer of *16 and Pregnant*, *Teen Mom*, and *Teen Mom 2*.

In chapter 4, "'If You Don't Tan, You're Pale': The Regional and Ethnic Other on MTV (2009–2013)," I chronicle a different set of popular reality identity series on MTV—*Jersey Shore* and *Buckwild*—which make the Otherness of its cast central to the series' appeal. I argue that these programs were successful because they entertained audiences through the spectacularization of certain identities, turning them into broad stereotypes about both Italian Americans and the working-class residents of Sissonville, West Virginia. In doing so, these cast members open themselves up to ridicule, the primary affect generated by their series. In these MTV series, whiteness seeks out fractures and corners, places of not-whiteness, that can offer some unique vision of the self that is not-white. Thus, both series enabled audiences who generally categorized as being "white" to locate a different identity for themselves.

Chapter 5, "'That Moment Is Here, Whether I Like It or Not': When MTV's Programming Fails (2013–2014)," looks at two failed series, which offers an interesting counterpoint to the success, longevity, and franchise potential of other identity series like *The Hills*, *Jersey Shore*, and *Teen Mom* and reveals some of the ways in which certain MTV-codified identities can fail to translate into reality TV success. Like *Jersey Shore* and *Buckwild*, MTV's *Washington Heights* featured racial or ethnic groups living in a clearly defined region of the United States who take pride in their identity. However, the Dominican American identities at the heart of *Washington Heights* were unsustainable as a serialized narrative because the identities presented on the series were too far afield from audience expectations and stereotypes about urban, Latinx youth. I also analyze another failed series, *Virgin Territory*, which aired for just one season. I argue that this series likewise failed because it did not conform to previously successful models of reality identity programming on MTV; the series featured nonwhite, nonheterosexual identities who were not aspirational or comical.

In the conclusion to this book, "*Catfish* and the Future of MTV's Reality Programming (2012–)," I focus on *Catfish*, which brings together two people who have never met in real life but who nevertheless have intense, romantic, virtual relationships. This self-reflexive series highlights the ways in which youth audiences are aware of and actively engaged in the apparatus of the social media platforms they use to construct their identities. I argue that *Catfish* offered concrete language for something so many internet users were experiencing, as well as an interlinked pair of new identities for its youth audiences: the Catfish (the deceiver) and the Hopeful (the deceived). MTV intervened in larger discourses about Millennials and identity throughout the 2000s by presenting identity as something that becomes possible only when (primarily white) people interact with those who are different from them, as something that can be achieved through making good (consumer) choices and avoiding risky behaviors (like unprotected sex), or as something that can be chosen (the Guido, the Redneck). *Catfish*'s focus on the fluidity and instability of identity contradicts earlier incarnations of MTV's reality identity cycle (discussed in chapters 2, 3, 4, and 5), which presented identity as fixed and easily defined. This chapter is supplemented by interviews I conducted with Max Joseph, cohost of *Catfish*, who offered his own theories about this series' appeal and the nature of online intimacy.

MTV's programming is an ideal artifact to study in relation to youth identity because the channel's target demographic remains stable throughout time; they are always chasing the same young audience, no matter how old they get. Analyzing the various (and often intersecting) tracks made by these youth cultures across the terrain of popular culture—mentioned in an admonishing editorial here and then glorified in a flashy movie there—can reveal how a particular identity is understood. As Sarah Thornton explains, the media is "crucial to the definition and distribution of cultural knowledge. . . . The difference between being in or out of fashion, high or low in subcultural capital, correlates in complex ways with degrees of media coverage, creation and exposure" (1997, 203). The insights about identity and youth culture of the twenty-first century found in this production cycle will make sense only if we return to MTV's origins and the need it claimed to fill in the lives of youth audiences. In the next chapter, I discuss the early years of MTV, as well as the various programming shifts it has made in its nearly forty years on the air in order to keep pace with its forever-young audience.

"It's Videos, Fool"
A Targeted History of MTV

(1981–2004)

When the twenty-four-hour music video–based cable channel known as MTV first debuted on August 2, 1981, its primary purpose was, according to former MTV president Bob Pittman, to build a "brand" and an "attitude" (qtd. in Anson 2000). The product sold by MTV was not pop music, but rather MTV itself. The channel sliced off a select demographic of twelve- to thirty-four-year-old, primarily white, suburban Americans, and then tailored this new product—music television—for that group. The channel's first commercial, which featured archival footage of Neil Armstrong planting a CGI-ed MTV flag into the moon's surface, was a signal that the channel was staking its claim in a new popular culture landscape. They were claiming this territory for youth audiences, which is why MTV is such an important resource for scholars studying American youth culture. The channel's mission is to define, brand, and sell youth culture to youth audiences. Although many different kinds of audiences have watched MTV over the last four decades, MTV's notion of "youth" is limited by its own notions of its target audience: white, suburban Americans, of the ages twelve to thirty-four. Nearly forty years after its premiere, MTV continues to play a vital role in the branding and construction of a specific segment of (mostly white) youth culture, even though its content has changed dramatically since its debut, a shift this book seeks to understand.

In order to appreciate the pivotal moment when MTV began creating and branding content for Millennial youth audiences in the 2000s, and it shifted from playing mostly music videos to mostly reality TV, it is first necessary to revisit the history of MTV. Specifically, why did MTV come to exist, what audience did it claim to serve, and what content did it offer that audience? What follows is an analysis of the historical, cultural, and industrial contexts within which MTV formed as a cable channel, as well as the strategies it deployed to become and remain, in the channel's own words, "the world's premier youth entertainment brand" (MTV 2020). I also outline the way MTV imagined its target youth demographic of Gen Xers and how the channel's project of studying and then branding by generations allowed MTV to convert what they knew about its (primarily white, middle-class) youth audiences into a measurable profit. This brief history of MTV's first two decades on the air (1981–2004) serves as a way to contextualize MTV's understanding of youth audiences of the 1980s (the so-called Generation X) versus its understanding of audiences of the 2000s (the so-called Millennials).

Teens and TV before MTV

What did American teenagers watch before they watched MTV? During the classic network era of American television (1950s to 1980s), the industry's central operating structure was an oligopoly composed of NBC, ABC, and CBS, which were themselves originally radio networks. These big three networks accounted for 95 percent of all prime-time viewing. Similar to the Hollywood studio system, this classic network era was efficient and stable. As Amanda Lotz explains, during the network era, most American homes had a single television with no remote control or playback devices: "This uniformity of use aided the industry's production processes because it enabled the industry to assume certain viewing conditions and rely on viewers to watch network-determined schedules" (2007, 51–52).[1] At this time, there was little to differentiate the TV content consumed by teenagers and the TV consumed by adult viewers; prior to the 1980s, TV programming was not yet focused on the targeting of niche audiences, particularly teenagers.[2] But a few exceptions existed. The Philadelphia-based *Bandstand* was launched in the mid-1950s as a showcase for rock 'n' roll hits and the latest teen dance crazes. In his history of the landmark series, John Jackson describes *American Bandstand* as "a rallying point around which America's

1.1 Dick Clark, the host of *American Bandstand*, with some teen participants on the show. *American Bandstand* was one of the first television programs aimed at teenagers.

first teenage constituency was able to connect" (1997, x).[3] In 1956, when the show's original host, Bob Horn, had to leave his job due to a sex scandal that later led to his arrest, Dick Clark, the host associated with the series' legacy, took over as emcee. Among many changes Clark made to the program were instituting a dress code for the show's teenage dancers (jackets, ties, and sweaters for the boys; dresses, sweaters, and long skirts for the girls) and banning "sexy" dances (Szatmary 1987, 56). According to Clark, these changes made the teen-centered series "acceptable to adults who were frightened by the teenage world and their music" (qtd. in Szatmary 1987, 55). Jackson notes that although *American Bandstand* featured the "largely black-derived idiom of rock 'n' roll," this was not reflected in the teenagers featured onscreen: "the show's studio audience remained segregated to the extent that viewers around the country did not have an inkling that Philadelphia contained one of the largest black populations in America" (1997, 57). This whitewashed approach to the controversial musical genre of rock 'n' roll clearly assuaged nervous, white, suburban parents, because *Bandstand* was renamed *American Bandstand*, that is, it became a nationally televised series, by the close of 1957 (Szatmary 1987, 55). *American Bandstand* remained on the air until 1989.[4]

American Bandstand's success among white, middle-class teenagers was the result of several factors, including the postwar baby boom, which led to a marked increase in adolescents in America's white suburbs, and the rising popularity of rock 'n' roll music among white suburban youth. Jackson (1997, ix) also credits the rise of nationwide programming, the result of coaxial cable linking the east and west coasts in 1951, with transforming the medium of television from one that was mostly used by an urban audience to one aimed at a wider audience. In the search for MTV's televisual precedent, as a channel offering content specifically aimed at and centering the tastes and interests of contemporary (mostly white, mostly middle-class) American youth, then *American Bandstand* is a likely candidate. ABC's success with teenage audiences, and the marketing opportunities this cash-flush demographic provided, convinced other networks to roll out content for teenagers. CBS added a "Teen Age Special" segment into Patti Page's weekly show, *The Big Record*, and *The Ed Sullivan Show* announced it would feature more acts that specifically appealed to teens. Similarly, NBC's *The Perry Como Show* increased the number of rock 'n' roll acts on the variety program (Jackson 1997, 74). These were all attempts to replicate some of *American Bandstand*'s success with teenage audiences.

Although there was not much television programming made explicitly for teenage audiences during the classic network era, there is plenty of evidence to suggest that teenagers still watched a lot of TV. As Aniko Bodroghkozy explains in a study of 1960s television and youth rebellion, "prime time figured in the social and cultural dislocations provoked by the student and youth movements of the 1960s" (2001, 3). Likewise, in her study of content-promotion hybrids throughout TV history, Jennifer Gillan notes how one of the teenage stars of *The Adventures of Ozzie & Harriet*, Ricky Nelson, was the spokesman of choice for advertisers like Coca-Cola, due to his strong appeal to teen audiences (2015, 51–52). The latter example suggests that advertisers were aware that certain TV stars had a strong teenage following and that teenage audiences were a demographic worth pursuing. Indeed, Sharon Ross and Louisa Stein call *The Adventures of Ozzie and Harriet* "one of the first full-on teen shows" (2008, 12). TV scholars also suggest that teenagers were avid watchers of soap operas in the 1970s, specifically ones like *Dark Shadows*, which had an intense teenage girl fandom. Sitcoms from the 1960s and 1970s, like *Gidget*, *The Many Loves of Dobie Gillis*, and *Happy Days*, also attracted teen viewers.[5] Elana Levine notes that during this time, teenage audiences "were at the forefront of many of the changes brought by the sexual revolution" (2007, 79). She also cites made-for-TV movies like *Dawn: Portrait of a Teenage Runaway* (NBC, 1976) as content that was watched by teenagers though not *explicitly made for* teenagers, in the same way that "teen" movies from the 1950s like *Rebel without a Cause* and *Blackboard Jungle* were big hits for postwar American teenagers but, as social problem films, were not initially made for a teenage audience. Thus, while there was not a lot of content being produced specifically *for* teenage audiences during the network era, by the 1970s the teenage audience was definitely on the minds of TV producers as well as the subject of public discourse on TV and its impact on children.

Another category of television programming aimed at teen audiences (as opposed to young children or adults) in the 1970s was the afterschool special. TV scholars, including Kirsten Pike and Amanda Keeler, have argued that the ABC *Afterschool Specials* represent some of the first American programming made explicitly for and enjoyed by contemporary teenage audiences. Keeler explains that, "out of this desire to appeal to this vast, untapped audience, ABC's *Specials* aimed to give teenagers their own niche programming that treated them with respect *by creating television stories about them and for them*" (2016, 485; emphasis mine). *Afterschool Specials* premiered in the fall of 1972 during the "afterschool block," just as its target audience, viewers ages eight to fourteen, were coming home from their afterschool activities (Keeler 2016, 485).[6] Pike traces the origins of these specials to an activist group called Action for Children's Television (ACT), established in 1968 to influence both television studios and their advertisers to rethink content aimed at children (2011, 132). ABC, "long known for its interest in capturing and catering its content to the lucrative youth market," was the only broadcast network in 1972 to respond to ACT's calls for reform, specifically by creating the "after school special" (2011, 135–136). These specials covered a range of topics in the tradition of the "social hygiene films" of the 1920s, instructing their viewers on how to most appropriately manage their social, sexual, and legal behaviors, which would in turn lead to the better functioning of the community as a whole (Keeler 2016, 486).[7] *Afterschool Specials* added a new element to daytime programming: content made for and about adolescents (Pike 2011, 144). By the 1980s, popular discourses about the developing relationship between teens and TV expressed concern that this generation was "raised on television" and their brains were preconditioned to having short attention spans. Therefore any television content aimed at attracting the teenage market would have to be uniquely suited to this alleged limited attention span, which was, ironically, blamed on television itself (Newman

2010, 590–591). Michael Newman points to *Sesame Street* as an early attempt to craft content to the more "limited" attention spans of child TV viewers by focusing on "movement, speed, [and] constantly refreshed views" (2010, 583–584). By the early 1970s there was an "association of brevity with a juvenile or unintelligent audience . . . reinforcing television's reputation as an 'idiot box,'" as well as concern that television was actively (and negatively) shaping attention spans (586–588).

At the same time that American parents and pediatricians fretted over the impact of television on the plastic brains of young viewers, television executives were concerned with ways to entice teens to watch *more* television. With limited programming offered for teenage viewers who, nevertheless, wanted to watch TV, Bob Pittman and John Lack, the driving forces behind the origin and development of MTV, saw an opportunity to provide advertisers targeting the youth market with a captive audience. As Rob Tannenbaum and Craig Marks explain in their history of MTV's "Golden Age" (1981–1992), "Teens were an untapped audience, an invisible power. MTV gave them what they wanted, and got them not only interested in, but obsessed by MTV, making it their clubhouse" (2011, xxxviii). In a 1990 *New York Times* editorial, Pittman retroactively argued for the significance and utility of the channel he helped to launch. He wrote, "The pre-TV adults are the 'one thing at a time' generation. . . . The TV babies, by contrast, seem to be processing information from different sources almost simultaneously." Pittman designates the generation gap between baby boomers (pre-TV adults) and Generation X (TV babies) as a "communication gap," one that MTV was, by Pittman's accounts, able to fill. Remote controls were not yet ubiquitous in the American home in 1981, so MTV also satisfied the need for cheap and plentiful programming that ran continuously, eliminating the need to get up and change the channel.[8] Videos ran twenty-four hours per day, seven days per week, so that a teenage viewer could consume content during hours not generally programmed for audiences in their age group. Music videos could be watched for five minutes or five hours, depending on how much time the viewer had to spare.

The Beginning of MTV

Martha Quinn, one of the very first of MTV's "veejays," or VJs, recalls the first time she ever heard about the channel, in July 1981: "I was at [my internship at WNBC] one afternoon when a guy in the office said, 'You should be a V.J.' I said, 'What's a V.J.?' And he said, 'It's just like being on the radio, but it's on television.' To which I replied, 'What do you do during the records?' He said, 'It's videos, fool.' I couldn't imagine what he was talking about" (qtd. in Anson 2000). Of course, music videos *do* predate MTV. Video-music clips can be traced all the way back to the 1940s and the brief vogue for short film clips of musical performances known as "soundies." Soundies were screened in nightclubs and restaurants on seven-foot-tall film juke-boxes called Panorams. These clips "represented the first systematic attempt to produce conceptual, short-form visualizations of recorded songs not intended for theatrical exhibition" (Lukow 1991, 6). Another pre-MTV venue for filmed musical performances was the Scopitone, a kind of coin-operated jukebox using 16-mm film, first developed in France. The Scopitone ultimately declined in the 1960s, due in part to the format's inability to draw in top acts (Sharpe 2006; Tannenbaum and Marks 2011). Pop music programs from the 1950s to the 1970s, like the aforementioned *American Bandstand*, *Shindig!*, *Hullabaloo*, and, later, *Soul Train*, which featured young people dancing to contemporary hits, are also historical antecedents to the modern music video (Lukow 1991, 6). Despite these precedents, Quinn was not alone in her ignorance of this new medium. Prior to the launch of MTV in 1981, television stations rarely aired music videos, because their short, discrete formats did not fit into the established model of thirty-minute and sixty-minute programming blocks.[9] Beginning in the early 1970s record companies began filming artists' performances and airing them in music stores, at clubs, or on television as a less expensive alternative to concert tours. But these videos were still not, at the time, considered as entertainment in their own right; they were commercials for the music that record companies wanted to sell (Banks 1996, 29). So when did things change?

Several industrial, technological, and cultural developments paved the way for music videos to become a valuable commodity in the 1980s. First, in 1975, the technology firm Telesonics began to test stereophonic audio systems in the Chicago area, and in 1984 the Federal Communications Commission (FCC) adopted multichannel television sound (MTS) as the industry standard for broadcast television (Dickstein 1975, 14). These developments led to the newly "enhanced audio capabilities of television." Studios were now on the hunt for content that could exploit this new technology (Banks 1996, 29).[10] Second, the record industry was experiencing an economic slump in the 1970s. Many industry insiders blamed this decline on commercial radio, which was playing mostly classic rock and therefore unwilling to take chances on new artists. Record companies were anxious for new media in which to promote emerging artists, and MTV was the right venue at the right time (31). Finally, the growth of cable television in US markets in the late 1970s and early 1980s made it feasible to offer channels and programming appealing to a niche, rather than a mass, audience (30). TV executives wanted to find content that would attract teenage viewers, who had yet to be adequately targeted by traditional network programming. This aspect of MTV, its ability to provide youth audiences with content they could watch at any time, for however long they liked, separated MTV's content from traditional network fare.

In the summer of 1979, Warner Communications Incorporated's Steve Ross and American Express's James Robinson III formed Warner-Amex Satellite Entertainment Company (WASEC). At the time, Warner Communications was heavily invested in the burgeoning technology of cable television, and it "envisioned cable television as a sales tool to deliver goods and services directly into the home." Ross and Robinson were on the hunt for cheap content for the various cable channels they were developing (Tannenbaum and Marks 2011). One option came from Elektra Records' founder Jac Holzman, who brought a selection of music videos to WASEC's chief operating officer, John Lack. As mentioned previously, every time an artist or group released an album, the record company would create a video clip of the group to promote it. These clips were freely distributed as part of the artist's or band's promotional materials. E. Ann Kaplan believes that these early rock videos should be called "rock promos" because "their short, four-minute span originally suited a promotional context, while the illogical image-change and generally 'avant-garde' techniques mimicked those long customary in many ads" (1987, 13). Holzman pointed out that using these free clips meant that MTV's primary content—music videos—had zero cost. Lack was intrigued by the pitch, not simply because the music-video content was free, but because it offered a different vision of music consumption; he recalls being impressed with how the medium was "not just about audio but had a visual component which would carry further the meaning of the song" (qtd. in Anson 2000). WASEC's president, Jack Schneider, and his team of Bob McGroarty, who ran marketing and sales, and Bob Pittman, director of WASEC's pay TV division, soon began exploring the option of a channel devoted entirely to showing music-video clips.[11] At *Billboard*'s first ever Video Music Conference in 1979, John Lack described WASEC's plans to start a twenty-four-hour music video channel, what he called "video radio" (qtd. in Marks 2017).

After securing financial backing for their music television channel, WASEC turned to extensive audience research that revealed, unsurprisingly, that "the average prospective viewer of MTV would be a suburban, white male with a commitment to rock music and an equally strong aversion to contemporary soul" (qtd. in Banks 1996, 34). For its first eighteen months on the air, MTV played only videos by white artists (Kraszewski 2017, 48). Pittman later explained that he made the decision to have MTV focus on (white) rock 'n' roll over (Black) R&B because "the audience was larger. . . . The mostly white rock audience was more excited about rock than the largely black audience was about contemporary rhythm and blues" (qtd. in Ed Levine 1983). These specious claims aside, Pittman's defense of his channel's white focus became a defining feature of MTV even years later when its video selection included more nonwhite artists and musical genres beyond rock 'n' roll.[12] MTV's reach was also initially limited by its mode of distribution: cable. In 1978, approximately 17 percent of American households had cable subscriptions. To have cable in the late 1970s or early 1980s meant that a household was close to a major city, or where towers were located (and thus able to receive signals), and wealthy enough to pay for a monthly cable subscription. Hence, even at its inception, MTV understood its target youth audience in a highly limited way (primarily white, middle-class or upper-middle-class, and suburban) and sought to offer a correspondingly limited vision of youth culture for them to consume (Banks 1996, 34).

On August 21, 1981, MTV aired its first broadcast, which opened with a close-up of the bottom of the space shuttle *Columbia* on its launchpad. In the right-hand corner of the frame, the letters "USA" appear on the bottom half of the shuttle. In the left-hand corner of the frame is MTV's animated logo, a burst of changing patterns and colors against the otherwise washed-out footage of the rocket launch. A voice-over from mission control begins the countdown to blastoff at twenty. This count occurs in real time, so there are moments of stillness during which birds chirp, blissfully unaware of the rocket that is about to launch. The frame fills with white smoke, followed by more footage of the rocket taking off, this time from an aerial view. The launchpad falls away and then dissolves into the famous, public-domain footage of Neil Armstrong stepping on to the moon's surface and planting an American flag there. Only, MTV's creative directors, Alan Goodman and Fred Seibert, digitally replaced the image of the American stars and stripes with the MTV logo. Then a voice-over intones, "Ladies and gentlemen: rock 'n' roll," with MTV's signature rock 'n' roll riff playing in the background. Kaplan explains the significance of such imagery in MTV's early marketing: "The idea is clear: MTV equals the men exploring outer space in its breaking of new territory, and also equals new technologies, the future" (1987, 18).

Former MTV CEO Tom Freston describes the image in a slightly different way: "We thought that was sort of a rock 'n' roll attitude: 'Let's take man's greatest moment technologically and rip it off'" (qtd. in Anson 2000). Both analyses work. The channel's logo on the flag, designed by Patti Rogoff, was of a large M with the letters TV spray-painted in the upper right-hand corner. Ironically, the original purpose of graffiti—to be the visual component to the physicality of breakdancing and the audio sounds of rap music—was once again buried by a channel that, initially at least, equated youth culture with *white* youth culture while simultaneously appropriating key markers of Black and Latinx youth culture.

After the moon man plants his flag, the first music video to air is "Video Killed the Radio Star" by the Buggles. When it was originally released in 1979, "Video Killed the Radio Star" was an international hit but barely cracked the Top 40 charts in America. As mentioned in the introduction, the video was selected to go first because of the timeliness of its themes about changing technologies and nostalgia for the past. MTV's first video also offered early evidence of the dreamlike narratives that the music video would become known for. "Video Killed the Radio Star" opens with a bright ball of light in the darkness. A young girl crouches before an old-fashioned radio and turns it on as a rotoscoped line drawing of Trevor Horne, the Buggles' lead singer, croons into a 1950s-era dynamic microphone. Old media is calling out to youth audiences, but there is something else, something new coming: music videos. Over the course of the video, the little girl is transformed into a grown woman in a sparkling leotard and pastel-colored tinsel hair. The implication here is that the child who listened to her favorite artists on the radio is now modern and all grown-up, watching music videos instead. This imagery is intercut with footage of the Buggles singing and playing their instruments in a futuristic, all-white room. Significantly, in this "modern" space, Horne's microphone is now a slim, almost imperceptible, fiber-optic model. On top of the keyboard is a color television that features two young women singing along to the chorus of "Video Killed the Radio Star." Even the subjects of the music video are themselves watching music videos! Also notable about this first video is the use of the lower-third graphics that offer the following information about the song: artist name, song title, album title, and record company. The music video was simultaneously revenue-generating entertainment *and* an advertisement for the artist and record company.

"Video Killed the Radio Star" is followed immediately by Pat Benatar's "You Better Run," making that the second video to air on MTV. "You Bet-

1.2 The MTV studio was intended to evoke the relaxed atmosphere of a teenager's bedroom.

ter Run" is a conventional American rock song, and its video is filmed inside an empty, derelict warehouse, making it quite different in both aesthetics and content than "Video Killed the Radio Star." "You Better Run" is composed entirely of close-ups, medium shots, and long shots of Benatar and her band performing.[13] After "You Better Run," the next image is of the MTV studio set. Mark Goodman, one of MTV's five original VJs, is shot in a medium close-up, framing his long, brown, curly hair. He has his arms crossed and resting on his knees, as if he is also sitting around watching TV. Goodman looks directly at the audience and declares, as the camera slowly tracks away to reveal the studio, "This is it. Welcome to MTV. Music Television. The world's first twenty-four-hour stereo video-music channel. Just moments ago, all of the VJs and crew here at MTV collectively hit our executive producer, Sue Steinberg, over the head with a bottle of champagne and behold! A new concept is born: the best of TV combined with the best of radio. Starting right now, you'll never look at music the same way again." Here the camera cuts away to a high-angle shot of Mark, slowly craning back until there is a cut to commercial. The channel's first commercial break is followed by introductions to the other four VJs: Nina Blackwood (the hip punk rocker in black leather), Alan Hunter (the blonde heartthrob to Mark's brunette), Martha Quinn (the relatable girl next door), and J. J. Jackson (the sole person of color, both in the studio and also among the videos). Each VJ appears relaxed and welcoming in their introductions, as if they've invited the viewer to come and hang out in their living room and watch videos with them. Executive producer Sue Steinberg wanted to make sure the VJ felt like a part of the audience (Anson 2000). Similarly, in a strategy aimed to differentiate itself from broadcast television, early MTV broadcasting constructed a casual aesthetic: poorly lit, cluttered sets resembling the bedroom of an American teenager (Banks 1996, 34).[14] After introductions, several other music videos aired: Rod Stewart's "She Won't Dance with Me," the Who's "You Better You Bet," PhD's "Little Suzi's on the Up," Cliff Richard's "We Don't Talk Anymore," and the Pretenders' "Brass in Pocket," among others. That was MTV's first hour on television.[15]

When MTV was first launched, Pittman famously described it as "a channel with no programs, no beginning, no middle, no end" (qtd. in Boyer 1988). It was to be an all-day music-video jukebox. In place of plots and characters, MTV's programming offered brief bursts of highly stylized, disjointed imagery. In her book-length study of MTV's first years on the air, Kaplan notes that MTV's first generation of music videos (pre-1987) abandon cause-and-effect narratives, as well as established codes of continuity editing (like the use of shot/reverse shot and eye-line matches). Therefore these first-generation videos are frequently self-reflexive—by presenting themselves as making-of videos or videos in which the image is altered by the subjects of the video (as in A-ha's "Take On Me")—and blur distinctions between the image onscreen and the self (Kaplan 1987, 33–45). According to Kaplan, this early stage of MTV's history "positions the spectator in the mode of constantly hoping that the next ad-segment (of whatever kind) will satisfy the desire for plenitude" (143). Because record companies were just starting to create video clips to accompany singles, MTV initially had just 125 clips to choose from (Banks 1996, 35). Most of those video clips came from British New Wave acts like Duran Duran, Culture Club, and Eurythmics, since the medium was already an established way to promote artists in Europe. They had readymade singles to air. Goodwin notes that "it was the distinctive look of the new Pop that gave MTV its 'cutting edge' kudos and established its visuals as nonnarrative, or antirealist, in the eyes of many cultural critics" (1992, 133). As a result, MTV found itself in a position of (somewhat unintentionally) introducing new artists to American teens, further solidifying its status as a hip source of new music for American viewers (Banks 1996, 35). This was the beginning of MTV's role as the arbiter of the cool and new, but only for a highly select audience of white, middle-to-upper-class youth audiences.

Within weeks of its premiere, MTV was selling trade ads in *Billboard* featuring quotes from satisfied record-store managers, who claimed to be selling albums of artists who received no radio play but heavy rotation on MTV (Anson 2000; Lukow 1991, 9). These sales served as concrete proof of MTV's reach as well as its ability to influence the taste and, more important, the buying habits of its young audience. Soon, music videos became a standard way for record companies to promote artists and their new singles. By 1983, just two years after MTV's rocket launch, "record companies are finding videos to be a more cost-effective, less time-consuming method of promoting their acts. A clip shown on MTV could be seen immediately in more than 12 million homes." By contrast, "a national tour might take six months and only reach 100,000 rock fans" (Ed Levine 1983). Within the first few years of its launch, and with the support of both the music industry and its fans, MTV became the go-to home of youth viewers in the early 1980s. In its first eighteen months of operations, the channel earned approximately $7 million in ad income (Kaplan 1987, 1).

In 1984 MTV became a public corporation and boasted between eighteen and twenty-two million viewers (Kaplan 1987, 2). That same year, MTV celebrated itself and its accomplishments by hosting the first Video Music Awards (VMAs). The show was cohosted by Dan Ackroyd, who had just starred in the blockbuster *Ghostbusters*, and Bette Midler, who was an established singer at the time but soon would have a big movie career (with the films *Down and Out in Beverly Hills, Outrageous Fortune*, and *Beaches*). At this very first awards show for the medium of music videos, the Cars' "You Might Think" took home the Video of the Year award and the Beatles, David Bowie, and Richard Lester were all given individual Video Vanguard awards, which highlight an artist's lifetime body of work (Sanchez 2018). Of course, this awards show is most famously remembered for a performance by a then-unknown pop star named Madonna, singing her new single "Like a Virgin." Madonna's initial vision for the performance involved a live Bengal tiger, and when this request was denied, she settled on a wedding theme, including a seventeen-foot-tall wedding cake and a white lace tulle skirt and bustier adorned with a belt featuring the phrase "BOY TOY" (Tannenbaum 2014). Some sitting in the audience that night believed that Madonna's salacious performance, in which she rolled around on the stage revealing her underwear, would end her career before it started. Instead, the boundary-pushing singer's 1984 VMA performance became one of the channel's most defining moments.[16] Madonna's onstage performance epitomized the value and utility of the music video to pop music; it demonstrated how a compelling pop song was not just about the music but also about the way the artist looks when she performs it. From that night forward, the VMAs were about pushing (and crossing over) boundaries, and scaring the censors (Mantzouranis 2020).[17] The excitement that Madonna's unscripted, seemingly authentic performance generated was a possible hint about the kind of content MTV would generate for Millennials, just twenty years later.

Dayparting and Stripping

Andrew Goodwin cites the years of 1983–1985 as MTV's "second launch" or "the true beginning of the new service." It was at this point when the channel was finally available in the crucial media markets of New York City and Los Angeles (1992, 135). Then, in 1984, the year of the first VMAs, the Cable Communications Policy Act was established. The Cable Act deregulated the industry and promoted the spread of cable use in America; between 1984 and 1992, the cable industry invested more than $15 billion in cable services (CCTA 2020). As MTV built its audience, and cable became available across the country, more and more cable providers began carrying the channel. MTV's ratings stayed on an upward trajectory throughout its first few years of operation. In 1985, just four years after the launch of the channel, MTV's original creator, WASEC, sold its controlling interest in MTV Networks to Viacom. MTV's ratings stagnated in 1986, losing 20 percent of its eighteen- to twenty-four-year-old viewers and 25 percent of its twelve- to seventeen-year-old viewers (Banks 1996, 126). The loss was attributed to the waning appeal of music videos (at this time MTV was still adhering to its original goal of playing music videos around the clock, with no larger structure or schedule) and to the fact that MTV's playlist was becoming more conservative and more like Top 40 radio. In other words, MTV was losing its edge. As a result, the channel had to begin adjusting its understanding of its core (white, suburban) audience and their desires, the first of many brand overhauls made by the channel in reaction to the changing needs of its always-aging and, therefore, always-changing audience.

Goodwin thought that 1986 marked the moment when MTV's programming shifted away from its structureless schedule (as a nonstop video jukebox) to "the development of more discrete program slots" (1992, 137). MTV aired videos according to a "dayparting" format that grouped music videos by genre or into distinct programs that aired on a schedule in order to better target specific audiences who watched the channel at specific times. Programs like *Club MTV*, which appealed primarily to young girls, aired in the afternoons, just as this demographic was coming home from school. By contrast, *Headbanger's Ball*, which focused mostly on punk and heavy metal music, aired late at night, when, presumably, the only people still awake and watching MTV were the kids who were up late drinking coffee or alcohol and smoking (Banks 1996, 124). In the late 1980s, MTV also began producing original nonmusic programming with its TV-centered game show *Remote Control*. Other programming at the time, including *Just Say Julie*, in which host Julie Brown did brief comedy bits, played music videos, and offered mean-spirited commentary on popular music videos and artists, and *Kevin Seal: Sporting Fool*, which focused on the host's attempts to participate in extreme sports like bungee jumping and white-water rafting, centered around former MTV VJs. *The Week in Rock*, hosted by Kurt Loder, was also added in 1987. This program, which eventually became known as *MTV News*, offered weekly reports on concerts, album releases, and other current events in popular music. Over time, the program began to cover social, political, and historical issues tied to pop music and to youth audiences in general. But as Jane Hall noted in a 1992 *Los Angeles Times* story on the program, the program's ultimate goal was the promotion of MTV and its products.[18] Goodwin believes that this moment marks MTV's "third phase," representing a "widening musical scope [heavy metal, rap music] and an accelerated movement toward a more traditional television schedule" (1992, 136). MTV's schedule became more predictable and less chaotic at this time.

I will highlight just one of these additions to MTV's dayparting schedule, *Yo! MTV Raps*, because it also usefully illuminates MTV's complicated relationship with Black artists and, by extension, Black youth audiences. As previously mentioned, WASEC's focus on white, middle-class, primarily male youth meant that MTV's playlist centered around rock music. This is, as Kaplan notes, "symptomatic of Reagan's America," in that "the largely white, middle-American audience to which MTV gears itself are uninterested in black bands" (1987, 30–31). This debate over what kind of music MTV would play came to a head with the burgeoning popularity of the African American performer Michael Jackson and the channel's refusal to play his videos. Walter Yetnikoff of CBS Records, Jackson's label at the time, threatened to boycott the channel and pull all CBS videos within twenty-four hours if MTV continued to block Black artists from its playlists.[19] Consequently, in

1.3 MTV launched *Yo! MTV Raps* in 1988 in response to the presence and commercial viability of the hip hop subculture in America.

1983 MTV aired videos from Michael Jackson's album *Thriller* (1982), starting with the hit "Billie Jean." Jackson's "Thriller" video (1983), a thirteen-minute homage to horror movies, went on to become one of the channel's biggest hits and a cultural phenomenon in its own right (Tannenbaum and Marks 2011, 144).[20]

Similar to the reaction to Michael Jackson's music at first, MTV was reluctant to embrace rap music, fearing it would "alienate" white, suburban, middle-class audiences. MTV's decision to launch *Yo! MTV Raps* in 1988 was a (late) recognition of the presence and commercial viability of the hip hop subculture in America. The buzz around hip hop (including rap music, breakdancing, and graffiti art) had already convinced American movie studios to exploit this subculture with a cycle of films that approached hip hop as *the* cultural form of the moment accessible to everyone, from the most seasoned inner-city b-boy (i.e., breakdancer) to the most isolated suburbanite, white and Black, male and female.[21] This widespread acceptance and embrace of hip hop culture were strongly tied to its redefinition as safe for white, middle-class consumption throughout the mid-1980s. As always, MTV did not begin a musical trend so much as it adopted the trend early enough so as to still appear fresh, hip, and in the know to a majority of its audience, the isolated, white, suburban teen whose only exposure to the music scene came from MTV or Top 40 radio programming. Hosted by Fab 5 Freddy, and later with Ed Lover and Doctor Dre, the new series featured rap music videos, interviews, comical ad libbing, and live performances by contemporary artists in the hip hop community. The opening credits in the pilot episode featured clips from contemporary rappers and their videos (though there were few available at the time), including Run-DMC and the Fresh Prince (aka Will Smith), but the majority of the footage was made up of clips from "It Takes Two" (1988) by Rob Base and DJ E-Z Rock. This single was on the *Billboard* Top 100, as well as *Billboard*'s Club and Hip-Hop Charts, thus marking it as accessible for MTV's white suburban viewers.

After the opening credits roll, the pilot opens with Run-DMC, wearing their signature black T-shirts and gold rope chains, live onstage. Run-DMC was the first of the new school rap artists to get a gold record and to receive a Grammy nomination (both in 1984). Like MTV's use of "It Takes Two" for the series' main theme, Run-DMC was selected to launch *Yo! MTV Raps* because of the group's balance between novelty and familiarity. The group had mainstream (i.e., white) success and yet was still enjoyed and embraced by Black audiences, which is MTV's sweet spot. MTV is not after the coolest kids in the room; they're after the kids who *want* to be the coolest kids in the room. This pilot episode pulled in one of MTV's largest audiences at the time. *Yo! MTV Raps* became a "how to" manual of hip hop style, allowing its mostly white, suburban, male viewers between the ages of sixteen and twenty-four to keep abreast of the latest urban slang and fashions (Samuels 2004, 152). The first video to air on *Yo! MTV Raps* was "Follow the Leader" (1988) by Eric B. and Rakim, which features the duo in tuxes, smoking cigars with other powerful-looking Black men. As with the choice of "Video Killed the Radio Star," the selection of "Follow the Leader" was a self-reflexive commentary on MTV itself. For example, in the first verse, Rakim raps, "Now stop and turn around and look / As you stare in the darkness, your knowledge is took / So keep staring, soon you suddenly see a star / You better follow it, cause it's the R / This is a lesson if you're guessing and if you're borrowing / Hurry hurry step right up and keep following the leader." Rakim is urging the audience to stay on pace with contemporary youth culture, to "hurry up" and "follow the leader." Here rap music becomes a sign of the modern and the new, just as music videos signified the future in "Video Killed the Radio Star." Soon, artists and groups like JJ Fad, LL Cool J, and Kool Moe Dee joined MTV's rotations with the likes of other, more established Black artists like Michael Jackson and Lionel Richie.[22]

In addition to its dayparting strategy of scheduling programming for specific audiences, MTV also built its target youth audience throughout the late 1980s and early 1990s with a strategy known as "stripping," which refers to the practice of airing episodes of the same TV series at the same time each day: "MTV's twenty-four-hour 'flow' [was] increasingly punctuated by regular slots organized around a predictable weekly schedule" (Goodwin 1992, 142–143). *Liquid Television* featured avant-garde and experimental short-form animation, all of which were commissioned by and created for MTV (in a joint producing venture with BBC 2). *House of Style*, hosted by supermodel Cindy Crawford, covered contemporary fashion, the world of models, and other topics related to the fashion industry. *The Ben Stiller Show* was a sketch comedy series featuring now-famous comedians like Stiller, Andy Dick, Janeane Garofalo, and Bob Odenkirk, which was later picked up by the-then fledgling broadcast television network Fox (which first launched in 1986). MTV still predominantly aired music videos at this time, but they were becoming increasingly expensive to produce; music videos were no longer the free content that convinced WASEC's James Robison III to commit $2 million back in 1979 (Tannenbaum and Marks 2011, 513). Many of the top video directors were moving into filmmaking. But the audience's tastes were also changing, as evidenced by the fact that the number of music videos airing on MTV dropped by 36 percent between 1995 and 2000. In a 2001 interview with *Billboard* magazine, then-MTV president Van Toffler explained, "Clearly, the novelty of just showing music videos has worn off. It's required us to reinvent ourselves to a contemporary audience. Music will remain the soul of MTV. . . . What matters most to us is pleasing our audience." This seems to be the lesson MTV executives must relearn every five or ten years: the youth audience is fickle because the moment a company figures out how to create content that pleases them, they age out of that content and fresh content then must be produced anew for the next group of young people (Tannenbaum and Marks 2011). It was time to appeal to the youth audiences who were starting to watch MTV in the 1990s for the first time, as the channel's original audience was aging out of the target demographic.

The End of MTV's Golden Age

Tannenbaum and Marks cite the year 1992 as the end of MTV's "Golden Age," a time in which music videos were MTV's primary content. In order to maintain its youth audience, who were losing interest in music videos, MTV needed to come up with more non-music-based programming options.[23] One tactic MTV sought for increasing viewership was to create some scripted teen dramas. Jonathan Murray and Mary-Ellis Bunim, cocreators of *The Real World*, were looking to produce a scripted drama about young people in the vein of the then-popular teen series *Beverly Hills 90210*. But the costs of creating original scripted programming—including money for writers, actors, and costume designers—was untenable for many independent producers; per-episode costs for scripted dramas ballooned in the 1980s, with above-the-line talent demanding increasingly higher wages. To solve this problem, Bunim and Murray did what so many other TV producers did at the time: they decided to make a reality show. The team drew on Murray's background in broadcast journalism and documentary filmmaking and on Bunim's background working on daytime soap operas (she was executive producer of series like *As the World Turns* and *Santa Barbara*) in order to create a dramatic series that was based on real life, rather than actors and scripts. Out of a pool of five hundred applicants, Murray and Bunim found seven "strangers" and paid them just $2,600 each to appear on the groundbreaking series known as *The Real World* (Blake 2011).

In chapter 2, I offer a detailed history and analysis of *The Real World*'s place in MTV's reality identity cycle as well as a discussion of its significance to the legacy of reality television as a whole. But for the purposes of this chapter's history of MTV, pre-2004, there are just a few things to keep mind about *The Real World*. First, *The Real World* was an outlier at the time of its inception. When the series premiered in 1991, there were no other series like it on MTV or on TV anywhere for that matter. In her succinct *Reality TV* (2012), Misha Kavka calls this era of programming (1989–1999) the first generation of modern reality TV. In this "camcorder era" of reality TV, the genre depended on two new technological developments: closed-circuit television (CCTV) and the home video camcorder. Both inventions provided American consumers with the technology to surveil themselves and others. As a result, US television during the 1980s was populated with tabloid series like *A Current Affair* as well as reality series focusing on crime and law enforcement, like *Cops* and *America's Most Wanted*. All of these programs were constructed out of this newly available surveillance footage. According to Kavka, in this "security-conscious" and "crime-focused" context, there was "a shift away from elite, institutional discourses of the self." That is, ordinary people captured on film speaking in "first person" became a signifier of authenticity (2012, ch. 2). But *The Real World* was different from these other, popular reality TV programs airing on network television because real people *willingly* placed themselves as subjects of a narrative that would later be created in an editing booth (they are not "caught" on camera).

Second, although, relatively speaking, viewership for *The Real World* was not particularly high as compared with other cable channels, it was a large viewership for MTV and the subject of much public discourse on documentary ethics and "kids today." To illustrate, a review by a *New York Times* critic, John J. O'Connor (1992), is representative of the many negative reviews published on other mainstream platforms like *USA Today* and the *Washington Post* about the show's premiere. After praising the series' innovative approach, O'Connor asks, "Should 'The Real World' be kept going much beyond these 13 episodes? I doubt it. There really isn't much happening."[24] There were some positive reviews of the series, such as Ken Tucker's (1992) in *Entertainment Weekly*, in which he opines, "*The Real World* proves to be by far the most beguiling and involving piece of programming MTV has ever offered." But *The Real World* did not gain widespread, national attention until 1994, when it cast a young, Latinx, HIV-positive man named Pedro Zamora to live with the other housemates. During this season, *The Real World* became MTV's highest-rated show, surpassing even *Beavis and Butthead* (Fretts 1995). Finally, the launch of *The Real World* is fascinating because it becomes the moment when MTV first turns to real young people playing themselves, as opposed to scripted content or music videos, to generate content. When the costs of videos, actors, and writers became too high, MTV turned to a cheaper source of entertainment: youth identities. Diversity and difference did the heavy lifting where story and character (which requires more money than the series' producers could afford) could not. *The Real World* is a series that both *predates and, eventually, makes up* MTV's reality identity cycle.

Total Request Live

Although *The Real World* was a success for MTV, overall ratings for the channel declined throughout the 1990s. MTV needed to better understand a new generation of MTV viewers, viewers who were not tuning in to music videos the way Generation X had. In response, the channel began to conduct in-depth ethnographic studies of American teens. *Total Request Live* (TRL), the video countdown program hosted by Carson Daly, which began to air in 1998, was an early application of MTV's audience-based research. Todd Cunningham, who was senior vice president of strategy and planning for MTV during the launch of TRL, explains: "There's no question that research played an integral and driving part in creating that show, in helping to showcase viewers, understanding the role of countdowns, understanding the role of a host who was approachable, who was accessible, who was someone who they believed in" (*Frontline* 2001). The resulting show played the top ten most-requested videos of the day, Monday through Thursday, a playlist determined by MTV's young audience. The show also provided a venue for live performances and celebrity guests promoting new albums, concert tours, or other projects. TRL served the dual function of bringing in viewers *and* providing artists and record labels with free promotions, making it, as *Rolling Stone* reporter Gavin Edwards (2000) put it, "an obligatory stop on a [musician's] promotional tour." But more important to the purposes of this book, TRL demonstrated how much Millennial audiences liked to be active participants in their own media consumption.

TRL was set inside the MTV studios in Times Square. The studio space was surrounded by floor-to-ceiling windows, allowing MTV to show off the massive crowds of screaming fans who would regularly throng Times Square in the hopes of getting a peek at their favorite Top 40 artist. MTV's cameras would often head out to these crowds so that the home audience could see close-ups of fans and their handmade signs professing love for performers like the young men of NSYNC or Christina Aguilera. In this way, TRL allowed fans to be a physical part of the entertainment they consumed. Fans could call in and tell the switchboard operators what their number one video pick was for the day, and their vote *would* count. Or, even better, fans could head to Times Square with a sign that might catch the attention of the cameras (or the artists themselves). By 2000 TRL was MTV's highest-rated daily show and, more important, was the highest-rated cable show for its time slot (Edwards 2000), reviving the ratings-starved channel. As one newspaper put it, "Just a year on the air, 'TRL' is the force behind an MTV ratings renaissance. More than 1 million youngsters tune in at 3:30 p.m. each weekday to hear their favorite music—and often hundreds of fans turn up on the Times Square street below MTV's studio to gape at Daly and his guests" (Bauder 1999). Ron Shapiro, who was the executive vice president of Atlantic Records, describes TRL's value this way: "A decade ago, a hit song on the radio was enough. . . . Now there's the Internet, PlayStations, a hundred channels—too much choice. We don't know where kids are. But I have yet to meet a nine- to sixteen-year-old who doesn't love TRL" (qtd. in Edwards 2000). TRL's influence on the charts was so robust that, according to a *Los Angeles Times* profile, "record companies would do almost anything . . . to get a clip into the daily Top 10 countdown" (Hochman 1999). MTV has

1.4 *Total Request Live* (TRL), the video countdown program hosted by Carson Daly, debuted in 1998.

always tried to generate identification between the performers at the center of their content and their young audiences for the purposes of selling more content (including albums but also artist-oriented swag) (Kaplan 1987, 19). But with the development and success of TRL, the channel was once again helping the record industry sell music to youth audiences.

Much of the rhetoric surrounding TRL, both within and outside MTV, celebrated the show's democratizing power; 1990s pop star Christina Aguilera recalls watching TRL before she was famous and wishing that she could one day appear on the show to promote her music: "I loved the energy and how so many *kids decide what the programming is*" (qtd. in Edwards 2000; emphasis mine). This utopian view of participatory media, with its power to interact, impact, and identify with the cultural products we consume, was common when shows like TRL and *American Idol* were first airing.[25] Nevertheless, as Mark Andrejevic explains, having the power "to decide" (and the very act of framing "choice" or "participation" as a benefit) does come with its costs. When a consumer calls into TRL or logs on to a social media account, in both cases to be heard and seen and to express one's tastes and therefore one's identity, this "laboratory" act also "creates secondary markets for demographic information that has been selected, sorted and packaged by middlemen" (2004, 257). As recent scandals from 2014 to 2018 concerning data breaches at prominent companies like Equifax, Uber, JP Morgan Chase, and Facebook, among others, have made all too clear, the dangers of this consumer model, which turns personal data into commodities, have become real.[26]

In a 1999 *Los Angeles Times* editorial, Cheryl Lu-Lien Tan described TRL as a turning point on MTV, when the channel went from broadcasting the performances of celebrity musicians to broadcasting the performances *of its youth audience*: "The show's cherubic host, Carson Daly, his audience and the thousands of screaming fans lining the streets outside are as important as the videos themselves." Tan does not see TRL as the cause of this shift, but rather as a symptom of MTV's new interests, one which she did not hail as wholly positive: "In the hype-focused culture reflected on MTV, the Everyman has assumed tremendous importance. Everyone is fascinating." Tan's negative view of the democratization of celebrity, which arrived in full force circa 2000 with the rise of unscripted television programming, is hardly unusual for the time, as I will discuss later in this chapter. Aguilera's neat narrative of success that led from watching TRL and dreaming of fame to eventually being on TRL *as* a famous person is not common, of course. But this narrative is at the core of much of MTV's programming at this time. Tan continues: "To this generation of viewers, simply watching the videos is not enough. . . . They want to inject themselves into the picture, too, because hey, who's cooler and more interesting than them?" To quote Cunningham again, a show like TRL helped to "showcase viewers," that is, to place them before the cameras, allowing them to watch themselves, alongside their favorite artists. MTV's ability to put the viewer in the place of the viewed would become central to the appeal of the reality identity cycle in 2004.

The seeds of MTV's reality identity cycle can also be found in the way TRL instructed its young audience members to have a specific kind of taste, to make that taste clear to others, and to also fight for or defend their tastes in the face of others who did not share their opinion. Edwards notes how the TRL countdown was initially dominated by pop acts like Britney Spears, Christina Aguilera, and "the boy bands" (NSYNC, the Backstreet Boys, 98 Degrees), a genre that catered strongly to young, middle-class, white girls. Over time, TRL's content began to change, molded explicitly by the voice of its audience. By 1998, rock bands like Limp Bizkit, Korn, and Blink-182, and rappers like DMX and Eminem, were regularly on the countdown, essentially pitting "pop fans against rock fans," a dichotomy that often boiled down to female fans versus male fans (Tan 1999). Korn fans of the late 1990s likely did not think rock music was something they would have to fight for until MTV provided a venue in which they might do so. In this case, a shared vision of "freedom," power, or "having a voice" led to the creation of identities that are not typically granted status as being legitimate identities. One of the main arguments of this book is that MTV's programming appealed to Millennial audiences in the late 1990s and early 2000s precisely because it provided opportunities to seek out, declare, or defend a new identity.

TRL was canceled in 2008, signaling the fundamental changes that were occurring in the music-video industry, namely that it was difficult to make audiences sit in front of a television waiting for videos to air when that audience knew they could go online and watch any video they liked on emerging platforms like YouTube, Vevo, and Daily Motion (NPR 2008). Van Toffler, then president of Viacom, explains this transition in generational terms: "When you give way from one generation to the next, from Gen X to the Millennials, you are going to see some blip in the ratings" (qtd. in Arango 2009). Toffler ties a drop in the network's ratings to a shift in its core youth demographic, with Millennials replacing Generation X. But some of the lessons learned through TRL's success remained. The tactics MTV employed to lure in its youth audience circa 1981, namely iconoclastic music that separated teenage tastes from that of their parents, were no longer appealing. Millennial youth audiences seemed to crave a different viewing experience. MTV spent the next few years trying to determine what, exactly, that viewing experience was. It is at this key moment that locating and branding youth identities, the living labor that is now so vital to the channel's success, became a central concern and focus for MTV.

Tabloid Celebrity in the 2000s: A Brief Detour

In order to understand the changing audience for MTV and its relationship with media content, it is important to revisit the way the concept of "celebrity" was also shifting in American popular culture at this time. Graeme Turner explains that it is possible to locate the "precise moment a public figure becomes a celebrity" to the moment when media coverage of their private lives exceeds coverage of their body of work (2014, 8). For film actors, this is the moment when the person becomes more interesting than the work they do on screen. As Richard Dyer explains, in his formative study of film stars, "A star image consists both of what we normally refer to as his or her 'image,' made up of screen roles and obviously stage-managed public appearances, and also of images of the manufacture of that 'image,' and of the real person who is the site or occasion of it" (1986, 7–8). In the context of reality television, the shift from public figure to celebrity creates a paradox: if the appeal of reality television is that it provides access to the real lives of ordinary people, what happens when ordinary people become celebrities for being "themselves"? Erin Meyers (2014) studies this phenomenon, noting that the tabloid's celebration of the "ordinary" person as "celebrity" poses a challenge to the reality series' goal of making the subject appear ordinary and relatable, which "has prompted a shift in the notions of 'private' and 'ordinary' within reality television." *Teen Mom*'s Amber Portwood is an "ordinary" woman, but the frame of reality television—the presence of cameras, microphones, nondiegetic music, and coherent editing—transforms the chaos of real life into a clear, emotionally resonant narrative. Meyers (2013) notes it is no coincidence that the rise of reality television and what she calls "private side discourses" circling around its stars in the late 1990s and early 2000s coincided with the expansion of print tabloid magazines like *Star, People, Us Weekly,* and *In Touch*. At this time, reality television and the tabloids existed in a mutually beneficial relationship wherein one industry fed on and perpetuated the other.[27] Reality television offered print journalists, and the paparazzi who supply their images, a new, seemingly endless well of stories to cover. The circulation and proliferation of print tabloids increased over the last two decades, in direct correlation to the popularity of reality television stars. For example, celebrity gossip magazine *Star* saw a 50 percent increase in subscriptions between 2003 and 2004 (Story 2005). This increase is especially noteworthy because the market for tabloids was in decline at the time.

A prime example of a seemingly talentless individual (one who does not sing, act, dance, or perform a skill) who became a "celebrity" just by being "herself" is Paris Hilton, a wealthy heir to the hotel magnate's fortune and an object of pop-culture fascination in the early 2000s.[28] In 2003 Hilton was a frequent paparazzi subject due to her partying, a leaked sex tape entitled *One Night in Paris* (2004), and a costarring role in the reality series *The Simple Life*. She was the first of many "ordinary" women who became celebrities due solely to their cultural visibility; Hilton was "famous for being famous." Julie Wilson notes that this new model of celebrity—of "famous for being famous"—was tied to a new way of thinking about the self. In being famous, reality TV celebrities acted as a how-to manual for becoming famous and audiences could consume this form of celebrity as entertainment but also as *instruction* (2014, 422). Appearing on *The Simple Life* accelerated and further refined Hilton's tabloid identity as an out-of-touch rich girl, and vice versa. Over the course of the series, Hilton and her costar, Nicole Richie, also playing the role of an out-of-touch rich girl (but with sharper edges), were filmed working a string of low-wage jobs: milking cows, flipping burgers, and auctioning cattle.[29] While performing these tasks, the women were usually dressed in expensive, designer clothing (always highly inappropriate for the task at hand) and loudly complaining about the indignity of the work they were performing as their coworkers (who actually did the work for a living) look on. The girls feigned ignorance over how "common" Americans lived, disingenuously asking if Walmart "sells walls" and if a grocery store sells clothing by the high-end designers Marc Jacobs and Chanel. Hilton's appeal was rooted in her embrace of her own wealth and dismissal of those who lacked it. This spectacle of white privilege would eventually become a liability in the wake of the 2008 Great Recession, but in the early 2000s, it was still charming enough to keep *The Simple Life* on the air for five seasons. The success of MTV's reality identity series is, in part, indebted to this intertwined relationship between reality TV and the tabloids; cast members on MTV series like *The Hills, Jersey Shore,* and *Teen Mom* appeared on the covers of print magazines like *Star, Us Weekly,* and *In Touch.* And the tabloids certainly benefited from MTV's series as well.[30] The private lives of reality TV stars—which are their public lives as well as their star identities—provided an endless stream of content.

Reality TV on MTV

As discussed earlier in this chapter, when ratings declined in the 1990s, MTV turned to the findings of the nearly two hundred studies it conducted about Millennial youth. One key finding was that this new generation of viewers loved to be on camera. Todd Cunningham explained, "Young people today are not the least bit afraid or ashamed to be in front of a camera. You put a camera in front of them and they're ready to be a star, just fascinated to be a celebrity" (*Frontline* 2001). This willingness to be recorded and studied was perhaps the network's first clue that reality television series featuring casts made up of individuals mirroring MTV viewers in age, temperament, and concerns might be exactly what MTV viewers wanted to see. Millennials, who came of age during the rise of social media, have been groomed for a life of performing for the gaze and consumption of others (Jayson 2007). They are comfortable projecting themselves into the world or, as Laura Grindstaff describes it, "self mediating" via social media, personal blogs, selfies, and, in the case of MTV programming, through winning a spot on a reality television show (2011a, 205). Information and communication technologies (ICTs), particularly social media, enable users to express their personal opinions and, just as important, consume the personal opinions of others. As a result, Millennials, more so than any previous generation, have had the opportunity to observe a wide variety of identities or have access to platforms from which and through which they can express these identities.

Some of the earliest unscripted content to appear on the channel after MTV conducted their in-depth ethnographies of Millennial youth were programs like *True Life, Jackass, Cribs, Sorority Life, Punk'd, Fraternity Life, Made, Making the Band, Surf Girls,* and *Rich Girls* (*Boston Herald* 2003).[31] The channel also dabbled in the wave of "celebreality" programming that was successful on other networks, with series like *The Osbournes, Run's House,* and *Newlyweds: Nick and Jessica* and its spin-off, *The Ashlee Simpson Show.*[32] It is worth noting that, around the same time that MTV was rolling out its unscripted programming, Black Entertainment Television (BET), a Viacom-owned cable network devoted to programming made for African American audiences, was doing the same (Klein 2009a). In other words, just as MTV was creating content that reified whiteness and white identity, BET was providing content that offered a similar viewing position for its primarily Black audiences.[33] For the sake of space, I will limit my discussions of MTV's earliest reality programs to just a few that are representative of series that are *direct precursors* to the start of MTV's reality identity cycle in 2004. The series that serve as blueprints for the reality identity cycle's later success center on the "ordinary celebrity," as articulated by Meyers, Wilson, and Grindstaff. In particular, MTV series like *Made, Rich Girls,* and *Sorority Life* work to codify identities claimed by the subjects or to train subjects to fit the contours of an identity they long to claim.

Case Study: *Made*

Made appeared on MTV's schedule in the early 2000s, during a general wave of reality gamedocs that centered around the display of an elite skill set.[34] In addition to their competition format (based primarily on the idea of weekly eliminations), these gamedocs demonstrated that certain careers take skill and time, *while also* instructing audiences on how to attain or at least mimic a similar set of skills (in far less time). The aforementioned series tell audiences that reality TV can make us into something else, something better, by showing us aspects of our identities that were previously hidden, or by helping us to develop newer and better identities. Laurie Ouellette began noticing a trend in reality TV of "do good" TV, or reality TV programming that aims to provide audiences with the knowledge or skills needed "to make the best choices in the service of their own well-being" in an ownership society. Shows like *The Biggest Loser* or *Extreme Makeover: Home Edition* train audiences to lose weight or renovate their homes. This programming "reveals the duties, pressures and instructions for the care of the self" (2006). MTV's programming in the early to mid-2000s similarly takes up the project of the care of the self, only tailored specifically to the needs of the teenage consumer. MTV's turn to reality programming mirrors the larger trend of what Misha Kavka describes as programming that promoted "the idea that something real could be gained from watching people labor under artificial constraints" (2012, 73), aka the second generation (1999–2005) of reality TV.

Made's opening credits feature different young people looking directly at the camera and proclaiming, "I wanna be *made*." In MTV's *Made*, everyday teens—who are out of shape, unpopular, clumsy, manic, and/or awkward—gain the opportunity to become the identity they most want to be (every episode uses the same line, spoken by each character, "If I could be made into one thing, it would be . . ."). This serves as the individual's moment of identity confession, or at least the moment where they admit to what identity they *wish* to claim. *Made* also revolves around careers or skills that, as almost every *Made* coach ever employed has admitted, takes a lifetime of work to perfect. Yet the series only allots about six weeks for the subject to master his or her new skill or identity. In *Made*, cast members have a few weeks to work with a special trainer who will help them transform into a new identity like a "cheerleader," a "BMX biker," a "homecoming queen," a "ladies' man," a "skater chick," and a "girly girl." In this way *Made* represents an opposing narrative to this genre of specialization embodied by competition series like *American Idol* or *The Apprentice*. *Made* posits that maybe the special and talented people on the television are not so special after all, or rather that with hard work, perseverance, a good attitude, and sincerity (traits the *Made* coaches consistently mention as either being present or lacking in their current apprentices), any "average Joe-teen" can be special, too (and on television). In her groundbreaking work on makeover TV, Brenda Weber argues that on these types of shows the self is defined by what one has the capacity to be, what she calls "the emerging self," rather than what one is (2009, 5). This emerging self becomes an ideal text to study because, as Weber notes, "makeovers intervene with class, race, and gender-inflected 'improvements' that gain legitimacy by speaking through the idiom of identity" (5). Preceding ratings leaders like *The Swan* and *The Biggest Loser*, *Made* is one of the earliest reality programs to highlight the neoliberal project of the self and the push to self-brand, by helping the subjects become the best version of themselves.

Of particular interest to the reality identity cycle's genealogy is *Made*'s focus on specific identity groups, like extreme sports enthusiasts (BMX bikers, snowboarders, skateboarders) or Black-oriented cultural performers (breakdancers and rappers). These episodes tell the narrative of an individual seemingly at odds with this subculture acquiring a (forced) admittance, culminating with a spectacle of co-optation, which MTV's audience is meant to see as a success. In this climactic scene, the subject "officially" performs their made-ness, followed by conclusions and analysis by the *Made* coach, the subject, and the subject's community. Most *Made* episodes aim to establish, quickly and clearly, who the subject is and why they are so far from their goal identity. For instance, in a season 6 episode entitled "Rapper," a bespectacled, awkward, teenage boy named Niles wishes to be made into a "battle rapper." In Niles's case, the contrast between dream identity and real identity is easy to make because he already fits into an identity category (white, middle-class, Jewish, and nonthreatening) that is both visually and culturally different from the one to which he aspires (Black, working-class, intimidating). Niles's peers disparage his dream to be a battle rapper based primarily on his identity, calling him "DJ Synagogue" and "DJ Dreidel." Though the degrees of "success" vary from episode to episode, the lesson of *Made* remains consistent: it is possible to assume any identity that is presented via popular culture, as long as the subject is willing to work hard and commit to their coach's instructions and then allow MTV to document it.

Case Study: *Rich Girls*

Like *Made*, *Rich Girls*, which debuted on MTV in 2003, is also about wish fulfillment and fantasy, albeit through very different methods. *Rich Girls* was a scripted reality series following the lives of Ally Hilfiger, the daughter of the famous designer and fashion-label owner Tommy Hilfiger, and Jaime Gleicher, an heir to a $10 million fortune. *Rich Girls* existed to showcase the massive class differences between wealthy people like Hilfiger and Gleicher and everybody else. *Rich Girls* was released in this environment of loving and hating the rich on reality TV (see also *The Simple Life*). Initial reviews of *Rich Girls* linked its cast members' performances and the "spoiled antics of heiresses on camera" to earlier incarnations like the Hiltons and Kardashians. An article about the series in October 2003 is characteristic of the series framing: "Two wealthy young women dash around New York City, mindlessly spending money while TV cameras follow them. . . . But they're not the notorious Hilton sisters. They're Ally Hilfiger and Jamie Gleicher, the teenage stars of MTV's latest reality series, 'Rich Girls'" (McFarland 2003). *Rich Girls* is watchable because its cast members say and do things that audiences love to hate: they are narcissistic, entitled, and clueless about the way the world functions differently for the obscenely wealthy.[35] MTV encouraged this viewing position with the series description on its website: "Get a firsthand look at their super-fabulous life when MTV follows two of the wealthiest teens on the planet to see how they spend their mountains of money." The series, which only lasted one season, focuses on the summer after the girls graduate from high school: they go to prom, shop in dozens of high-end boutiques across New York City, and vacation in Nantucket and the West Indies.

Public discourses naturally focused on the show's contribution to a larger trend on television of depicting young and wealthy characters. A sampling of national headlines about the series premiere in October 2003 highlight this focus: "Clueless Rich Girls Take Primetime by Storm"; "With a Rich Girl Here and a Rich Girl There"; ""Puttin' on the Rich: The New Trend in Following the Money Is with a TV Camera"; "Poor Little Rich Kids: Wealthy Offspring Flaunt Riches with Little Sympathy"; "Heir Heads—Reality TV Is Obsessed with People Trying to Get Rich"; and "Specials on HBO and MTV May Be a Little Too Rich for Some Viewers."[36] The appeal of *Rich Girls* is the subjects' astounding wealth and their blasé attitude toward their wealth. Being rich is effortless and fun, and the audience gets to watch, feel envy, and maybe also enjoy the schadenfreude that comes from seeing people embarrass themselves on television. François Jost attributes the popularity of series like *The Simple Life* to how it "provides by proxy a popular vengeance: the stars are deposed from Olympe, decreased, and undergo work as a punishment" (2011, 41). Similarly, part of the appeal of *Rich Girls* is the way the girls embarrass themselves by revealing their ignorance of the world or their petty concerns. Although it was canceled after one season, several aspects of *Rich Girls* would go on to form the template for future MTV reality identity series: the focus on an insulated community, the maintenance of the fourth wall, and building a series around the strong (and often off-putting) personalities of the cast members. Although early press placed the series in the genealogy of celebreality, the series is very much a precursor of *Laguna Beach* and *The Hills*.[37]

MTV's *Sorority Life* also offers a profile of a particular identity—that of the college sorority pledge enrolled at University of California at Davis circa 2002. During the pledging process, a group of differentiated people are asked to form a group identity (i.e., the pledge class). The pledge process is about declaring loyalty, physically, mentally, and emotionally, to a single identity, the sisterhood. Sigma Alpha Epsilon Pi, the sorority profiled in *Sorority Life*, is interesting in this regard because it is small compared to other sororities at UC Davis, and, therefore, the group has heretofore been unaccustomed to having their pick of rushees. Many of the sisters (correctly) attribute the abundance of new potential pledges to the presence of MTV's cameras. Since the sorority already had a clear identity for itself before the arrival of MTV's cameras—it was founded to provide a community for Jewish women on campus—the main narrative in *Sorority Life* is figuring out which women are there to become pledges and which women are there just to be on MTV. For example, Becca, the Sigma Alpha Epsilon Pi pledge master, describes the new pledges as "pretty and blonde and tall" and worries that these identities might be "different from the majority of the girls we have right now." Here the camera cuts to a wall on which there are several group pictures of the Sigma sisters, who appear to be mostly dark-haired and petite. As if to put a point on it, there is a Star of David nestled among these pictures. What Becca is describing, but what she cannot quite articulate directly, is that none of these potential pledges are Jewish (or even Jewish-looking), but they are still rushing a Jewish-identified sorority. The sisters of Sigma want to build a pledge class of committed young women, but this is at odds with the needs of the reality TV production.

Laura Grindstaff, who was employed by UC Davis when *Sorority Life* filmed there, had the opportunity to interview many of the young women involved in the series. She found that many of them wanted to be on a reality show, not to become a Sigma or even to be famous: "A structural tension existed between [pledges and sisters] that was amplified if not wholly introduced by the fact that the pledge process was being taped for television" (2014, 335). This ambiguity dogs the series but also offers a useful way of understanding how MTV saw identity through the lens of reality TV, and how this would later be developed in the reality identity cycle. The pledge process is traditionally about molding a group of individuals to simulate the values of the larger organization, but due to the presence of MTV's cameras, the series instead highlighted the various, competing identities appearing on camera. In order to make filming and storytelling manageable, MTV placed just six of Sigma's new pledge class into their own *Real World*–style house, an act that opposes the very purpose of pledging: to create a shared sense of identity among the group of strangers. Thus, identities are established early and clearly in the series: Jordan is a tomboy who has never had many female friends; Jessica is overweight and Latinx and therefore believes she could bring a "different perspective" to the sorority; and Mara's chronic sports injuries mean she has to abandon one identity (a UC Davis gymnast) and take on a new one (a Sigma). Five of the six are white. Thus, as Grindstaff notes, "Being white and middle class, they felt free to represent no one but themselves in their pursuit of media exposure" (2014, 336). Those five women ultimately used the experience of being on the show as a personal life experience (or an opportunity to break into the world of entertainment), rather than as a way to speak for their identity community. By contrast, Jessica felt the burden of her identity (Latinx) during the production and consequently tried to behave in a manner that might best represent her identity group on television (336). Participants like pledge Jessica and sister Becca participate in the hopes that the experience will serve to offer better representation of their identities (as Latinx or Jews), while the other white cast members on *Sorority Life* were there to be on TV. *Sorority Life* thus offers a preview of the way MTV offered nonwhite cast members limited parameters for their identity, while white cast members retained the "right to be various" (Dyer 1997, 49).

After the release of *Sorority Life*, MTV released more reality series, all profiling a specific youth identity (wealthy teenagers, aspiring models, profane young men, and pregnant teenagers), including *Laguna Beach: The Real OC, My Super Sweet Sixteen, 8th & Ocean, The Hills, From Gs to Gents, 16 and Pregnant*, and *Teen Mom*. In 2008 *The Hills* became MTV's and basic cable's highest-rated program (Gorman 2008). In 2010, MTV officially dropped "Music Television" from its corporate logo. Just three decades after the channel was first launched in 1981 as a twenty-four-hour music-video jukebox, showing its target youth audience the music, slang, and fashion that defined a generation, it transitioned into an identity workbook, in the form of reality TV, that offered youth audiences (aka Millennials) different ways to be and exist in an increasingly identity-focused world. MTV, which had always been about courting youth audiences, was officially out of the music video business and in the reality TV business.[38]

Conclusions

While it is impossible to create blanket definitions about groups of people who happen to have been born at the same time and in the same place, I have laid out how the radical changes in MTV's programming are tied to generational shifts and the kinds of technology available to them. Millennials' view of their experiences in and expectations of the world are largely conditioned by having come of age during the dawn of social media. Millennial consumers seek out consumption experiences that are shareable, tweetable, Instagram-able, and Snapchat-able. With its reality identity cycle, MTV found a way to let Millennials be the star of the content they consume, as they consume it. MTV was exploiting a trend that would dominate the market's approach to Millennials. Whether it's social media, "made-for-Instagram" exhibits, selfie sticks, or MTV programming, it is clear that the cultural products made for Millennial youth have centered around fulfilling a single need: the need to define identity and to make it knowable through technology.[39] These products attempt to answer these questions: Who am I? What do I stand for? How do I express that identity to others? This drive was central to the launch of MTV back in 1981, but the first time MTV attempted to analyze and codify identities was in *The Real World* in 1992. In the next chapter I trace the roots of *The Real World* and chat with the series cocreator and coproducer, Jonathan Murray, as well as two former *Real World* cast members, Irene McGee and Paula Maronek, whose identities are still understood in the cultural zeitgeist through the way they were defined when they were in their early twenties.[40] I demonstrate that *The Real World* introduced the all-important concept of "diversity" to MTV's audiences, defining it as a racial, ethnic, sexual, or gendered difference that primarily exists to help white, straight, cisgendered Americans to understand them, and not the other way around.

"This Is the True Story . . ."

The Real World and MTV's Turn to Identity

T‌*he Real World* was released in the wake of intense ideological debates about identity in American life revolving around race (the Rodney King beating [1991], the Los Angeles protests in response to the Rodney King verdict [1992], increasing fears over the alleged criminality of urban Black youth sparked by the crack cocaine epidemic [circa 1981–1990s]), gender (Clarence Thomas's Supreme Court confirmation hearings and the national conversation about sexual harassment [1991], the "Year of the Woman" in Congress [1992], the beginning of Third Wave feminism), and sexual expression (the end of the "free love" movement of the 1960s and 1970s, the beginning of the AIDS epidemic [circa 1981]). Therefore, when the series premiered on MTV in 1992, it promised viewers a rare opportunity to see American youth grapple with the very questions of racial, gendered, and sexual identity and difference that contemporary Americans were struggling to articulate. Indeed, *The Real World* always opens with the same statement, with different cast members reciting a few words each: "This is the true story of seven strangers picked to live in a house and find out what happens when people stop being nice and start getting real." The series exposed a generation of (mostly white, mostly middle-class, mostly suburban)

American youth (ages twelve to thirty-four in 1992) to a variety of identities that they might not otherwise encounter in their daily, more segregated lives. Henry Jenkins describes reality television as "a mediated space that offers audiences a chance to see different people performing themselves on and off stage and to see themselves at the same time" (2006, 129). *The Real World*, and the dozens of identity-focused reality series that MTV eventually created following its success, gave its young audiences a point of entry into their own identities. In particular, *The Real World* operates under the premise that it is only necessary for individuals to claim, name, and explain their identities to others (and in front of a camera) for there to be understanding and discourse. This particular approach was further codified in the 2000s via social media and rising reality television consumption, and it accounts for the success of later MTV programs like *The Hills* and *Jersey Shore*.

When asked about how he approached casting the first few seasons of *The Real World* with his late partner, Mary-Ellis Bunim, Jonathan Murray told me that the concept of what he calls "diversity" was always central to casting decisions. *The Real World* was premised on the belief that casting a diversity of identities is enough to generate a compelling, serialized narrative filled with tensions, conflicts, and important social messages for its audience: "I think it's healthy to live in a diverse world. It's healthy to interact with a diverse group of people; I think you grow a lot. And for us that growth isn't always neat and clean. It's messy and, quite honestly, messy growth is good television." *The Real World* proved that casting a diversity of youth identities, and watching them interact, was an inexpensive and compelling television formula. Historically, the series' most explosive interactions were rooted in race-based conflict, often with a white roommate consciously or unconsciously uttering a racial slur. These moments are cathartic but not necessarily redemptive. Jon Kraszewski argues that on *The Real World*, particularly in the first half of its time on air, conversations about topics like race rarely lead to any discernible change. Instead, the series "portray[s] race as a project of self-management where individuals would rely upon themselves, not the government and the welfare state, to succeed in society" (2010, 140). Some examples include Julie Gentry, a white woman, asking Heather Gardner, who is Black, if her beeper meant she was a drug dealer in season 1 (New York); Davis Mallory, who is white, calling his Black roommate, Tyrie Ballard, a "n*gger" during a drunken, late-night fight in season 18 (Denver); or white cast member Jordan Wiseley making "monkey noises" intended as a racial slur against his Black roommates, Nia Moore and Marlon Williams, in season 28 (Portland). In all cases there were tears, confessions before the camera, and (occasionally sincere) apologies.

The Real World's emphasis on confession and visible suffering functions according to the codes of the melodrama in that these actions are characterized by the belief that guilt and innocence can be uncovered, displayed, and rendered unambiguous. According to Linda Williams, the protagonist of the melodrama, much like the defendant of the courtroom drama, must undergo a visible trial or ordeal for the "truth" of his or her guilt or innocence to be understood by the jury or audience (1998, 81). Thus, revelation and testimony become primary markers of authenticity in series like *The Real World*. The serious conversations about identity generated by the series' premise are also intended to be a learning experience for audiences, which might then "induce attitudinal and behavioral changes in targeted audiences" (Ouellette 2018, 152). How *The Real World* constructs what racism looks like is the way the series pins intolerance to identity. One is racist because one is from the South. One is sexist because one is a male jock. One is homophobic because one is a Christian. This shorthand facilitates the series' narrative economy and allows cast members to serve as synecdoches for their identity groups and their presumed belief systems. Intolerance is often positioned as something that cannot be helped, and the solutions offered to the problem of intolerance are always individual-based, never systemic (Kraszewski 2017, 208).

This chapter asserts that *The Real World*, which premiered in 1992, popularized the format of first-person confessional reality TV and set the stage for the fascination with and normalization of the culture of self-branding and self-disclosure that characterizes Millennial youth culture and its popular discourses, particularly MTV's reality programming, in the 2000s. It is devoted exclusively to the history, origins, and antecedents of *The Real World* and how this series set the stage for the boom in identity programming that MTV fostered and from which it profited throughout the early 2000s and 2010s. This history and analysis are supplemented by interviews I conducted with *The Real World*'s cocreator, Jonathan Murray, who is one of the series' strongest advocates; Irene McGee, an alum of *The Real World: Seattle*, who is also one of the series' strongest critics; and Paula Beckert (formally Meronek), an alum of *The Real World: Key West* and multiple seasons of MTV's *The Challenge*. Beckert's testimony offers an interesting counterpoint to the interviews I conducted with both McGee and Murray.

When I asked Jonathan Murray about which TV series inspired the creation of *The Real World*, he cited the documentary *7 Up!* (Paul Almond, 1964) and the films in the *Up* series that followed it. The first film in this series followed the lives of twenty seven-year-old British children, chosen to represent a variety of social classes. Michael Apted, who went on to direct the rest of the *Up* series, claimed to have been inspired to get involved with the project based on Francis Xavier's claim, "Give me a child until he is seven and I will give you the man" (qtd. in Fox 2015). After the initial film was released on the British channel ITV, Apted returned to the same original subjects once every seven years. The most recent entry in the series, released in 2019, chronicles the lives of the participants at age sixty-three. Reflecting on the series, Murray told me, "If you look at the first *7 Up* series, they brought all these little kids together from different socioeconomic backgrounds; they bring them together to meet each other, to shoot their opening sequence—and then they flash to each kid in their home in their home community and they do their little bio package, which is what reality TV shows do today." Like Apted, Bunim and Murray originally planned to bring together a (limited) range of identities (rich, poor, urban, rural) and document them over time in order to see what this experimental structure might reveal about the clash of these diverse identities. Both projects also employ the "objective" documentary camera to uncover the hidden beliefs inside and between human subjects.

Of course, the term "reality TV" was not used to denote this type of content until the late 1980s, when nonfiction programming became a cost-cutting strategy to counter economic shifts in the TV industry (including the rising costs of production, a glut in programming, and labor unrest, leading to the 1988 Writers' Guild strike).[1] Jon Kraszewski warns that TV scholars have "projected the category of reality television onto texts" of the past but he also notes that "the fact that these programs were classified through other genres when they were initially released does not disqualify them from historical analysis as reality television programs" (2017, 16–17). Indeed, retroactively labeling some pre-1980s nonfiction TV as "reality TV" will allow me to reconstruct the programming that set the stage for MTV's reality identity cycle decades later.[2] To that end, I begin my prehistory of *The Real World* with Allen Funt's *Candid Camera*, one of the earliest examples of American reality TV programming.[3] Hidden-camera series like *Candid Camera* and *Truth or Consequences* created simulated situations to see how everyday people would react within them.[4] Anna McCarthy finds that the first American TV audiences saw this programming as a high-minded use of modern technology for the greater good that was "understood as working in the service of socially liberal models of culture" (2009, 26). This use of hidden cameras could promote model forms of citizenship by showing how people act in group situations; it was a way to learn about human behavior and a model for teaching viewers what to do or not do. In this context, TV was a tool for the production of social knowledge, if wielded properly.

Hidden camera–based programming appeared on television at a time when American audiences were seeking out more realist forms of entertainment as they grappled with the ethical questions that arose as a result of the unthinkable atrocities of World War II, like "What would cause a person to join the Nazi party?" or "What would drive the US government to obliterate two Japanese cities with the atomic bomb"? Voyeurism was the answer to many of these big questions. As Misha Kavka details in her history of reality TV, Funt's work made the idea of surveillance feel less like a threat and more like entertainment (2012, ch. 1). Hidden cameras and carefully controlled scenarios would help Americans know the unknowable. This new use of TV promised to unlock the secrets to human behavior, both good and evil, and this knowledge might lead to some control over an uncertain world. Thus, even in its earliest days, there was a fine line between television and the social sciences, between entertainment and education, between exploitation and social betterment, between reality TV and documentary, an opposition Neil Harris has called the "operational aesthetic," or the tension between the educating and entertaining aspects of a text (1981, 57).

The 1948 premiere of *Candid Camera* marked the moment when TV became a location where popular culture and social science overlapped. Prominent social psychologists of the time, such as Stanley Milgram, the lead researcher behind the notorious Yale obedience experiments, expressed interest in Funt's work. In 1977, Milgram even wrote a paper about *Candid Camera*, citing its value for understanding human behavior in controlled circumstances. Similarly, Philip Zimbardo, (in)famous for conducting the Stanford prison experiment in 1971, compared Funt to Sigmund Freud, while Cornell social psychologist James Maas convinced Funt to donate *Candid Camera* footage to the university so that it could be studied (Kavka 2012, ch. 1). *Candid Camera*'s mission of finding out "what happens when" offers the patina of scientific legitimacy because it's not just entertainment, it's also *science*. According to Jon Kraszewski, *Candid Camera* "was part of a post–World War II television cultural moment that embraced the medium

2.1 Allen Funt's *Candid Camera* was one of the earliest examples of American "reality TV" programming.

for its ability to convey realism, but *Candid Camera* challenged what realism was and how real life could operate" (2017, 26). This postwar context, in which documentary technology is associated with truth, shaped the way audiences understood a program like *Candid Camera*.

Candid Camera's success and positive reception was therefore inextricable from postwar America's newfound obsession with unlocking the motivations behind why people do what they do, to learn about people in ways that would have been impossible prior to the development of lighter, cheaper, and more portable 16-mm cameras, and portable sound equipment, such as the Nagra tape recorder. These new technologies, developed during World War II, fostered a concomitant desire to capture the reality of the world, without the interference of large, unwieldy equipment (Kraszewski 2017, 36). The technological developments that allowed Allen Funt to hide cameras in public mailboxes, also enabled journalists like Edward R. Murrow to produce made-for-television exposé documentaries on major social crises like the Red Scare and the war in Korea for *See It Now*, which was itself an adaptation of the radio series *Hear It Now*. CBS also created a series of game shows that manipulated the new mass medium of television to make human subjects knowable to the American viewing audience.[5] Series like *What's My Line, I've Got a Secret*, and *To Tell the Truth* addressed the demand for truth, voyeurism, and the revelation of previously hidden aspects of human character (McCarthy 2009, 27). More and more American homes had televisions in the 1950s, firmly linking the burgeoning medium with other democratizing technologies of the postwar era (Kraszewski 2017, 30).

In addition to the *Up* series, Jonathan Murray cited *An American Family* (1973) as a major influence on *The Real World*. *An American Family* focused on the Louds, a white, upper-middle-class family of seven who lived in Santa Barbara, California. According to a PBS press release, the series offered "a unique panorama of contemporary American life" (qtd. in Ruoff 2002, xxii). Producer Craig Gilbert's approach to his subjects was influenced by nonfiction writers like Joan Didion, Truman Capote, and Norman Mailer, whose profiles of their subjects went beyond a mere recording of facts and explored the so-called hidden nature of the subjects being profiled. This, too, was Gilbert's goal as he filmed the Loud family for seven months. For example, unlike *Candid Camera* or Milgram's infamous experiments, *An American Family* documents its subjects within their homes (Kavka 2012, ch. 1). Gilbert, sound and camera engineers Susan and Alan Raymond, and the rest of the crew worked in the Loud home for seven months, incorporated into the rhythms of the family's daily existence. Because the participants in a documentary or a reality series are, to use Bill Nichols's term, "social actors," rather than actual actors, there is always the potential exploitation of the subject (2001, 9), and *An American Family* was no exception. The commercial needs of TV are, in many cases, at odds with the discourse of sobriety and its implied objectivity. For example, many viewers and critics attributed the breakdown of the Loud marriage to the presence of the TV cameras and crew, despite the fact that both Pat and Bill claim that their marriage was rocky well before the cameras began rolling (Nichols 2001, 6; see also Ruoff 2002, 111). By bringing a camera *into the home*, the series rendered the boundary between private and public spaces more tenuous than ever. Indeed, the series raised questions about the ethics of this kind of production. At what point do these relationships break down and how will that alter the documentary? Likewise, how does the act of filmmaking impact the lives of the subjects?

The first episode of *An American Family* aired January 11, 1973, in the 9 p.m. slot and ran for twelve weeks. It was a massive hit for PBS, averaging ten million viewers per episode, the highest ratings of the decade for a public television series. During our interview Jonathan Murray recalled the impact the PBS series had on him when he was growing up: "I thought it was fascinating to see how the filmmakers [behind *An American Family*] made a dramatic series, about this family's life, how they edited it together in different episodes. They went about filming the typical American family, having no idea how this would mirror American society in the 70s, with the breakdown of the American family, kids coming out of the closet, divorce . . ." Over the course of the series, Bill's interest in his work and inability to see that his wife was unhappy clashed with Pat's desire for a more emotionally fulfilling and exciting life, culminating in their separation and divorce. Bill's inability to understand the interior lives and identities of his own family also manifested itself in his disputes with Kevin over his future career; Kevin wanted to please his father but also had no desire to enter Bill's strip-mining business. And, to be sure, Lance's decision to move to New York and live in the Chelsea Hotel, as well as his fashion choices and mannerisms, all signified aspects of a gay identity in the 1970s. In *An American Family*, every subject had a clearly defined story arc and was a well-formed character who interacted and generated drama over the course of the reality TV season.

An American Family provided PBS audiences with an opportunity to consume a documentary profile of an American family as if it were a fictional series; real lives were converted into a spectacle for the audience's entertainment. As Susan Murray notes in her essay on the intersection of documentary and reality TV in *An American Family*, the series carried a "social weight" inherited from its public television context and its claims to documentary realism, "a rhetorical stance that can be mobilized in an effort to endorse or authenticate a particular television text and attract an audience who cherishes liberal notions of social responsibility or public service" (2009, 44). The series overtly laid claim to scientific standards by asking cultural anthropologist Margaret Mead to watch and review the series for *TV Guide*. Not surprisingly, Mead's high-profile endorsement was used in PBS's publicity materials for the series and highlights a long-standing trend in conceptualizations of a particular brand of reality TV: the belief that its controversial existence is justified by its perceived prosocial or scientific pur-

2.2 Jonathan Murray cited *An American Family,* which chronicled the lives of the Louds, a Caucasian, upper-middle-class family of seven, as a major influence on *The Real World.*

pose (42–43). *An American Family* also mimicked Bill Nichols's "discourse of sobriety," in which "style is second to content" and objectivity is stressed, to appeal to viewers' ideas about what "authenticity" looks like (2001, 166). For example, according to Susan Raymond, the sound recordist for the 1973 series, "We really believed rigidly in 'fly on the wall' observation. It's a very Zen exercise to diminish your presence as best you can" (qtd. in Kraszewski 2017, 36). Jon Kraszewski argues that in replicating the "style and philosophy" of Direct Cinema, *An American Family* marked the moment when the new genre of reality television moved "away from the authored world of Allen Funt to an authorless world where cast members become more known than producers" (2017, 47).[6] The "fly on the wall" approach to the subject resulted in aligning personality and character development with the developing genre of reality television.

In his book-length study of the PBS series, Jeffrey Ruoff (2002) describes *An American Family* as being controversial at the time of its release. Reviews and editorials in prominent mainstream publications ranging from *Time* magazine to *Newsweek* to *The Atlantic* fretted over what *An American Family* was revealing about hot-button issues in America like the rising divorce rate, the generation gap, the sexual revolution, and the state of the (middle-class, white) American family (105–107). A review in *Time* argued that *An American Family* was an indication of the nation's "compulsion to confess" (106), while a review in *The Atlantic* claimed that the Louds were a "a symbol of the disintegration and purposeless[ness] in American life" (112). In a logical Catch-22, the Louds were characterized as being deviant for agreeing to participate in the series, while much of this criticism *also* implied that participating in the series is what *made* them deviant. This push and pull between empathy and revulsion, identification and critique, may be one of *An American Family*'s strongest legacies passed down to *The Real World*. Complex people were converted into simpler, more TV-friendly versions of themselves so that they could appear as characters, to love and to hate, in a real-life soap opera. In 1992, *The Real World* would employ the same strategy, eschewing the cost of writers and actors, and rely on the natural drama generated by human bodies when they are placed into a shared space, along with a camera and sound crew.

Producing the Real

At the time of *The Real World*'s release, reality television was primarily represented by true-crime series like *Cops* and *America's Most Wanted*, which relied on footage from closed-circuit television or handheld cameras. Sensational, commercial, and potentially exploitative or manipulative infotainment series like *Hard Copy* and *A Current Affair* also relied on the covert camcorder footage sent in by viewers, in addition to covering celebrity news and some current events. Kavka labels the years 1989–1999 as reality TV's first generation, the "camcorder era." This era is marked by the deregulation of the government and the rise of neoliberalism (as characterized by the policies of Ronald Reagan), a focus on the linked ideas of security and surveillance, and a series of production-based crises (such as the 1988 Writers Guild strike) (Kavka 2012, ch. 1). Jon Dovey (2000) theorizes that, at this moment in television history, the interaction between camera and subject is "fundamentally altered" (61) due to the development of inexpensive portable recording technology. This relationship was now shifted from being "predicated on a subject outnumbered and physically intimidated by the apparatus to one based upon a more equal footing" (61). Dovey explains that because the apparatus was smaller, it was less threatening and more integrated into everyday life, effectively normalizing the act of recording "everyday people," turning those recordings into a form of entertainment. Television was no longer the province of a select, elite group of entertainers. Misha Kavka describes this shift as a moment when the "'truth' seemed to be spoken no longer by those in power, but by ordinary people speaking in the 'first person'" (2012, ch. 1). *The Real World* emerged from a context in which programming based on real people "being themselves" and speaking in the "first person" on camera not only was entertainment, but also promised access to a form of truth not accessible through scripted programming.

For the first ten to fifteen years of its existence, *The Real World* employed Bill Nichols's discourse of sobriety as a way to claim legitimacy for its content. It *looked* like a documentary. *The Real World*'s cinematographers tend to rely on wide-angle lenses to capture as much of the mise-en-scène as possible within the borders of the television frame. The camera remains familiar with the subject, relying on close-ups and medium shots even when the subjects leave their homes and head into the world beyond their living quarters. This cinematography creates a sense of intimacy between viewer and subject because the audience sees cast members at their best (dressed up for a night at the club) and at their worst (the morning after, when they are hung over). They are filmed with visible blemishes and their sometimes-smeary eye makeup remains untouched. The roommates can be seen yelling at their roommates but also comforting them. After all, as the series' title indicates, this is the "real world," where not everything is black or white.

Nichols's discourse of sobriety also requires minimal interactions between filmmaker and subject, which is why *The Real World* initially maintained the fourth wall as a way to demonstrate that the people being filmed were not coached or prompted. Murray told me, "My late partner Mary-Ellis had come out of daytime soaps" and that their intention had always been to present the stories and characters in *The Real World* "the way scripted drama is presented." The stitches connecting the cast of real people to the apparatus (projector/camera/screen) behind the show could not be visible. Murray explained that the maintenance of the fourth wall was important both for the audience as well as for the cast members: "You don't want [the cast] to be constantly reminded they're on a television show." Here Murray links authenticity with cast members somehow forgetting they are on camera, or not caring that they are on camera "so that they'll relax and enjoy themselves and lower their guard." *The Real World* residences, in locations ranging from Honolulu to Los Angeles to New Orleans to Key West, were designed for maximum surveillance. This near-constant surveillance (with wireless mics being removed only for showers) is the primary strategy used for capturing a "real" moment. If every moment is recorded, at some point people will "stop being polite and start getting real," as its opening credits promise.

Even though the underlying ideology of *The Real World* is that only by concealing the apparatus can the casts' *true* stories really come out, in many cases, maintaining the fourth wall made the scenarios depicted in episodes *more* artificial than they would have been in real life. Former *Real World* cast member Irene McGee told me that the show's strict rules about no contact between cast and crew led to uncomfortable exchanges in which cast members would have to act as if they were not being filmed by a large crew of people who followed them everywhere. She explains that the crew was "trained to not have eye contact with you and not look at you, you know, if you're joking around [they are trained to] not laugh, it's a real mindfuck." The performances of *The Real World*'s cast were also influenced by the rules and requirements of production to ensure that cast and crew behaved in ways that were amenable to the needs of the complicated production process. For example, if cast members wanted to leave the house, they had to first clear it with the show's producers.[7] This gave producers a chance to get clearance from the businesses the cast members wished to patronize and to get a crew mobilized to follow them. Cast members who refused to comply with this arrangement would be fined by the production. During season 20, *The Real World: Hollywood* cast member Joey was so frustrated by a fine imposed by the crew that he left the house, abandoned the cameras, and returned later with a new tattoo that read "Fuck MTV." Due to this constrained living situation, arguments among the roommates often were more heated and explosive then they would be under normal circumstances.

The Real World also creates an artificial social environment where cast members receive continual, real-time feedback on their identity performances. For example, during our interview, McGee described how a simple task, like going to the drugstore with a roommate, could become loaded with conflict, based on the behavior of the very large crew that followed the cast members around. If the crew abandoned one cast member to follow another, McGee explains, that meant you were less interesting or compelling than your roommate. The camera's presence or absence was an implicit judgment, not just of the cast member's "performance" but of who they were as people. McGee explains: "You'll be having a conversation and then all of a sudden the camera leaves. . . . It's not like a camera, it's an entire crew! You don't know if they were taking a lunch break or if you were just boring." This system also created a kind of competition within the reality series' attention economy. Cast members who were always being followed by MTV's crews were clearly the "most interesting" subjects and would get the most airtime. This feedback loop is remarkably similar to the instant rewards that contemporary social media users gain or lose in real time when they perform their identities online. Before social media taught its users to view everything they do or see as filtered through the eyes of an audience (Andrejevic 2014, 46), or later, through a "Facebook eye" (Jurgenson 2012), *The Real World* was teaching viewers how to be interesting enough to cultivate a monetizable identity.

Diversity on *The Real World*

Although the concept behind *The Real World* dates back to earlier TV series like *Candid Camera* and *An American Family*, it nevertheless marks the first time that a TV series was based on the premise of placing seven hand-picked, "diverse" strangers to share a living space and hang out, talk, and find ways to amuse themselves.[8] It was the result of trying to find a cost-effective method for producing a scripted teen series modeled on the success of series like *Beverly Hills 90210*. Unable to afford writers or professional actors (or sets or costumes), Bunim and Murray decided to produce a reality TV series for MTV instead. Murray explained it this way: "So I've always been fascinated by how different people interact with each other. When [Mary-Ellis Bunim] and I were going to do an unscripted series, the only way to ensure drama was to cast seven different people. . . . The story engine would come out of putting seven diverse people together, that there would be conflict, and out of that conflict would come growth, and that would be our story arc." Murray described *The Real World* as a setting that allowed a group of young people the opportunity to live and work with individuals whom they might otherwise never meet in their own limited social and family circles. His belief is that the series is more than entertainment; it's an opportunity to learn. The drama for this series would be generated through the clashes between the varied identities selected to be in the first cast. *The Real World* had the price tag of a documentary but the narrative certainty of a scripted drama. Despite various changes to its format—the introduction of a "job" that all seven roommates must do together in season 5 (*The Real World: Miami*), the pairing of cast members with their exes in season 29 (*The Real World: Ex-plosion*), and the forced revelation of cast secrets in season 30 (*The Real World: Skeletons*)—*The Real World*'s basic goal has remained consistent since its debut: to find out "what happens when people stop being polite and start getting real." To get "real," the show needed "diversity."

During our interview I asked Murray to define how he understood this oft-used term, "diversity," when it came to casting his long-running series. I already shared this quote in the introduction; however, it bears repeating because this particular understanding of identity and diversity eventually shaped MTV's reality series in the 2000s: "Diversity for me is people from different backgrounds, it can be socioeconomic, it can be regional, it can be racial, it can be gender orientation, it can be disability, it can be outlook on the world—whether you're a pessimist or an optimist—it is the full rainbow of types of people."[9] Here, Murray is arguing that identity could also extend beyond race and ethnicity to something like whether one is from the city or the country or whether one is optimistic or pessimistic. In this way, *The Real World* opened up a range of possible identities for MTV's largely white, suburban youth audience, who may not have thought of themselves as even *having* an identity. For example, McGee, who is white with dark, curly hair, was certain that she was cast on *The Real World: Seattle* (1998) because of her hair type: "When Murray says he casts for diversity, I think he means how like it was [considered] 'diverse' back then to have Benetton ads with people who weren't white with blonde hair. He casted for 'diversity' by casting someone with naturally curly hair." McGee's observation may be hyperbolic, but it addresses one of the key effects of a series like *The Real World* and, by extension, the reality identity cycle that followed in the 2000s: the series generated a possible worldview in which even white, suburban youth were able to "find an identity" for themselves.

Lacking a script to follow, *The Real World* participants are expected to perform the self on television, to make the internal external. They must, as Laura Grindstaff notes, "exteriorize" their inner lives by offering their private selves up for public consumption (2014, 330). Murray described it this way: the cast is filmed in the process of "figuring out their identity" and "trying out different ideas about who they are." As discussed in the introduction, a central convention of *The Real World* is a moment of identity confession, the moment when a reality show cast member makes an *invisible* identity visible or draws attention to an already visible identity as their new roommates and MTV's cameras bear witness. Once established on camera, these identities can clash, which is the engine of the series' narrative.

Season 2 of *The Real World*, set in Los Angeles, offers a useful way to understand how Murray and Bunim used casting, as well as editing, to generate conflict among the series' diverse cast. The series opens with pairs of the cast members meeting and traveling to their new, shared living arrangement, sometimes stopping to pick up another cast member along the way. In season 2, Dominic Griffin (white, straight, British, cisgendered) and Tami Akbar (Black, straight, American cisgendered) are sent to pick up Jon Brennan (white, straight, Southern, cisgendered) at his home. While the first two cast members are introduced with long shots, Jon is revealed in pieces: a cowboy hat, tapping cowboy boots, a large silver belt buckle, and a medium shot of Jon from behind, carrying a guitar case. Without any other details, Jon's identity is made clear: he's a Southerner, a cowboy, or both. When Dominic and Tami ring the Brennan family doorbell, it plays "The Battle Hymn of the Republic." When they hear this, Tami and Dominic double over in laughter and look directly at the camera in a rare, early moment of direct address in the series. Jon opens the door with the greeting "Wassup!" Here the episode cuts to Dominic's recollection of this moment in a voice-over, a significant rhetorical move that highlights Dominic's prejudices and assumptions about white Southerners: "Jon, being the third party, was a little shocked. He opened the door going, 'Yeehaw! Come on in.'" Dominic's voice-over continues, comparing Jon to the cowboy characters he has seen in American movies: "You really don't think there's this person with a hat, who talks like that." Clearly, Dominic's expectations for who and what Jon is condition and warp his memory of their meeting (Jon said "Wassup!," not "Yeehaw!"). Jon's recollection of this first meeting is strikingly similar to Dominic's, in that he is equally surprised by his new roommates' appearance: "When [Dominic] first walked in, I was like, 'This guy is *so* weird and he's gonna freak me out. I'm just gonna stay away from him.'" Although Dominic is, like Jon, white, male, heterosexual, and cisgendered, he is "weird" due to his unnaturally dark, spiky hair, distressed jeans, and British accent, all stereotypes of a street punk. Dominic, like Jon, is an identity, a character playing the role he was cast to play; he was selected by the producers to pick up Jon precisely because he appears to be Jon's cultural opposite. Similarly, Tami, a Black woman, feels ill at ease in a white, Southern home that proudly displays a Confederate flag . . . which is *exactly* why she was selected to accompany Dominic to Jon's house. As in an episode of *Candid Camera*, reality TV producers want to find out "what happens" when a Black woman rings the doorbell of a Confederate history enthusiast. Embedded in this televised crucible of diversity is MTV's belief that bearing witness to difference somehow generates tolerance.

When I interviewed Paula Beckert, another *Real World* alum, she agreed with Murray's perspective about the series' social value. Beckert, who suffered from an eating disorder, alcoholism, and an abusive boyfriend during her time on *The Real World*, told me that appearing on the show "was the best thing that ever happened" to her: "I went in [to the experience] very weak but I came out of it very strong. . . . Before, it was like, you could live with those skeletons in your closet. On the show, *everybody saw mine*. There's no hiding any more. . . . The crazy part is, especially for people who are hiding their own mess, it's like I made them so uncomfortable. I was free now. Like, 'This is what I am, take it or leave it.'" For Beckert, the experience of being surrounded by cameras and microphones, coupled with the requirement to reflect on the self during confessionals, forced her to come to terms with her own problems. She told me, "When you have people legit calling you out [on the show], if everybody's saying, 'You walk like a duck and you quack like a duck,' then it's like, 'Fuck, I'm a duck. I better get my shit together.'" Instead of seeing the show's twenty-four-hour surveillance as an invasion of privacy, Beckert saw it as the only way to root out the destructive identities she had been trying to hide. She needed to see her identity reflected through the eyes of her castmates, MTV's cameras, and, later, the MTV audience in order to understand that she had some personal problems to address. For

Beckert, surveillance and identity performance were/are therapeutic. She told me that all cast members must go on the show prepared to be in an "uncomfortable place": "It's called *The Real World*, it's not *Hey, Live with Six Other People Who Will Be Nice to You*. Like, clearly [the production staff] is going to put you with people who are going to test/push/pull, otherwise it would be a boring season."[10] Beckert felt that by agreeing to be on a series like *The Real World*, a cast member has to be open to being emotionally exposed on camera.

However, when I asked McGee what she thought about Murray's claims that the series prompted important dialogue about important social issues, she told me, "I'm sure he puts himself to bed at night telling himself all those things. I mean, to some degree it's true, right? I do think that certain things happened in ways that probably never would have existed had there not been reality TV."[11] Still, McGee felt that the conflicts generated among the cast members had less to do with their diverse identities and more to do with the conditions of filming a reality series, which placed cast members in a pressure cooker of a living situation, with little to do and plenty of alcohol: "I think the narrative [when I was on the show] was that you're cast against diverse people—so here's a Black person and here's somebody from the KKK—and you think to some extent, '*That's* why people are fighting.' But, really, it's quite impossible to be friends with anyone. Like, you're really set up to fight."[12] The very different perspectives espoused by Murray, Beckert, and McGee on *The Real World*'s social value and therapeutic possibilities highlight how the series effectively collapses the boundaries between "fighting" and "dialogue," between "difference" and "polarities," and between cast members "being real" and "playing a role."

After speaking with just three people who were involved in the making of *The Real World*, it is also clear that they all have different definitions of "diversity" as well as what is or is not beneficial to someone's personal growth. Murray's definition of diversity offers an opportunity for individuals without a strong sense of identity, like middle-class, white people, to see themselves as something, a presence rather than an absence. But McGee sees this approach to casting as simply setting individuals up to fight: can an avowed racist really learn and grow in his beliefs by having a Black roommate for three months? But one thing Murray, McGee, and Beckert all seem to agree on is the fact that *The Real World* is fueled by the interactions between people who perceive themselves as being different from one another. Conflict on reality TV is possible only when people with different, but clear-cut, identities are placed in the same space.

The Real World Begins

The first season of *The Real World* was filmed in a SoHo loft in New York City from February 1992 through May 1992. Just three days after the first group of seven strangers packed their bags and left the loft, the series premiered on MTV. This rapid turnaround time is indicative of the loose structure of the first season of thirteen episodes, each twenty-two minutes in length; Murray and Bunim were still not sure what they were creating and neither were the cast or crew. The first group of roommates was composed entirely of youth involved in arts or performance: a Black, heterosexual poet (Kevin Powell); a white, heterosexual model (Eric Nies); a white, homosexual painter (Norman Korpi); a white, heterosexual musician (Andre Comeau); a white, heterosexual singer (Rebecca Blasband); a white, heterosexual dancer (Julie Gentry); and a Black, heterosexual rapper (Heather Gardner). All cast members were cisgendered. This inaugural cast was paid very little to appear on the show (just $2,600 per person), but the opportunity to be on TV and make important media contacts in New York was clearly their motivation for appearing on the invasive series (Blake 2011).

This first season was not very well received by TV critics, who found it dull and navel-gazing. A TV critic for *USA Today* wrote that "watching *The Real World*, which fails as documentary (too phony) and as entertainment (too dull), it's hard to tell who's using who more" (quoted in Wu 2016, 242). The *Washington Post*'s Tom Shales (1992) complained: "The program dutifully reflects the MTV gospel, which says that above all else one should express oneself, even if there's nothing much to express or the ability to express it. Never mind neighborhood or community or society. Ask not what you can do for your country, ask what your country can do for you." In other words, early critics of the series were most frustrated by the very thing that would ultimately secure *The Real World*'s success: its simultaneous efforts to gaze inwardly at the self and then to project that self outward for others to watch. The narcissism that so riled the series' early critics would eventually become its raison d'être.

However, as mentioned in chapter 1, ratings for the series skyrocketed in season 3, *The Real World: San Francisco*, due to its casting of a young, HIV-positive, Latinx man named Pedro Zamora (Fretts 1995). In 1994, HIV treatments were still largely experimental; being diagnosed with HIV was widely considered a death sentence. Since HIV disproportionally impacted gay men and IV drug users, two highly marginalized identity groups, Americans were terrified of the disease and incorrectly believed it was commen-

2.3 The first season of *The Real World* was filmed in a SoHo loft in New York City from February 1992 through May 1992.

surate with moral laxity ("HIV and AIDS" 2001). Season 3 cast members like Rachel Campos were initially worried about the risk factors involved in living with someone who is HIV-positive, and the series used her concern as an opportunity to teach American youth about the disease and how it is (and how it is not) transmitted from person to person. Pedro became an object of difference—as gay, as Latinx, and as HIV-positive—for nearly every member of the cast. Although the season 3 roommates are depicted in the pilot episode, "Planes, Trains and Paddywagons," as *surprised* by Pedro's health status, Murray told me that everyone on the cast knew about Pedro's medical condition in advance: "the cast knew someone who was HIV+ was to be a roommate, they just didn't know who it would be."[13]

Murray remains (rightly) proud of MTV's pivotal casting decision, claiming that "San Francisco . . . *sort of rose above just entertainment*, because of Pedro's involvement with the season. . . . I played a big role in putting him on the show and I spent time with him before he went on, to make sure it was something he was comfortable doing. I had had friends who died of AIDS because I had lived in New York as a gay man in the mid-80s" (emphasis mine). Bunim and Murray hoped that putting Pedro on *The Real World* would educate Americans about HIV and AIDS, and they were correct. Zamora was an activist prior to being cast on the series (in 1991 he testified before Congress to demand better HIV/AIDS education programs in the United States) (Israel 1994) and, as José Esteban Muñoz argues, Zamora used his time on *The Real World* to be a "televisual activist" since he was one of the only Latinx, gay, and/or HIV-positive figures on American television at the time (1998, 206). Throughout his short time in the public eye (he died on November 11, 1994), Zamora was the subject of countless newspaper articles and magazine profiles and was invited to appear on mainstream talk shows like *Oprah* and *Phil Donahue* (Vaillancourt 1994). Zamora received thousands of letters a week from people around the world who credited him with humanizing the LGBT community and the HIV-positive community, which, for many Americans at the time, were two conflated groups (Muñoz 1998, 193). Pedro used the performance of his identity to advocate on behalf of the marginalized communities (LGBT, Latinx, and HIV-positive) to which he belonged: "Although his housemates and cast members from other seasons used the video confessionals to weigh in on domestic squabbles, Pedro used them to perform the self for others," an act that, according to José Muñoz, "convert[s] identity into a 'poetics of defense'" (1998, 198). Pedro represented one of the few cases in which a cast member on MTV's reality identity series was able to (successfully) harness the performance of identity for impactful, educational, and activist purposes.

However, coexisting with the agenda to educate the audience, producers of season 3 of *The Real World* were also constrained by the demand that the program be entertaining. To achieve this delicate balance between entertainment and education, the operational aesthetic described by Neil Harris, Bunim and Murray made sure to cast someone who was combative, insensitive, and willing to be the devil to Pedro's angel. Enter David "Puck" Rainey, a heterosexual, white, male bike courier, covered in tattoos and very much in love with himself. Puck's identity was that of someone who was "who he was" and who did not care if his words or actions upset his more "politically correct" roommates. Murray makes clear why he decided to cast Puck in this season: "To me that was like a perfect play, a three-act play, and it all took place over twelve hours. . . . So we always wanted to focus on the roommates, their stories, and we didn't want anything to sort of distract from that." While it is clear that the casting of Pedro was a genuine attempt to put a personal face on the AIDS crisis in America, there is something cynical about having Pedro live with a bully like Puck, a loaded weapon ready to take aim at Pedro's identity as an HIV-positive gay man. Pedro's illness and Puck's indifference to it were part of a "three-act play" that was not written by paid writers and performed by paid actors, but generated by the clash between two people who were selected to live together based on their capacity for conflict.

2.4 Viewership for *The Real World: San Francisco* (1994) rose with the casting of a young, HIV-positive, Latinx man named Pedro Zamora.

The Real World's obsession with identity—finding it, cultivating it, and living it—is perhaps best exemplified in a season 3 episode entitled "White Like Me." Hunter Hargraves offers a compelling reading of this episode in terms of how it defines white identity as the absence of cultural markers (Hargraves 2014, 288). I would add that this episode is also important because it serves, in many ways, as *The Real World*'s thesis statement on identity in relation to youth culture. In this episode, Cory Murphy, a twenty-year-old, white, heterosexual, cisgendered woman, has an existential crisis after attending a spoken-word poetry event that her roommate, Mohammed Bilal, a Black, heterosexual, cisgendered man, participates in. The evening's theme is "Black Love," and it features different Black poets and writers reading work that is, in the words of the evening's emcee, grounded "in our Africanness, our Blackness." As a montage of images of Black artists performing plays onscreen, Cory's voice-over explains, "Seeing *him* come together with *his* people, and sort through those feelings is an incredible thing."

In the next scene, which takes place back at the house, Cory reflects on the evening, concluding, "I've never felt so white in my life." Being in the presence of Black people who write, speak, and think about what it means to be Black forces Cory to think about *what* she is, and to her terror, she believes that she might not be *anything*. Cory tells her roommates, who are seated around the kitchen, "I thought, 'Gosh, I am so freaking boring.' I have no major cause, no really close connection to my culture and my history and my race." This moment illuminates one primary way whiteness was understood at the beginning of *The Real World*'s tenure in the early 1990s: as an absence. Cory looks at her skin color, her history, and her culture as something to which she has no connection, mainly because her life and environment have so far never demanded that she see herself *as* having a culture, a history, or a race. Her culture is the dominant culture and her history, the dominant history. As such, it remains invisible to her, even though she (unknowingly) reaps the benefits of this identity every day. As Richard Dyer notes, whiteness has had the privilege of seeing itself as neutral, as the default, and as "unmarked, unspecific, universal" (1997, 45). It makes sense, then, that Cory, who is just starting to see herself *as* white, calls herself "boring" and "ordinary."

Cory's sense of being "identity-less" is exacerbated by the fact that her nonwhite cast members on season 3 have strong racial and ethnic identities, as well as defined life goals: Pam Ling is an Asian American medical student; Mohammed Bilal is a Black poet; Pedro Zamora is a homosexual, Latinx, HIV-positive activist; and Rachel Campos is Latinx and a Republican activist. Cory does not know what she wants to do with her life and implicitly connects that with her so-called "boring" (lack of a) racial identity, thus conflating identity with vocation and purpose. Hargraves notes that for Cory, "articulating a nonwhite identity becomes associated with movement, a directionality that the boring white subject apparently cannot achieve" (2014, 288). The other two white cast members, Judd Winick and Puck Rainey, are also different from Cory since they, like their nonwhite roommates, have a strong sense of identity and purpose. Judd is a sensitive, liberal cartoonist, and Puck is a brash, anarchist bike courier who is eventually thrown out of the house for his antagonistic behavior. Still, even a negative identity, like being the house bully, is an identity.

Being cast on *The Real World* and meeting people her age with such clear and strong identities has forced Cory to question what it means to be white, possibly for the first time. Cory lacked a context as well as a vocabulary for talking about these complex issues and is confused and uncomfortable. Judd, who is older than Cory and, it would appear, more knowledgeable about how to speak about race and identity, tries to warn Cory not to "covet the struggle" of her nonwhite roommates. Cory responds with "sometimes when there's not a defining feature that makes you stop and think about what your life means, it's easy to be carried along by the flow." This may be the most nakedly honest definition of identity offered in any episode of *The Real World*. It was as if Cory looked around the fishbowl in which she was placed, noted the Black poet and the Latinx Republican and the Asian medical student, and wondered: so why am *I* here? What Cory could not see was that she is there for the same reason, that she, too, is filling a representational gap; Cory is the young, naïve, straight, white woman of her season. In this episode, MTV launched an idea for its youth audiences, best articulated by Judd, who tells her, "You're not boring or ordinary because you haven't had to overcome something." This statement is key: as Black and Latinx and Asian kids began to see their identities, not as something to overcome or transcend, but to embrace and channel, white kids, who have generally never had their life struggles linked with their identities as white kids, wondered what *they* were. They wanted "in" on having an identity, too. In the 1990s, white youth were starting ask what *their* "defining feature" was, and could it be something unrelated to racial or ethnic oppression? *The Real World* seemed to tell its audience "yes."

Season 3's approach to race is very much tied to the colorblind ideologies that were so strongly promoted in American media in the 1980s and 1990s.[14] For example, in the same episode, Cory approaches Mohammed's girlfriend, Stephanie, who is a light-skinned, African American, cisgendered woman, and asks her if she is "part white." Cory is surprised and saddened to discover that this question upsets Stephanie. Later, Cory tells Pedro and his boyfriend, Sean, "It's weird how you can do some things that mean nothing to you, but they are so offensive to other people." Cory is confused because her experiences on *The Real World* have taught her that identity is important, especially to people of color, but her identity-based questions are viewed negatively. Mohammed later discusses the incident with Cory at the dinner table, where she openly weeps, clearly overwhelmed by her inability to navigate the multicultural world into which she has been cast. In an attempt to comfort Cory, Pam admits that she only recently discovered that the term "Oriental" should be used to describe objects, not people, while Pedro explains how he is never sure which people prefer to be called "Hispanic" and which people prefer the term "Latino," and, as a result, he is not always sure how to refer to himself.[15] These moments, in which individuals with seemingly clear identities admit to their own confusion over identity and identity labeling, are comforting to Cory. The episode implies that a white woman like Cory, who is navigating a world composed of different races, ethnicities, sexualities, and religions, must learn to listen and also be comfortable with making mistakes and learning from them. Toward the end of the episode, Cory admits, "What once seemed normal and real and absolute is just crumbling into a bunch of questions." Although Cory complains about not having an identity, being cast on *The Real World* has forced her to come to terms with that previously invisible identity—whiteness— and what that means. Her whiteness, which once felt "normal" or invisible, is rendered knowable and visible (Cory was also quite lucky to have such understanding and patient roommates, who allowed her to make mistakes and learn from them). Once MTV launches its reality identity cycle in 2004, the crumbling whiteness that so troubles Cory in this episode will be recuperated, and the process of asking questions and learning from one's peers will disappear from the series entirely.

The Formula Shifts

The Real World maintained its standard formula for the series—bringing together seven young people who differ in race, gender, ethnicity, religion, sexuality, and region—for its first seven seasons. But, in season 8, when Ruthie Alcaide, a self-identified bisexual, adopted, Filipina woman joined the series, it began to rely more heavily on issues like addiction and other mental health concerns.[16] While Ruthie was obviously cast on *The Real World: Hawaii* for her diverse traits, there was another aspect of her identity that was not fully visible until after the series started filming: Ruthie was an alcoholic.[17] Here it is important to pause and point out that, on *The Real World*, cast members have large stretches of time during which they have little to do but drink alcohol and socialize in a monitored environment. Beckert told me, "You're literally going crazy—there's no music, no TV, there's a phone, kind of, but everything's recorded. So, you make your own entertainment." This is why cast members sometimes dress up in homemade costumes, have "weird parties," or host talent shows. They are bored, and MTV's cameras are waiting for something to happen. McGee adds, "Alcohol is a tool used in [reality TV]. . . . When we showed up [at the Seattle house] there was free alcohol. . . . They don't give you free food when you show up, just free alcohol." Alcohol gives everyone on set, the cast and the crew, something to do. However, in season 8 of *The Real World*, Ruthie's use of alcohol gives *everyone* on the set something to do.

Ruthie's identity as an alcoholic is established immediately in the season premiere, when, on their second night in the house, Ruthie becomes highly intoxicated partying at a club, passes out, and must be taken to the hospital. From that episode forward, Ruthie's story line is focused on her problems with alcohol, with each of her roommates comforting her and urging her to get some help. By episode 9, an MTV producer and director must intervene, breaking the fourth wall to speak to Ruthie directly about her alcoholism. In the past producers have only been visible in cases of a sexual transgression (season 1) or physical violence (season 2).[18] But in season 8 the producers appeared onscreen to ask Ruthie to see an addiction counselor. Her antics only become more extreme after this discussion until, in episode 13, the roommates stage an intervention and give Ruthie an ultimatum: go to a rehabilitation center or leave the show for good. Ruthie agrees to go to rehab and returns to the series just five episodes later. Ruthie's identity as Asian and gay certainly set her apart from other roommates like Amaya Brecher, Colin Mortensen, Kaia Beck, and Matt Simon who were all straight and white, but it was her alcoholism—and the drama it generated among her roommates— that drove the series' drama.

After *Hawaii*, MTV cast three more seasons of *The Real World*, in New Orleans, New York City (again), and Chicago, all of which created considerably less buzz than *Hawaii*, presumably due to the absence of a breakout character like Ruthie. The series producers therefore made changes to the casting for *The Real World: Las Vegas* (2002–2003). This season featured the usual cast of attractive twentysomethings, all cisgendered and heterosexual: among them, a conservative, white Southerner (Trishelle Cannatella); a mixed-race, urban woman raised by a single mother (Arissa Hill); and a white, middle-class man raised in a two-parent home in Pennsylvania (Frank Roessler). But, perhaps due to its hedonistic Las Vegas setting—the roommates lived in a penthouse suite in the Palms Casino and Resort—the season focused more on the outrageous antics of the cast than on their ability to learn and grow from exposure to one another.[19] The diverse cast members still had their distinct identities, but those identities were almost beside the point; Trishelle may be a conservative Southerner, but her greatest asset is her willingness to get very intoxicated.[20] More than any other season, alcohol is central to the generation of plotlines and drama in *The Real World: Las Vegas*.

For example, in the season premiere, after all seven roommates have arrived, there is a knock at the door and a room service attendant brings in bottles of champagne and seven glasses, courtesy of Palms owner George Maloof. Maloof also invites the group for rooftop cocktails, a formal dinner (with more alcohol), and then, finally, spa treatments (with still more alcohol). Although the idea of getting a massage at midnight, after three hours of drinking, may seem odd to some, it makes more sense when the cast appears in matching white robes and then drunkenly enter a hot tub together. Via this planned itinerary, MTV has artificially created what occurred naturally on the *Hawaii* premiere: drunk, naked swimming. Arissa observes, "I live in a house with people who have no problem with getting down in a Jacuzzi with mad people watching."

Sex was also key to MTV's new formula for *The Real World* in its twelfth season. In the first few minutes of the premiere, it is clear that the producers are priming the sexual pump. The first words from Steven Hill, a white man whose main identity marker is his impending divorce, are "Sex is very important to me. I'm really comfortable being a sexual person. . . . If one of my roommates is really hot, I don't know what I'm gonna do." The last part of his statement is odd, given that nearly all the women who have been cast on previous seasons of *The Real World* have been young, physically fit, heterosexual, and conventionally attractive. This soundbite is immediately contrasted with Trishelle's confessional, during which she expresses excitement about meeting new men, but also adds, "Sex is really not that important to me." The nature of both Steven's and Trishelle's statements on the importance, or lack thereof, of sex in their lives would indicate that producers asked each cast member the same question: "How important is sex to you?"

Later, when Steven and Trishelle arrive at their penthouse suite, there is a montage of their new living space, a convention of every *Real World* premiere. In addition to ornate bedrooms, blue-tiled bathrooms with mood lighting, and a basket of toiletries from the high-end cosmetics line The Body Shop, the camera focuses in on a basketful of Durex-brand condoms. The camera lingers on Steven as he picks up the condom's instructions, feigning confusion, "How do you *do* this?" In episode 3, Steven and Trishelle do ultimately have sex with each other, but, ironically, fail to use one of the free, display condoms that Steven mocked in episode 1. This is not to say that sex was not important in previous seasons of *The Real World*, but, rather, that sex was established as a framing narrative of *Las Vegas* and remained a constant plot point for the season. *The Real World*'s new focus on girls (and guys) gone wild was very much a reaction to the cultural climate of the time, when there was a renewed focus and interest in the offscreen lives of celebrities and their bad behaviors and the rise of people who were famous for being famous, like Paris Hilton.[21] *The Real World: Las Vegas* scratched both itches simultaneously: the cast members were not celebrities, but their wild antics made them compelling TV subjects who then became celebrities based on their willingness to perform these antics for MTV's camera.

After *Las Vegas*, having an interesting identity was no longer the sole prerequisite to being cast on *The Real World*; all future cast members needed was to be able to party on camera. It should not be surprising then that the former *Real World* cast members I interviewed for this book expressed a nostalgia for earlier incarnations of the series, believing that the original mission of the series had been compromised by seasons like *Las Vegas*. Beckert told me, "I can't speak for everyone [but] my experience for me was, I think, very different from the experiences of people who were on *The Real World* later. I just wanted that real experience from *The Real World* that I grew up with, like in the '90s, like the Pedros. You know, when they were in New York, those things. That's why this show was so forward. It was like the shit. Now it's turned into this muddled . . . people wanting to be on TV to be a *version* of themselves." McGee agrees that the goals and purposes of *The Real World* have changed since she appeared on the series. "When I was on *The Real World* there was still some authenticity to the process," she told me. Whether or not the previous seasons of *The Real World* were truly "more authentic" than the post-*Vegas* seasons, both McGee and Beckert feel that there is more artificiality to the onscreen performances than in the past, as well as more overt grabs for fame. Beckert explained, "If you're only looking to get bar gigs and get famous, then go on *Jersey Shore*! Because [*The Real World*] isn't *that*." Both women attribute the series' perceived decline to an absence of authenticity and an emphasis on sensational performances.

The Real World in the Postdocumentary Context

It is worth recalling that, in its initial seasons, *The Real World* firmly maintained the illusion of a fourth wall. These shows were real, but not so real that the audiences got to see how the series were made, and the incredible amount of mechanical, intellectual, and, most important, emotional labor that goes into creating a single episode. However, after so many years of reality TV viewing, the rules about what was perceived as real or authentic had shifted. Whereas once the existence of video footage meant that a real event had occurred somewhere, most contemporary reality TV viewers inherently understand the constructedness of the shows they watch. Today, few audience members believe that "reality television" is "real." John Corner claims that this shift, something he calls the "postdocumentary context," can be attributed to the way the "documentary status" was weakened by fictional adoptions of a "documentary look" (i.e., the aesthetics of *Arrested Development* or *The Office*) and the documentary's adoption of the conventions of fiction (i.e., *The Hills'* use of continuity editing) (2002, 263–266). Tom Mole (2004) calls the consequent fascination with and focus on the mechanics of production a "hypertrophic shift" in reality television, highlighting an anxiety over the maintenance of or control over the diegesis.

In this postdocumentary context, a time of increased self-consciousness and performativity on the part of the reality TV cast as well as the production (Corner 2002, 264), *The Real World* had to change its formula to maintain audience interest. As Gareth Palmer explains, "The reflexivity of reality television, the apparent exposure of its processes, is also illustrative of the way in which the brand can reflect on itself and make adjustments so that potential users can feel more comfortable within its boundaries" (2011, 136). The "kids gone wild" formula that had goosed *The Real World's* ratings in 2002 became stale and led to stagnating viewership. Thus, one change was the decision to purposefully break the fourth wall, in yet another bid to rebuild its waning audience. Murray explained it to me this way: "We wanted to sort of try to reinforce that our show was real. That we're not giving them lines, we're trying to be flies on the wall, so we decided to pull back the interviewer, seeing the cameras try to capture the story, just those things." Thus, in the self-reflexive, later seasons of *The Real World*, audiences could hear producers asking cast members questions offscreen, and cast members began referencing aspects of the series that had previously been hidden, such as their scheduled interviews and requirements to complete regular confessionals. In these later seasons, the production process is made (partially) visible because the assumption is that the audiences are already aware of the production. As Mark Andrejevic reminds us, with the rise of reality television programming we see consumers summoned to participate in the "rationalization of their own consumption" (2004, 66). That is, this final stage of MTV's reality identity cycle asks the audience to participate in the process of making reality TV. We can only consume these series—and enjoy them—if the series remind us that none of us are actually fooled by their performance of reality.

Breaking the fourth wall also liberated *The Real World* from the obligation to be a neutral observer; the pretense to being purely observational was gone. In these later seasons of *The Real World*, producers actively manipulate both plot and character through the introduction of new cast members at random moments in the season. For example, in 2014, MTV released season 29, *The Real World: Ex-plosion*, which is the first season to *not* be named after the city in which it is filmed. For the first month of this new season, the cast members have a fairly conventional *Real World* experience: they get to know each other, get drunk, and hook up. But after a group vacation the roommates return to a home populated by several of their ex-boyfriends and ex-girlfriends. Drama ensues. In the seasons that follow, including *The Real World: Skeletons*, *The Real World: Go Big or Go Home*, and *The Real World Seattle: Bad Blood*, the production team creates similar interferences for the cast (by bringing in people from their past or forcing previous cast members to room with former rivals), and the fourth wall remains broken (Angelo 2014). When people in the *actual* real world first meet strangers, they generally try to be on their best behavior—to rein in bad traits and appear normal and pleasing. However, the point of *The Real World* is to move past that awkward period of politeness between strangers and get right into the good stuff (to stop being polite and start getting real). In season 30, producers forced these conversations to occur much sooner by bringing in "skeletons" from each cast member's past. The self-branding and acts of identity confession that each cast member engaged in and that might have allowed them to avoid conflicts in the house are short-circuited.

In his analysis of *Celebrity Big Brother* that aired on the United Kingdom's Channel 4, Andrew Tolson discusses how the series relies on the creation and continuation of "oppositional arguments," that is, confrontational arguments "designed to dispute a position held by another speaker" (2011, 48). Tolson points out that these types of reality series tend to rely on this type of argumentation, which is "extremely 'aggravated' and without much in the way of mitigation, either at the level of ordinary conversation or provided by the format in which it occurs" (49). In season 30, *Real World: Skeletons*, for example, the cast members all have "skeletons" in their "real life" closets. That is, like most humans who have reached the age of twenty, the cast members of *Skeletons* have ex-lovers and ex-friends, estranged family members and co-parents, in their past. What makes these cast members unique enough for a place on reality TV, however, is that their human skeletons were willing to go on television to humiliate, intimidate, or otherwise surprise them. For example, in episode 6, Tony (a white, cisgendered man) and his fellow castmate, Madison Walls (a white cisgendered woman) have just had sex for the first time. Both cast members are happy with this turn of events. But rather than revel in this new love, the producers take advantage of the duo's happiness and exploit its dramatic potential by introducing Tony's (first) skeleton, his ex-girlfriend, Elizabeth, soon after. Elizabeth's sudden presence will make it very difficult for the romance between Madison and Tony to continue to bloom. In a different season of *the Real World*, Tony could self-brand in his relationship with Madison; his narrative would be that of a man who falls in love with a girl who is, as he notes in his confessional, just his "type." Getting cast on the same season, and having a relationship, was "meant to be." But the introduction of Elizabeth effectively bars this script from playing out; Tony must now pause his new "drama" with Madison in order to retread the problems and "drama" he left at home (Elizabeth tells the camera that she was in a great relationship with Tony until he broke up with her to be on *The Real World*). When Tony questions Elizabeth's motivations for surprising him on the show, she explains that getting to fly to Chicago for free and be on TV (however briefly) was a great opportunity. This offends Tony, who snaps, "I don't want you to see me as no opportunity."

Later, Tony is surprised with yet *another* skeleton, who is *another* ex-girlfriend, Alyssa. Now he is faced with the truly uncomfortable situation of simultaneously dealing with three different women who all believe he is *their* man. By the end of the night, in which Tony drinks heavily and flirts with/enrages all three of his "girlfriends," the reality TV subject reaches his limit. He goes into a bathroom and begins repeatedly punching holes in the walls of his home/set. He screams, "*They* put me in this shit! *They* don't expect me to do this!" Here the "they" are not Tony's ex-girlfriends but, rather, MTV's producers. By destroying a piece of the set, Tony is attempting to vent his rage against the series' producers, who have placed him in such a difficult emotional situation. However, as Tony's punching of the walls demonstrates, there is no way to punish the producers for their offenses. There is no scenario—other than a scripted sitcom—in which a person would be forced to live in a house with two ex-girlfriends and a current lover. This is not a "real-world" situation but, does it, as Murray claims, reinforce "that the show is real"? The cast members agreed to put themselves in this social experiment; they signed on the dotted line and have no choice but to endure it or leave the series. Such contradictions highlight the ways in which identity series' claims to the more aggrandized half of Neil Harris's operational aesthetic obfuscate their existence as exploitation.

Season 30 of *The Real World* is premised on the idea that if you place two warring parties into a room and force them to talk, a compromise, a form of "truth," will be generated. But this is a very specific definition of "truth"—the truth sought by the season 30 cast members is emotional resolution. These heated arguments, while, at best, useless and, at worst, harmful for its participants, nevertheless make for excellent television. This appears to be MTV's tactic for saving its flailing reality franchise: to offer "more real" realness through an acknowledgment of the apparatus. Other long-running MTV reality identity series, like *Teen Mom*, have also recently turned to self-reflexivity, direct address of the camera, and an overall revelation of the production apparatus in their final seasons. While both *The Real World* and *Teen Mom* initially aimed to conceal the apparatus in an attempt to maintain a "fly on the wall," observational mode of storytelling, rooted in the ideas of the Direct Cinema movement, their final seasons abandon this pretense altogether.[22]

Conclusions

When *The Real World* premiered on MTV in 1992, it was widely praised for encouraging difficult conversations about race, sexual identity, and mental health among its cast members. In its first season, the series featured its young cast discussing racial stereotypes and prejudices and the harm that they cause. In my interview with Murray, he repeatedly emphasized the redeeming social value of *The Real World*: "We were old-fashioned liberals who believed that people had more in common with each other than they think they do, and if they just dropped their walls and were stuck in a house together, maybe they'll realize that." For example, *The Real World*'s Rachel Campos-Duffy explained, in an interview conducted decades after her time on the series, that the seemingly transparent structure of *The Real World*— the idea that audiences were seeing the real actions of real people—allowed viewers to make connections to characters in ways unthinkable before the rise of reality TV: "Because the show feels so personal, people felt like they knew us. People felt like they really knew Pedro or they really knew me or they really knew Puck" (qtd. in Arthur 2014). Rachel credits *The Real World*'s "transparency" for its ability to educate and connect with audiences; however, as time would tell, viewers stopped believing in this transparency. As a result, *The Real World* offered audiences an experience that was "more real than real." The legacy of the show, according to its creator and many of its cast members, was and is its ability to facilitate dialogue between a "diverse" group of young people. By selecting a range of identities— men and women, gay and straight, Black and white, urban and rural—and requiring them to engage in a kind of televised talk therapy, perhaps the wide gaps between the rest of Americans, sitting in front of their televisions, could be breached. Likewise, *The Real World* was the first MTV program to encourage public acts of self-branding and to portray identity confession as desirable. This idea that it is desirable and therapeutic to be known and defined publicly will come to frame MTV's reality identity cycle of the 2000s. In the next chapter I examine the first entries in MTV's reality identity cycle, which focus almost exclusively on white women, including *Laguna Beach*, *The Hills, The City, 16 and Pregnant*, and *Teen Mom*, in order to understand exactly what kinds of identities were represented during this period in MTV's programming and how and why they resonated with MTV's viewers.

3

"She's Gonna Always Be Known as the Girl Who Didn't Go to Paris"

(2004–2013)

Can-Do and At-Risk White Girls on MTV

A s discussed in the previous chapter, *The Real World* was the first American reality series to select a group of strangers to live together in order to film the drama resulting from surveilling the intimate details of the cast's daily lives. In this first generation of reality TV, what Misha Kavka calls "the camcorder era," the presence of the camera was enough to prompt the kind of revelatory interactions required for entertaining the audience. The second generation, dominated by series like *Survivor* and *Big Brother*, relies on rules, eliminations, and the performance of tasks that vary in their required skill sets in order to entertain. In these series, the main drama arises from an artificial competition inside a controlled environment that creates the "opportunity for self-revelation" (Kavka 2012, ch. 3). This generation of reality TV is followed by but also coincides with the popularity of both celebrity-centered MTV series, like *The Osbournes*, and MTV series focusing on "ordinary" people, like *My Super Sweet Sixteen*. Kavka argues that these reality TV series do not rely on the drama generated by the interaction of seven strangers, nor do these series demand that cast members follow certain rules of engagement in order to receive a final prize. The appeal of this form of reality TV lies in simply watching individuals perform themselves. Within this third generation of reality TV, identity becomes especially salient since casting decisions were (and are) the engines of the narratives. These casting decisions "set up racial, sexual, and sociopolitical flash-points by casting participants as the raw material for dramatic narratives" (Kavka 2012). This is why Benjamin Wallace (2013) refers to reality television as "an extractive industry," in that it records, amplifies, and repeats identities, converting them from lived experiences into "corporate brands." Within this environment MTV premiered the first series in what would become MTV's reality identity cycle, *Laguna Beach: The Real Orange County*, in 2004. While previous MTV reality programs like *The Real World*, *Made*, and *True Life* were engaged with questions of identity prior to 2004, *Laguna Beach* is the first program on MTV to monetize the practice of self-branding and to rely on this process to generate the content of each episode.

In this chapter I argue that upper-class, cisgendered, heterosexual, white women, like *Laguna Beach / The Hills'* Lauren Conrad (aka LC), are characterized by the control they have over the stories MTV told about them. Their stories are aspirational—audiences are encouraged to dress, consume, and behave like LC and her wealthy, white female peer group. As I mentioned in chapter 1, MTV has always envisioned its audience as white, suburban youth, so the channel's focus on this racial demographic is not surprising. But why did MTV focus almost exclusively on female-centered casts? Because, as Anita Harris argues, "It is primarily as consumer citizens that youth are offered a place in contemporary social life, and it is girls above all who are held up as the exemplars of this new citizenship" (2004b, 163).[1] Young women are reliable consumers, and the products they consume can be easily advertised on the TV screen as they center on image. The young women featured in series like *Laguna Beach* are, by Harris's definition, high-achieving "Can-Do Girls," who can use their celebrity status to build successful careers (2004a, 4). But this is not true for all cisgendered, heterosexual, white women featured on MTV at this time. *16 and Pregnant / Teen Mom's* Farrah Abraham is unable to build a career based on her celebrity identity, because it is associated with negative representations of delinquent motherhood and her overall failure to live up to gendered expectations of white womanhood. Laurie Ouellette argues that series like *Teen Mom* "[hold] its female subjects accountable for their successes and failures" (2014b, 253). Cast members like Farrah are, therefore, examples of Harris's "At-Risk Girls" and serve as warnings to MTV's primarily white, female viewers: do not be this girl. Throughout this chapter I apply Harris's schematic of the Can-Do Girl / At-Risk Girl to the identities modeled on MTV series like *The Hills* and *Teen Mom*.[2]

Although MTV would go on to profile other identity groups, like the self-branded Guidos of *Jersey Shore* and the Rednecks of *Buckwild*, this initial phase of the channel's identity cycle presents a successful prototype for later iterations: the spectacularizing of youth identity for the purposes of modeling behaviors of what to do or not do to be a successful example of a particular, highly coded identity. MTV programs focusing on young, white, heterosexual, cisgendered women, like *Laguna Beach, The Hills, The City, 16 and Pregnant*, and *Teen Mom*, exist mainly to model appropriate behaviors and consumption patterns for audiences who share the same racial, gender, and sexual characteristics. On occasion, certain Teen Moms, like Maci Bookout, rehabilitate their image to the point where they are *also* able to model appropriate behaviors and consumption patterns for the target audience. Indeed, the women who appear on *16 and Pregnant* and *Teen Mom* generally serve an educational purpose, teaching viewers about the importance of birth control or, alternatively, how to make the best of an unwanted pregnancy.

The Can-Do Girls of *Laguna Beach: The Real Orange County, The Hills,* and *The City*

Laguna Beach, which ran for three seasons on MTV, was created to capitalize on a popular, scripted Fox series in the mid-2000s, *The O.C.* (hence its bulky subtitle, *The Real Orange County*). Like the fictional Fox series, *Laguna Beach* follows the lives of several wealthy, attractive, white teenagers residing in picturesque Orange County, California. *Laguna Beach* was on the air at the apex of the American real-estate "bubble" of the early 2000s. Meredith Blake describes it as a moment when Southern California neighborhoods like Laguna Beach and Newport Beach "succeeded in taking over Beverly Hills' long-held dominance in the collective imagination as a bizarre, sun-soaked parallel universe populated by trophy wives and sexually precocious teenagers with designer wardrobes" (Adams et al. 2012). *Laguna Beach* was MTV's cost-effective way to capitalize on these popular mythologies about Southern California and part of the larger industry trend of developing formats for "unscripted, directorless" television (McCarthy 2004).

As discussed in chapter 1, reality TV was a cost-cutting solution to the problems faced by TV producers in the late 1980s because it allowed producers to cast nonunion actors, bypass Hollywood agents, and avoid striking writers, all at once. A cluster of factors in the early 2000s, including the global success of reality TV programming, the launch of social media platforms, the consequent monetization of self-branding, and the rise of "ordinary celebrity," led to a noticeable rise in the production of reality TV. Reality series like *Laguna Beach* could mimic the expensive look and feel of scripted network series like *The O.C.*, but for a fraction of the cost.

In the fall of 2003, series creator Liz Gateley pitched the concept for *Laguna Beach* to the families of teenagers attending Laguna Beach High School. According to press releases, the series was billed as a "positive opportunity" to be in an MTV program about "getting into college, working, family life and activities such as surfing or music" (qtd. in L. Smith 2005). The Laguna Beach parents were wary of MTV's presence in their city, particularly after the media storm that followed the infamous Super Bowl XXXVIII halftime show, produced by MTV. The 2004 halftime show featured Janet Jackson, who performed a medley of some of her biggest hits. Toward the end of Jackson's performance, pop star Justin Timberlake joined her onstage to perform his hit song "Rock Your Body" (2002), which includes the verse "I'm gonna have you naked / By the end of this song." Timberlake illustrated this lyric by tearing at the front of Jackson's bustier, revealing a portion of her right breast (including, most salaciously, her nipple) to 140 million viewers. There was much discussion (in a landscape not yet dominated by social media) about whether or not the exposed nipple was an accident or a planned publicity stunt.[3] Regardless, three days after the controversial Super Bowl halftime show aired, Laguna Beach parents demanded that the school board rescind their contract with MTV. Due to what became known as "Nipplegate," parents felt that "MTV wasn't responsible enough to be allowed to film students on campus at Laguna Beach High School." Even though this meant losing tens of thousands of dollars in scholarship money for its students, MTV's crews and cameras were prohibited from recording on the grounds of the high school (Susman 2004). The resulting series focused almost exclusively on the teens' interpersonal dramas. In place of classes and college prep was gossip, innuendo, and betrayal.

How could an entire TV series be fueled by the petty arguments of wealthy, white high school girls? This was a key question of much of the early public discourses surrounding *Laguna Beach*'s 2004 premiere. In a review of the series, the *New York Times*' Virginia Heffernan (2004) marvels at the way the series transforms the quotidian experiences of affectless teen-agers into compelling narratives: "No fiction show does as well at evoking, so forcefully, the hot, tribal mentality of high school kids who might just redeem their adolescence with sex. Hooking up with the right person to-night might just make their teenage years no longer boring or wasteful, but lovely and romantic and rad." Naturally, one critic's passion can be another one's poison. The *Chicago Tribune*'s TV critic, Maureen Ryan (2004), called the series surprisingly "lifeless" and described it as focusing on the prob-lems of "not-very-compelling teens . . . [who] range from uninteresting to mind-numbingly boring." Critics were divided about this strange new mix of real people interacting in scripted scenarios, but nevertheless the series was a success, coming in first in its cable time slot (Tuesdays at 10:30 p.m. EST) and among its target demographic of twelve- to thirty-four-year-olds (Rochlin 2005). By the end of season 2, *Laguna Beach* was averaging 3.1 mil-lion viewers, which nearly rivaled MTV powerhouse *The Real World*'s view-ership in 2005 (L. Smith 2005). But unlike *The Real World*, which brought together a range of "diverse" identities to see how they might interact, *La-guna Beach* focused exclusively on one identity: the wealthy, white Can-Do Girl.

What is the Can-Do Girl? In 2004, the year of *Laguna Beach*'s premiere, she was an empowered and confident (cisgendered, heterosexual, white) young woman whose success was tied to her consumption habits as well as her life choices. Harris argues that Can-Do Girls have "glamorous careers and luxurious consumer lifestyles, financial independence, and high stan-dards of physical beauty and grooming" (2004a, 18). While the Can-Do Girl is usually always-already successful, it is her *potential* success that is mar-keted and sold back to audiences in a neoliberal, postfeminist economy (18). The narrative of the Can-Do Girl, which Harris traces back to the 1990s-era embrace of "girl power," is "a sexy, brash, and individualized expression of ambition, power and success, neatly captured, for example, in the image of Britney Spears" (17). Under this new regime, the Can-Do Girl, finally free of the barriers once imposed by gender, is able to find economic and per-sonal success through a combination of hard work, determination, and nat-ural talent. *Laguna Beach* focuses on Can-Do Girl LC, who knows how to have fun, but not too much fun. She's smart but not a nerd. Her achieve-ments are the product of effort yet she appears to do everything effortlessly. LC also has, according to her on-again/off-again boyfriend, Stephen Col-letti, the "sickest view" from the massive house that her dad, an architect, is building, with an entire closet dedicated just to her shoes and purses. By

2008, with the onslaught of the Great Recession, such images would be obscene, but in 2004 they were still entertaining and escapist.

Undeniably, a large part of *Laguna Beach*'s appeal was its remarkable aesthetics. The show looked so similar to other contemporary, serialized television shows like *The O.C.* that, when it first premiered, many viewers were confused about whether the show was scripted or reality TV. This liminal aesthetic was not accidental, but rather usefully mirrored its cast members' positions as wealthy, white Can-Do Girls living in a world free of economic hardship or social injustice. The picturesque settings of *The Hills* connote luxury and privilege. When outdoor spaces, like the beach or the expensive properties where cast members live, are featured, "it is mostly through montages, car rides, or exterior shots to set up where an indoor scene will take place" (Kraszewski 2017, 60). Series producer Adam DiVello wanted the tones to be warm and sunny, with lots of reds and oranges, to reflect this beachy milieu. The use of high key lighting also ensures that every subject appears in the most flattering light possible, and its widescreen framing (16:9 aspect ratio) is reminiscent of classic cinematic spectacles such as Westerns, musicals, and melodramas. Widescreen is used to capture the lush California mise-en-scène of beaches, palm tree–lined hills, and rows and rows of pricey boutique stores. The program is also filmed with telephoto lenses, creating a limited depth of field. Series colorist Paul Roman claims that he would digitally "paint" the faces of the girls and then "defocus" the background, so that LC and her friends stood out even more prominently against the settings (Kaufman 2008). These Can-Do Girls are literally the most important thing in the frame, reinforcing the belief that the self must be broadcast and documented exhaustively to an audience of observers.

In a reality series like *The Real World*, audiences have been trained to ignore style in favor of content; the camera is dependent on the whims of the subject.[4] It doesn't matter how that three-way in the hot tub is framed; all that matters is that the three-way in the hot tub has been caught on camera. By contrast, in *Laguna Beach*, as well as its spin-offs, *The Hills* and *The City*, the camera holds primacy over its subjects. The women are told where to stand and what conversations to have. The cameras remain stationary because the action has been preplanned—it already knows where it's going. *Laguna Beach* depicts events and conversations that could or would have occurred in real life but portrays them with the best possible lighting and against the most breathtaking California backdrops. Its image of real life has been airbrushed, color-corrected, and soundtracked with a compelling pop hit. Anna McCarthy adds that the "show's commitment to narrative form and continuity over the pretense of spontaneous action" works to "position the teenage cast as improvising actors rather than sociological subjects" (2004). This is how the girls' often-banal conversations take on the weighted quality of the melodrama's script.

This premeditated cinematography and mise-en-scène is necessary because, as Elana Levine has thoughtfully explained, the producers must "literally create conflict, 'drama,' narrative out of the thinness of the shows' premises." In other words, *Laguna Beach* relies on a careful combination of nondiegetic music, editing, and lingering close-ups to create drama and emotion where little would otherwise exist. Levine also notes the way *Laguna Beach* takes up the conventions of the televisual soap opera, such as the "egg," or "the shot at the end of many daytime soap scenes in which an actor holds an expression for several beats until the scene fades out." This technique is effective because soap opera viewers "spend so much time with the [series] characters that they learn to read into their faces" (2006). This tactic can be seen as early as the series pilot episode, in which LC and her friends Christina Schuller, Morgan Olsen, and Lo Bosworth plan an end-of-the year formal, which they decide to call "A Black and White Affair." The party is an opportunity for the series' producers to take a love triangle, which had been simmering offscreen, and make it dramatically visible. Will Stephen, LC's on-again/off-again love interest, stay at LC's party or leave with his ostracized, current girlfriend, Kristin Cavallari? Kristin prevails in this particular battle over Stephen (there will be many more to come), and as she, Stephen, and their crew ditch the party and file into their car, the camera cuts to LC staring longingly out into the middle distance, a perfect egg for the end of the pilot. Lauren does not need to emote; she can simply exist and the mechanisms of reality TV, like sad pop music playing on the soundtrack, will do the rest.

The *Laguna Beach* opening credit sequence is backed by Hilary Duff's single "Come Clean" (2003). Duff's lyrics center on the themes of perfection and revelation: "Cause perfect didn't feel so perfect / Trying to fit a square into a circle / Was no lie / I defy." Paired with the honey-toned glamour shots of LC, Lo, Stephen, and many other cast members who did not make it past season 1 (RIP Morgan and Christina), this opening sequence promises the viewer an opportunity to see why these young lives—so beautiful, so exciting, so *white*—may not be as "perfect" as they seem. These opening credits also establish another goal of the series: the chance to see underneath this veneer of perfection. Duff sings, "I'm shedding / Shedding every color /

3.1 *Laguna Beach*'s pilot episode focuses on LC and her friends hosting an end-of-the-year formal, which provides a staging ground for the conflict between LC and Kristin.

Trying to find a pigment of truth / Beneath my skin." As with the first days of reality television and *Candid Camera*, *Laguna Beach* guarantees access to the deepest recesses of the human soul via the miracle of portable television equipment. The opening credits promise to reveal all about its young, photogenic, white cast, and that revelation is freeing and exhilarating, like Duff singing, "Let the rain fall down / I'm coming clean, I'm coming clean." What the series fails to note is that Can-Do Girls like LC are in control of the identities they perform onscreen and the stories that are told about them because they are constantly informed about the process. They may be told where to stand, but they also know in advance what conversations they will be having with friends and lovers before they have them, and they can always be sure their makeup will look perfect through it all. This is LC's version of "coming clean." Later in this chapter I will discuss how coming clean differentially impacts young white women in MTV's reality identity cycle.

In *Laguna Beach*, LC's Can-Do spirit is primarily evident in her success in the one economy that matters to a wealthy, white, cisgender, conventionally attractive, heterosexual teenage girl: social capital. Unlike her dramatic foil, the antagonist Kristin, LC is liked by everyone who appears onscreen (except for Kristin). The stark contrast between the rivals is also established in the pilot episode during a scene in which LC, Lo, Morgan, and Christina crowd into a single bathroom to get ready for the aforementioned Black and

White Affair. The girls discuss their dresses, which leads Lo to lament that she has been unable to locate a "cute, white dress" for the event because "they're all trashy and tacky and . . ." Her dialogue is cut off, followed by a cut to a close-up of a woman's foot in an open-toed black heel. The camera tilts up to reveal that this foot belongs to Kristin, who is, naturally, wearing a *white dress*. Later, when LC discovers what Kristin is wearing at the party, she whispers to Lo, "I like that we're all wearing black and Kristin's wearing white. How ironic!" In a different scene, Stephen tells his friends, as they inexplicably lounge and chat about girl trouble in a vintage furniture store, "Kristin's like a really good girl to hook up with and have fun with . . . we can have so much fun. But coming [down to] the boyfriend/girlfriend stuff, Lauren would be, like, a better girl." Beautiful, rich, nice, smart, *and* wife material, LC offers an aspirational identity of white girlhood that is never explicitly hailed as such. Despite its blinding whiteness, the series performs as if it were colorblind.[5] The professionally and physically successful white femininity at the heart of *Laguna Beach* is itself a product sold to and consumed by MTV's audiences.

After LC graduates from high school and moves to Los Angeles for fashion school, MTV follows her story with a new reality series, *The Hills*, in 2006.[6] In this series, however, the Can-Do Girl is identified onscreen as "Lauren," instead of "LC," to indicate a new maturity. As *Lauren* speeds down the road in her convertible in the series' opening credits, the viewer is encouraged to see her life as one open to infinite possibilities. *The Hills'* theme song, "Unwritten" by Natasha Bedingfield, underscores the series' investment in Harris's Can-Do Girl ideology with lyrics like "Live your life with arms wide open / Today is where your book begins / The rest is still unwritten." Although viewers understand that Lauren hails from Orange County, and that her career trajectory on *The Hills* is at least partially (if not wholly) the result of the fact that she starred in *Laguna Beach* (itself an opportunity that came about only by virtue of winning the socioeconomic lottery), her success is nevertheless positioned as something Lauren has constructed and earned for herself. All of the young women featured on *The Hills* wear clothing, carry purses, and live in neighborhoods that would be prohibitively expensive for anyone other than the wealthiest of Americans, but the series never explicitly addresses the girls' uniquely privileged class position. Lauren's project of the self, a serialized narrative running for several seasons, is successful under the postfeminist meritocracy advertised in and supported by *The Hills* (and which was previously supported by *Laguna Beach*). When Lauren is onscreen, only the *results* of her labor are shown—the curled hair, the glossed lip, the manicured fingernails—rather than the time and money required to maintain that high level of personal grooming. Alice Marwick labels this specific self-branding persona the "edited self": "This edited self must remain business-friendly and carefully monitored, despite social media culture's advocacy of transparency and openness. The edited self is an entrepreneur whose product is a neatly packaged, performed identity" (2013, 195). Similarly, in *The Hills*, the upper-class, white glamour worker is presented as labor-free, while Lauren's clothing line and lifestyle brand promise that this "glamour-worker mode of feminine subjectivity" could be available to all girls, if they shop at Kohl's.[7]

If *Laguna Beach* was about high school and the promise of the future, *The Hills* is about adulthood and what life might be like for a Can-Do Girl living in Los Angeles in the early 2000s. In this way, the show is an example of what Chuck Kleinhans (2008) has called a "projective drama," that is, "the dramatic presentation of a situation that the core audience views in anticipation that they will be in a similar situation sometime in the future."[8] *The Hills* provides its viewers with a fantasy model of young adulthood, in which fulfilling work is easily obtained, every night offers a new chance to party in a chic club, and everyone is filmed against the golden hues of a Southern California sunset. As Nancy Franklin (2008) put it in her review of the series for the *New Yorker*, "For younger viewers—who are the intended audience for the series—it may be a soothing fantasy about coming of age, and give them the sense that even after they leave their parents' house they will still be the center of attention, the way these girls are." The girls on *The Hills* never express concerns over paying their rents, finding employment in the first crushing years of the Great Recession, or even engaging in the world that (presumably) exists beyond the borders of Los Angeles's club circuit. On *The Hills*, success in life and work boils down to one quality: the choice to regulate (and to conceal the regulation of) the female body. Lauren's life is perfect because she makes the right choices, and she makes the right choices because her life is perfect. Under this postfeminist ideology, women who make the right choices are rewarded, while those who don't get exactly what they deserve. Postfeminism fetishizes the concept of "choice," specifically focusing on the choice of which consumer products will help the individual be the "best" version of herself. It is premised on the belief that if a woman fails (in work, love, or grooming), it is due to her own shortcomings, not to her gender (or class or race, or any other intersection of identities, which are never mentioned).[9] Rosalind Gill (2007) suggests that rather than a definition, then, "postfeminism" should be viewed as a "sensibility" shaping the media we consume and the way we consume it, as well as the way we regulate and view our personal lives and choices.

This is precisely why the various career paths featured on *The Hills*—magazine intern, fashion stylist, party planner—are easily obtained by each Can-Do Girl on the series, notwithstanding the fact that they have yet to complete college. Furthermore, in the world fashioned by *The Hills*, labor is beautiful and glamorous. Using this distracting fantasy of beautiful labor, *The Hills* elides addressing the class position of its subjects, portraying their comfort, wealth, and social and economic success as a given and as natural. In his *Rolling Stone* cover story about *The Hills* Jason Gay (2008) also notes the similarities between Lauren and television's other "career women": "Like with Mary Tyler Moore or Carrie Bradshaw, viewers relate to Lauren because she's a searcher—for true love, the perfect job and friends that never let her down." However, in scripted television series that depict young, professional, white, cisgendered, heterosexual, female protagonists, like the main female lead characters in *The Mary Tyler Moore Show*, *Ally McBeal*, or *Sex and the City*, winning a promotion at work is depicted as a challenge that must be surmounted by the eager but determined heroine. The protagonists' achievements in the workplace have value because they labored to attain them, *especially* because they are women. By contrast, in *The Hills*, winning a promotion at work or obtaining a new job is as easy as asking for it. For example, Whitney Port, who is depicted as being the most capable and hard-working of *The Hills* cast, decides in season 3, episode 20, "Back to L.A.," that she would like to leave her current position at *Teen Vogue* in order to pursue a career in "styling" at the People's Revolution, a "full service branding company" for designers. While it is likely that Whitney's interview was edited down for time and interest, it is presented to the viewer as a complete event in which she explains she is capable of "styling" things, but she neither offers specifics nor is requested to be more specific in describing her abilities. As soon as Whitney finishes speaking, Kelly Cutrone, owner of the aforementioned full-service branding company, offers her the job.[10] There are no ellipses in the editing to indicate that story time has somehow exceeded screen time; instead it creates the impression that Whitney was awarded her new job based solely on her image as a well-groomed, stylish Can-Do Girl. The viewer must ignore the knowledge that Whitney probably got the job because she is on TV. As Allison Hearn argues, this representation of the effortlessness of well-paid labor, and the upward trajectory of the Can-Do Girl, stands in stark contrast to the low-wage labor that creates the series (that, in turn, continues to add to the success of the Can-Do Girl) (2010, 69).

Similarly, *The Hills* never acknowledged that Lauren's success was due not to her skill and drive, but to her wealth, her contacts, and MTV's cameras. Lauren's identity as a Can-Do Girl serves as an explanation for her grand success, and it becomes a self-fulfilling prophecy. In this way, reality television "glosses over the connections and disjunctures between the cultural performances enacted by individual bodies and the institutional power arrangements that the bodies encode" (Grindstaff 2011a, 202). This dynamic is particularly notable in the season 1 finale of *The Hills*, "Timing Is Everything," in which Lauren is offered a fashion internship with *Teen Vogue* in Paris *just after* her commitment-phobic boyfriend, Jason Wahler, asks her to live with him for the summer. The Can-Do Girl must choose between her dream career and her dream relationship. The episode builds tension, not revealing Lauren's pivotal decision until the finale's last scene, where we see Lauren and Jason standing on the balcony of his swank summer rental, hugging and staring off into the middle distance. In the real world, an ambitious woman in her early twenties like Lauren, who moves to Los Angeles in the hopes of making it in the world of fashion, would likely *never* turn down such a spectacular internship opportunity in Paris. Choosing love is the stuff of romantic comedies, not part of a rational career woman's ambitions, which is precisely the point. Giving up her internship for love only serves to make Lauren *better* at her job, her *real* job that is, which is being the star of *The Hills*.[11] Nevertheless, this finale implies that young women are truly "free" to choose any path they like: love, professional success, and anything else they set their minds to. The rest, as Natasha Bedingfield tells us, is still unwritten.

What this finale leaves out is the fact that Lauren is able to forgo her "big break," a summer fashion internship in Paris, because it is not truly her "big break." Lauren's big break has already happened (back in 1986 when she was born into the wealthy Conrad family, and again in 2004 when she was cast for *Laguna Beach*). Lauren knows that choosing love will not pigeonhole her as lazy or unprofessional (as it might with a different reality TV subject, such as *Teen Mom*'s Amber Portwood). As Beverley Skeggs notes, only those who are financially and culturally privileged have the luxury of not considering that privilege in their self-presentation (1997, 1).[12] Lauren's "choice" of Jason over a job opportunity is dislocated from its real-world repercussions; Lauren is financially comfortable enough to choose love. Viewers can see Lauren as a potential role model, even if their own invisible class positions make this impossible. Lauren, the postfeminist poster girl of MTV's reality identity series, is successful and happy in life due to the choices she makes: from her choice in boyfriends to the ways she mediates the "drama" in her life. Lauren's success or failure in each episode is rooted in Lauren; she is the maker of her own destiny. Thus, when Lisa Love, Lauren's boss, wistfully says, "She's gonna always be known as the girl who didn't go to Paris," it is disingenuous. Lauren will *not* be defined by this regrettable decision because she has so many more opportunities ahead of her. The rest is always unwritten for a Can-Do Girl like Lauren.

By 2008, *The Hills* was MTV's and basic cable's highest-rated program, as well as the top cable "time-shifted" show (Gorman 2008). This success encouraged MTV to produce another series profiling Can-Do Girls, *The City*. *The City* focused on the life of *The Hills* alum and former Lauren sidekick Whitney Port as she leaves the sunny bosom of Los Angeles for a job in the cutthroat New York City fashion industry. In *The City*, there are ample opportunities to showcase images of clothing, shoes, handbags, and accessories, because the series is filmed at department stores, the offices of fashion magazines, photo shoots, industry parties, and behind the scenes of runway shows. *The City* immerses viewers in a virtual, urban—almost tactile—shopping environment. Cast members frequently draw attention to each other's fashion choices, commenting on specific details like the color of a shirt, the cut of a dress, and makeup choices. For instance, in season 1, episode 16, "It's All Who You Know," Whitney has lunch with Samantha, a buyer for Bergdorf Goodman, and compliments her application of blue eyeliner by exclaiming, "You're so daring! I would never put that on!" Later in the same episode, Kelly Cutrone, Whitney's boss and mentor, questions one of Whitney's design sketches: "Asymmetrical? I think it's going out." Episode 20, "Friends and Foe-Workers," filmed at Miami's fashion week, confirms that "futuristic" looks are "in" for spring 2010. In all three cases, drawing attention to costuming alerts *The City*'s viewing audience (females ages twelve to thirty-four) about what is in and what is out in contemporary fashion (Weprin 2009).

Rather than using establishing shots to locate characters in a specific geographical locale, episodes of *The City* frequently open with establishing shots of high-end clothing and jewelry stores (Bulgari, Louis Vuitton, Ralph Lauren) or of anonymous but trendy New York City residents, while loving close-ups of expensive clothing items occasionally even serve as transitions between scenes. Rather than orienting the characters in space, such shots place them in a generalized "fashion world," as if New York City itself was merely the colorful backdrop for a fashion editorial. It is fitting, then, that the final shot of the season 1 spring finale, "I Lost Myself in Us," in which Whitney breaks up with her on-again/off-again boyfriend, Jay Lyon, was of a pair of purple ankle boots. As previously mentioned, emotional climaxes on programs like *Laguna Beach* and *The Hills* are often punctuated with a close-up on the heroine's face, a device known as the egg. But as Whitney leaves Jay in the street and dramatically reenters the doors of Diane von Fürstenberg's store, where she works (a visual rendering of Whitney's decision to choose a career over romance), we see a close-up of her purple, high-heeled booties. Here the display of fashion triumphs over narrative: the viewer must read meaning into these shoes, rather than Whitney's facial expressions. The editors' decision to make a pair of shoes the final shot of the spring season speaks to the very blankness of *The City*'s cast, who, much like fashion models, exist as unobtrusive frames for the display of clothing and goods.

The series' prioritizing of consumption is illustrated at the close of each episode, when viewers were instructed to go to MTV.com where they could locate and purchase items worn by cast members.[13] Fans could "go shopping" with Whitney and her (white, cisgendered, heterosexual) roommate, Roxy Olin, at their favorite New York City boutiques or check out the most versatile fall handbags with Whitney's (white, cisgendered, heterosexual) coworker, socialite Olivia Palermo. The series offered a multiplatform shopping experience that allowed viewers to first passively experience the world of New York City fashion through their television screens and then to actively search out and purchase these fashions for themselves, alongside Whitney, as they sit behind their computers. *The City* therefore took the static premise of the fashion magazine—to sell an image or lifestyle to its readers via the alluring display of fashion—and put it into the context of a reality program (Klein 2010). Audiences are presented with the *sense* of freedom of choice—to live a life like Whitney's, one need only *choose* to dress like her. This opens *The City* up to endless marketing opportunities—from the products Whitney uses onscreen to the music that scores her dreamy date (which is filmed with a telephoto lens for maximum privacy but also maximum voyeurism). Of the three Can-Do Girl–centered series discussed thus far, *The City* is the most brazen in its efforts to sell products to viewers, but not necessarily the most effective. Ultimately *The City* was not nearly as popular as *The Hills* or *Laguna Beach*, and it was canceled after just two seasons.

As with *Laguna Beach, The Hills'* Hollywood movie aesthetics mimics its glamorous content. Kraszewski argues that reality television's ability to depict Los Angeles as an "elite" and "beautiful" space, a move that "eradicates the poor from cities," is generated through a reliance on montages of long and aerial shots (2017, 61). Much as the series hides the labor and privilege that support Lauren's rarefied lifestyle, it likewise hides the economic inequality that structures the city of Los Angeles.[14] Los Angeles houses thousands of homeless people, but TV critics, like James Poniewozik (2008), described *The Hills* as "possibly the best-looking series on television. It doesn't just look better than life. It looks better than TV." *Laguna Beach* cinematographers were instructed that each shot should "look like a postcard [from the beach]," but when Lauren Conrad made her big move out of *Laguna Beach* and into *The Hills*, the palette had to be "cooler," with more silver and blue tones, to indicate that her new work environment was less welcoming (Kaufman 2008). Virginia Heffernan (2004) describes the transition thusly: "sand and surf have given way to steel and glass." *The Hills'* cinematographer, Hisham Abed, cites Michael Mann as an influence, claiming that *The Hills'* aesthetic is an attempt to emulate the look of film on television" (qtd. in Gay 2008, 44). The decision to use various telephoto lenses allowed the show's cinematographers to maintain a distance from their subjects. According to Abed, "This is a 180 in terms of the visual approach with a lot of reality shows. . . . We use longer lenses and stay away as far as possible, within limits, to give the subjects an emotional distance from the camera and make them more free to speak" (qtd. in Kaufman 2008).

In keeping with the aesthetics of classical Hollywood style, *Laguna Beach, The Hills*, and *The City* firmly maintained the fourth wall. This stylistic choice was difficult to maintain, however, as the series' stars appeared all over gossip magazines in the mid-2000s (see Klein 2009b). According to the former president of programming at MTV, Tony DiSanto, "We want viewers to watch Lauren and the girls as the characters we know instead of in a show about *being* the stars of *The Hills*" (qtd. in Armstrong 2007). DiSanto's distinction is key. Rather than allowing the tabloids and the cult of celebrity to dominate and eventually overtake the show—as it did with other successful MTV reality programs like *Newlyweds: Nick and Jessica* and *The Osbournes*—DiSanto wants the plotlines of his show to work in concert with the tabloids. For example, in an August 2008 interview, Lauren

Conrad describes how the show's producers worked to keep her status as a reality TV star separate from her nonfamous *Hills* persona: "We'll be filming at a restaurant and it will be us at a table, three cameras, and then a row of photographers behind the cameras" (qtd. in Stack 2008). Here Lauren's celebrity is pushed, literally, to the borders of the television frame. Consequently, in season 3 the show's producers do not wallow in Lauren's alleged sex-tape scandal or explicitly discuss the alleged roles of Lauren's ex-BFF, Heidi Montag, or Heidi's boyfriend, Spencer Pratt, in creating it.[15] To do so would be—to use DiSanto's terms—transforming the series into a show about what it is like to be a *star* of *The Hills*. When cast members are on-screen, they never mention the fact that they are being filmed, or that they are engaged in or affected by activities resulting from their involvement in an immensely popular reality television show.[16]

But by season 6, the world inside *The Hills* had effectively merged with the world outside *The Hills*. The series had become, as DiSanto feared it would, "a show about what it's like being the stars of *The Hills*." The first five seasons' avoidance of extradiegetic narrative stands in contrast to *The Hills*' final season in 2010, during which MTV ruptured its reality identity cycle's closed-circuit world. It is only during this season that cast members began to talk about what it was like to star in *The Hills* within the diegesis of *The Hills*. For example, in the first few minutes of the season 6 premiere, "Put On a Happy Face," Spencer's younger sister, Stephanie Pratt, sits down for lunch with Lauren's bestie, Lo, and launches into a frank discussion about the time she recently spent in a drug rehabilitation facility. She concludes, "I'm only twenty-three and I've been to jail twice? I mean, that's not normal." This conversation was unusual in that, in past seasons, any personal scandal that occurred off-season and which was covered at length by the tabloids, such as Stephanie's run-ins with the law, would not be featured in the diegesis of the series. These stories would be treated just like Lauren's alleged sex tape, an unarticulated, absent presence. But in season 6 of *The Hills*, this is no longer possible because the show began to explicitly acknowledge the cast members' extradiegetic behaviors, like jail or plastic surgery, which had previously been documented only by the tabloids. Later in that same season 6 episode, Heidi, still physically and emotionally fragile from her well-documented ten plastic surgery procedures, flies to Colorado to visit her mother, Darlene Egelhoff.[17] Upon seeing her daughter's altered visage for the first time, with its artificially raised brows and swollen lips, Darlene begins to cry. "No one in the world could have looked like Heidi Montag," her mother tells her, mourning the loss of the daughter she knew before she was cast on a hit reality TV series. Despite their inability to live up to the behaviors modeled by the Can-Do Girls surrounding them, Stephanie and Heidi are still *not* At-Risk Girls. Their biggest penalty is to play the role of "villain" in the melodrama of the series, a role that Montag and her husband were able to monetize throughout the 2010s.[18] Their race and class privilege always prevent a truly devastating fall; social embarrassment is the only penalty for the transgressions of these white women.

In these two scenes, the extradiegetic world has penetrated the formerly impermeable borders of *The Hills*' diegetic world—cast members are admitting to mistakes they made *outside* of the diegesis and crying over them *inside* the diegesis. This opening up of the world behind the scenes becomes quite literal in *The Hills*' series finale. After checking in with each major cast member, the series closes on two of the original members of the cast, Kristin Cavallari and Brody Jenner.[19] Kristin tells Brody she has to go, and he tells her, "I hope you find what you're looking for." The camera cuts to a long shot of the two reality TV stars embracing, with the Hollywood sign visible in the hills behind them. A lo-fi version of the series' title song, "Unwritten," plays softly, almost imperceptibly, in the background, like the ghost of Lauren Conrad haunting the set. Kristin gets into the backseat of a car with dark-tinted windows, and Brody closes the door for her. There is a close-up of Kristin looking out the window, a fitting ending to a series that opened with Lauren (not Kristin) driving into the world of *The Hills*. As Brody watches the car drive away, looking forlorn, the camera cranes backward and the sunny California backdrop that frames this scene begins to slide offscreen to the right. After the camera cuts to a final reverse shot of Kristin driving off, the next shot is of Brody against the visibly fake backdrop, and behind it are cameras, bright lights, and a full production crew. Brody turns to look behind him but shows no surprise at seeing "the man behind the curtain." As the camera continues to crane upward, revealing more and more of the set, Brody begins to clap, and the crew joins him. They are applauding the end of a successful shoot and an end of an era. The irony of this revealing, self-reflexive moment is that it is itself wholly constructed, a reality TV sleight of hand that, ironically, wished to unveil the sleight of hand of reality TV. This "shocking" ending was *The Hills*' creator Adam DiVello's attempt at self-referentiality; they pulled back the curtain, but behind it was simply another curtain. As with *The Real World*, *The Hills* had to change its production in order to appeal to the evolving reality television audience, who were savvy about the constructedness of the text as well as its stars.[20]

In *Future Girl,* Anita Harris argues that the decision to delay motherhood is often a major determining factor in terms of whether or not a girl will become a Can-Do Girl: "The linking of success with delayed motherhood is taken extremely seriously by young women on the can-do track, who perceive young motherhood as an unthinkable waste and tragedy" (2004a, 23). Women must, eventually, procreate, in order to truly "have it all," but children must be had at "the right time," that is, after an education and a meaningful career are secured (24). Just as Can-Do Girls are branded by their "good" choices, At-Risk Girls, as Harris calls them, are branded by their "bad" choices. Narratives surrounding At-Risk Girls emphasize how the consequences of their choices to do drugs, to drop out of school, or to get pregnant at the "wrong" time reverberate through their lives. Their only salvation lies in learning from their mistakes and, ideally, discouraging other girls from making the same bad choices. The young women appearing in *16 and Pregnant* and *Teen Mom* have failed the first test of Can-Do Girlness: delaying motherhood for an appropriate period of time. Thus, the differences between white girls featured on MTV's reality series boils down to which white girls made the "right" choices and which ones made the "wrong" choices.

In a press release for the new MTV series DiSanto explained, "'16 & Pregnant' follows the journey of six young women going through an immensely life changing experience at such a young age. . . . *This is the real* secret life of an American teenager" (qtd. in Garber-Paul 2009; emphasis mine). As with *Laguna Beach* and *Beverly Hills 90210, 16 and Pregnant* was MTV's attempt to create a reality TV version of a successful network series, ABC Family's *The Secret Life of the American Teenager.* And as with previous reality series like *The Real World* and *True Life, 16 and Pregnant* is framed as taking on a useful, prosocial role. For example, MTV's press releases trumpeting the premiere of *16 and Pregnant* in 2009 highlight how the channel worked with both the National Campaign to Prevent Teen and Unplanned Pregnancy and the Kaiser Family Foundation.[21] The National Campaign developed discussion materials to accompany each episode, along with online resources about birth control (and abstinence), sex, and dating, on the website www.stayteen.org. The Kaiser Family Foundation partnered with MTV on a campaign entitled "It's Your (Sex) Life," which, according to MTV's press release, "promotes responsible decision making about sex, offers insight into what to do if you think you could be pregnant, are pregnant, had unprotected sex, and how to choose and use contraception properly" (Viacom

2009). By including links to these resources alongside the series, teen pregnancy reality TV series like *Teen Mom, 16 and Pregnant*, and others work to
"instill the practice of making life choices reflexively and wisely" (Ouellette
2014b, 241). These advertised collaborations offer a patina of public service
to what was otherwise another attempt by MTV to capitalize on the success
of contemporary scripted, teen-targeted television[22]

What is key for this chapter's comparison between Can-Do Girl series
(like *Laguna Beach* and *The Hills*) and At-Risk Girl series (like *16 and Pregnant* and *Teen Mom*) is that these series tell the stories of only white girls.
Laurie Ouellette links this omission in *Teen Mom* to the discourses surrounding teen pregnancy education and advocacy throughout the 1960s
and 1970s: "The racial and class privilege ascribed to the teenage mother was
crucial to the expansion of rights and public services"; *however*, when teen
pregnancy was associated with nonwhite women, "the provision of public
resources for young single mothers was contested" (2014b, 238–239). As the
goal of these series was to use the At-Risk Girl, the Teen Mom, as a figure the
audience could pity but also learn from, MTV followed the advocacy model
established decades ago by casting primarily white teens. When I asked *16
and Pregnant / Teen Mom* creator and producer Dia Sokol Savage about this
omission specifically in our interview, she responded at length.[23] Sokol Savage's explanation ultimately boils down to one key (albeit depressing) observation: "The world of television reflects the world around us, which is . . .
kind of racist. . . . There is definitely a perception that Black audiences will
watch white stories and white audiences will not watch Black stories." Sokol Savage added that they had pushed "very, very hard" to cast a woman of
color on *Teen Mom*, but that ultimately the network made all final decisions
about casting, which did not include any young women of color.

Sokol Savage also told me that *16 and Pregnant* was cast in such a way
that the viewers would be able to "see themselves" in the girls. She summarizes the ideal Teen Mom cast member as "the girl next door, shoulda
known better, somebody who feels very much like a typical American teen,
who should have known better but didn't. . . . There was a blind spot . . .
not being thoughtful, a birth control malfunction. . . . It didn't really fit our
show to follow a girl who had *tried* to get pregnant" (emphasis mine). In
other words, when casting for the series, producers were looking for Can-
Do Girls who find themselves swimming in the At-Risk pool. If the women
were already on the wrong life track—whether because of drugs or crime
or lack of schooling—then a pregnancy would not be the sole factor in their
fall from grace. Instead, the series serves as a cautionary tale that all young

(white) girls are just one roll in the hay away from a life of hardship. If MTV reality identity series like *The Hills* and *The City* provide the sunny side of postfeminism—white female consumers curating their edited self through wardrobe selection, makeup, and other consumption habits to convey a vision of empowered femininity—*16 and Pregnant* and *Teen Mom* offer its inverse: the hard limits of postfeminism's narratives of choice. *16 and Pregnant* and *Teen Mom* invite a dual gaze; they generate empathy for the teens but also indict the girls for being in these predicaments in the first place. To quote Sokol Savage again, they should have known better.

The pilot episode of *16 and Pregnant* introduces Maci Bookout, who will go on to be one of the teen-pregnancy-focused franchise's biggest stars, appearing in seven seasons of *Teen Mom*, publishing books, touring American colleges as a paid speaker, and starting her own clothing company.[24] But in order to find true happiness and success, Maci first needed to learn from her mistakes, as all At-Risk Girls must do. Her redemption begins in the first episode of *16 and Pregnant*, which opens with an aerial shot of an orange notebook covered in doodles signifying key aspects of Maci's identity: dirtbike racing, softball, and little hearts with the initials "M + R" (for Ryan, her then-boyfriend). The cover of the notebook flips, with corresponding sound effects, to the blue-lined paper inside the notebook. On the pages is a line sketch of Maci as her voice-over explains, "Hey, my name is Maci. I'm sixteen; I live in Chattanooga, Tennessee; and I'm a total overachiever." A shot of Maci buying ice cream with two friends cuts to a medium shot of Maci sitting at a desk, doing homework. She continues: "I get good grades, I play softball, and I'm even on the cheerleading squad. But don't let that fool you—I do have a wild side. I'm all about dirt bikes." This voice-over is paired with shots of Maci playing softball, still photographs of her in her cheerleading uniform, and, finally, action shots of Maci riding her dirt bike.

Thus far, Maci's story seems to follow that of other Can-Do Girls featured on MTV—she's a happy (white, heterosexual, middle-class, cisgendered) high school student with a busy academic, extracurricular, romantic, and social life. But as Maci explains, "All my friends are psyched for senior year but I'm graduating early and moving in with Ryan because . . ." Here the camera cuts to a medium close-up of a smiling Ryan and Maci posing for a photo. Only their faces are visible in this shot. As Maci continues her narration, the camera tracks down to reveal her very large pregnant belly: ". . . I'm pregnant." With these words, the image then dissolves into a rotoscoped version of the same image, drawn onto the pages of the orange notebook. The page turns to reveal the series title, *16 and Pregnant*. As this opening to the series demonstrates, although Maci has many interests and activities, the most important feature of her identity, mentioned at the end of her introduction, is that she is both sixteen *and* pregnant. The animated sketches serve as transitions between segments of the series, with the roto-scoped images of the girls dissolving into actual footage of the subjects. In this way, *16 and Pregnant* aims to merge the lighthearted aesthetic of the high school doodle with the stark reality of teen motherhood.

Although Sokol Savage noted the series was aiming to tell the stories of women for whom teen motherhood was an unexpected, At-Risk detour on an otherwise Can-Do trajectory (i.e., middle- to upper-middle-class white women who made a single "mistake"), the series does profile some working-class subjects, like Amber Portwood and Caitlynn Lowell. Amber and the father of her child, Gary Shirley, were both working-class, high school drop-outs when they were cast for *Sixteen and Pregnant*. In other words, Amber was an At-Risk Girl well before she got pregnant. Sokol Savage told me: "You know Amber and Gary don't really fit into the MTV demo, but the two of them and their dynamic, they were just so funny together. That was before things were really bad between them. . . . I could just listen to them talk for hours and hours. They cracked me up even though they weren't really surrounded by a big supportive family." Sokol Savage described Amber and Gary as "not that kind of teen from that typical family," which made them "a harder sell" to MTV. Ironically, Amber is far more representative of American teenage mothers than her *Teen Mom* castmates, since financial instability is central to the incidence and the effects of teenage pregnancy. Indeed, one of the three biggest risk factors for becoming a teen parent is poverty; almost two-thirds of the families started by pregnant teenagers are classified as poor, and about one in four teen mothers will go on welfare within three years of their child's birth (Schuyler Center for Analysis and Advocacy 2008). For many of the women profiled on the series (Amber, Janelle, Caitlyn, Briana), their At-Risk status is a result of their own economic precarity, yet class does not play an explicit role in the series' discourse about teen motherhood.[25]

Amber's At-Risk status has served to define her identity throughout her many years on MTV, with her parenting constantly under scrutiny. In early seasons of *Teen Mom*, Amber is mostly portrayed in repose: listening to her iPod in bed, texting on the couch, or chatting with friends. Gary complains that his daughter's clothing and crib sheets are dirty and that Amber "sleeps all day." Amber also develops an addiction to prescription pills and finds it impossible to complete her GED. Sharon Varallo (2008) argues that the new ideology of intensive mothering, which demands that mothers expend

3.2 The cast of *Teen Mom*, portrayed as At-Risk Girls, must demonstrate that they have learned from past mistakes.

a tremendous amount of time, energy, and money in raising their children, relies on a class-based rhetoric of choice. Under this neoliberal framework, if your child fails, it is because you, as a mother, *chose* not to do enough to help them succeed. Indeed, Amber is perpetually depicted as choosing not to do "enough." After a season 2 episode aired, in which Amber physically assaults Gary, one of many such incidents caught on camera and replayed on the show, the young mother is charged with domestic violence. As a result, Amber is prohibited from having contact with Gary. Her daughter, Leah, becomes a ward of the state of Indiana, a plot that composes the bulk of Amber's season 3 story line. Season 4 opens with Amber's lengthy, court-mandated stay in a rehab facility for substance abuse and anger management. By placing the motherhood choices of these girls on display, *Teen Mom* reinforces the ideology of intensive motherhood and its narratives, inviting viewers to judge these young mothers for their "failures."

Had *Teen Mom* wrapped for good in 2012, Amber's status as an At-Risk Girl would be cemented. But after a three-year hiatus, MTV began to film a new season of the series, season 5, which provided Amber with another opportunity to make the "right choices," rebrand herself, and make the arduous transition from At-Risk Girl to Can-Do Girl. After spending a year and a half in jail, followed by drug rehabilitation and years of therapy, Amber begins season 5 of *Teen Mom* sober and with her GED in hand. She is also in a serious, monogamous relationship with a fellow recovered addict, Matt Baeir. Still, Amber is constantly on the lookout for stressors and triggers that could push her back into At-Risk territory, frequently voicing her fears that she will relapse and lose control of herself. She expresses resentment when she finds herself in life circumstances that might send her backward on her otherwise forward-moving narrative of progress. While the Can-Do Girl appears to effortlessly manage and control her body so that it complies with social norms and expectations for women, Amber, the At-Risk Girl, struggles to control her appetites and desires. For example, one of Amber's main story arcs in season 5 of *Teen Mom* centers on her desire to lose the weight she gained while she was getting sober. She explains that she once believed she could get sober and lose weight at the same time, but now that she's sober, she understands that you can only "do one thing at a time." Amber used to rely on heavy drug use to keep her weight in control, but she now understands that she needs to see a weight-loss specialist; being on *Teen Mom* has taught the moms that there is a counselor or specialist for every problem. Over the course of season 5, Amber is filmed drinking foamy green weight-loss shakes, eating meal replacement bars, and cooking green beans that make her daughter, Leah (who is happily eating macaroni and cheese), audibly retch. Although these activities annoy Amber, she is determined to be better, to become a Can-Do Girl. She just needs to try harder.

This drive for self-progress is also reflected in the fact that, in season 6, Amber and Matt purchase a home in a wealthier part of town, moving from a more working-class neighborhood to an upper-middle-class environment (a move that could be facilitated only by the paycheck Amber receives for being a star on *Teen Mom*). Amber often remarks that she feels out of place in such a neighborhood and worries about fitting in. Later she announces, as a smiling furniture store clerk looks on, "This is our big 'F.U.' to the people who said we wouldn't make it." That is, Amber's progress toward an acceptably bourgeois existence, marked by her sobriety, a healthy weight, and, now, a home in an expensive neighborhood with high-end furnishings, is for the benefit of MTV's cameras and the implied judgmental audience who tracks her every move. Occasionally it appears as if Amber wants these things less for herself than for her identity on *Teen Mom*. She admits to Matt that the reason she wants to lose the weight she has gained is because she perceives herself as a role model for *Teen Mom* fans: "I have people watching me. If I gain all this weight, what kind of role model am I?"[26] Here, Amber describes herself in the third person; she is watching herself through MTV's camera-eye, and she is aware of her tenuous position. Being a Can-Do Girl requires a high level of effortless self-surveillance and self-branding.

While Amber's status is that of the At-Risk Girl who is making a tenuous transition to a Can-Do status, *16 and Pregnant* / *Teen Mom*'s Farrah Abraham is its reverse. In *16 and Pregnant*, Farrah is memorable because her daughter's father, Derek Underwood, died in a car accident before the child, Sophia, was born. This trauma indelibly marks Farrah's story line as she often bursts into tears at the mention of Derek's name and brings Sophia to visit his grave multiple times throughout the *Teen Mom* series. Farrah's other defining trait is her caustic relationship with her mother, Debra, and father, Michael. They fight incessantly, with most of the fights caused by Farrah's hair-trigger temper and sensitivity. Farrah's fights do not land her in jail; they just upset her parents and Sophia. Even with these frequent fights and constant drama, Farrah remains an example of the At-Risk Girl who is in the process of transforming into a Can-Do Girl; she finishes school, pursues multiple business opportunities, and becomes an entrepreneur. Farrah, like Maci, and to a lesser extent, Amber, is smartly converting her MTV fame into a lifelong income. That's what a Can-Do Girl does.

Unfortunately, Farrah's entrepreneurship, a mark of her turn to respectability after being labeled a wayward teenage mother, goes too far just after season 4, when she agrees to star in a pornographic film titled *Farrah Superstar: Backdoor Teen Mom* (2013). The film costarred James Deen, a famous (or infamous) adult film star. Unused footage from that shoot was then used to make a second pornographic film featuring Farrah, a sequel called *Farrah 2: Backdoor and More* (2014). The tabloids reported that Farrah earned $1.5 million for the shoot, but Vivid Video, the producers of the films, marketed it as a "leaked" sex tape (à la Kim Kardashian), a narrative Farrah would continue to uphold, for obvious reasons (*Radar Online* 2013). Farrah was nominated for AVN awards (from the magazine *Adult Video News*), including "Best Anal Sex Scene" and "Best Celebrity Sex Tape." But Farrah's movie debut was more poorly received by her former *Teen Mom* castmates, who did not wish to appear on the series with a "porn star" when they returned to shoot season 5 in 2015. In advance of the season premiere, the Teen Moms gave interviews to various tabloids noting that they didn't want their children to appear on a series "where someone's talking about sex toys" (qtd. in E. Lee 2014). Although all of the Teen Moms have turned to some form of entrepreneurship, as evidenced by the small businesses founded by Maci

3.3 When she starred in *Backdoor Teen Mom*, a pornographic film, *Teen Mom*'s Farrah Abraham disrupted her narrative of redemption.

3.4 *Teen Mom*'s Maci Bookout successfully navigated the transition from At-Risk Girl to Can-Do Girl by promoting her autobiography on college speaking tours.

and Amber, Farrah's move into sex work is marked as a violation of the acceptable range of employment possibilities for a Teen Mom. Her choice to use pornography as a way to monetize her fifteen minutes of fame is scandalous because Farrah's status as a Teen Mom—her identity—is the basis for the kink.

When Farrah began her time on 16 and Pregnant, she was presented as an upper-middle-class girl next door who made one mistake: sex before marriage. Her task was to redeem that mistake through overcoming the obstacles generated by teen motherhood: she must get her diploma, cultivate a rewarding and respectable career, be beautiful and desirable (but not too desirable!), and, it goes without saying, be a perfect mother. But the serialized nature of the stories presented on Teen Mom, which requires that characters grow and change over time, is, ironically, what threatens their status on the series that built their fame in the first place. Farrah's participation in a pornographic film reversed this narrative of moral progress. Farrah misread her identity's narrative, seeking a kind of fame that, while monetarily stable, was too outside the normative femininity she was expected to embrace and that Teen Mom promotes. Farrah did not appear in the first four episodes of season 5 of Teen Mom, and, in order to return to the series, she had to disavow her past as a sex worker and continue the narrative she began in previous seasons of Teen Mom.

The At-Risk Girl and the Fourth Wall

When the original cast of Teen Mom, Maci Bookout, Catelynn Lowell, Farrah Abraham, and Amber Portwood, finished their work on season 4, the assumption was that they had just filmed the series finale. As in previous iterations of MTV's reality identity series, their celebrity status or even the fact that that they were on a successful TV show was never mentioned within the diegesis of Teen Mom.[27] As Sokol Savage told me, "At the pinnacle of Teen Mom, we were filming around all the paparazzi being there. And even that was a bit of a challenge for us to do." This avoidance of the extradiegetic world led to a disconnect between the mundanity of the diegesis and the extradiegetic celebrity of the cast, just as it did with The Hills. When MTV decided to give the original Teen Mom cast another season, Sokol Savage realized that something about the way the show was structured would need to change, asking herself, "How can I accurately tell you about Maci's life without telling you that she goes around and tours and talks to people about being Maci from Teen Mom?" Sokol Savage described the massive changes to the series between season 4 and season 5 in this way: "For the years and years we were making this show, we would always laugh amongst ourselves because the *real* story is not the scene we just filmed, the story is the four-hour conversation that I just had to even get this woman [to speak], to basically remind them of why they're on the show, why they're sharing their stories. Sometimes I'm like, 'That's where all the drama is.'" Sokol Savage, the crew, and the Teen Moms themselves decided that their next season would reveal the apparatus and acknowledge the fact that they were, in fact, filming a reality series because "we want to be able to see it *all*."[28]

For example, in season 5, episode 13, Amber takes her daughter, Leah, to the park and a little girl approaches Leah cautiously, asking for her name. When the child learns her name is Leah, she gets excited and exclaims, "You're from *Teen Mom!*" Later in this episode, at Catelynn and Tyler's joint bachelor/bachelorette party, the group heads to a strip club. Caitlynn ends up having a lengthy heart-to-heart with one of the club's dancers because, like all *Teen Mom* fans, she knows all the intimate details of the last seven years of Caitlynn's life. While such interactions likely happened routinely during shoots in the previous seasons, such footage would never make it to the air because it violated the implicit terms of the series: to conceal the apparatus. Many of the moms even worked service industry jobs, despite the fact that their paychecks from MTV more than covered their bills, as a way to maintain the illusion that they were regular, struggling, single moms. Season 5 gives up this ruse entirely.

Another good example of this breaking of the fourth wall occurs in season 5, episode 11, when Tyler Baltierra's father, Butch, has finished a four-year prison sentence at Macomb Correctional Institution. At this point, Butch was a veteran of four seasons of *Teen Mom* and well versed in the production's requirements, like not looking directly at or speaking to the camera. After picking up his father, Tyler pulls over in a parking lot so Butch can change into more comfortable clothing. As he changes, Kiki, a co-executive producer on the series, speaks from offscreen: "Yeah, so the new thing on the show, Butch, is . . ." and Tyler jumps in to finish, "You can look at cameras, you can talk to cameras, you can talk to anyone behind . . ." Then Kiki interrupts Tyler: "We can be on camera now, with you guys." Butch smiles and looks directly at the camera, before declaring, "Hello, world!" He is gleeful about this opportunity to finally acknowledge an aspect of his own reality that had never been revealed on *Teen Mom*: that he is surrounded by cameras tracking his every move and word. Now, instead of denying that being on a reality show is, in fact, their primary means of employment, cast members can discuss the "job" of being reality TV stars quite openly. Beginning in season 5, *Teen Mom* audiences could watch the cast going on promotional tours, getting makeup applied before appearing on a talk show, and experiencing the overall process behind being a Teen Mom on MTV.

While such a gimmick is one way to keep a reality TV franchise fresh (see chapter 2's discussion of self-reflexivity in *The Real World*), *Teen Mom* takes this reflexivity a step further, not just by exposing the presence and existence of cameras and crews, but by exposing the emotional labor used to cajole a cast member into sharing her most private and intimate moments and feelings with the world. For example, in the season 5 finale episode Amber is upset because Gary, the father of her daughter, is pushing back against her attempts to get more time with Leah. Heather, a producer who has an especially close relationship with Amber, says, "I heard you texted with Gary." Amber snaps, "I'm not talking about that right now." As Heather gently presses on, bringing up the topic in different ways, Amber becomes increasingly agitated, insisting that she is not in the "mood" to discuss Gary or the custody battle. Finally, Amber explodes, saying, "That's the shit I don't like right there!"—much like Tony did on *The Real World: Skeletons*.[29] This moment illustrated an interesting ethical quandary for a production like *Teen Mom*. On the one hand, it is Amber's job—her contractual agreement—to talk about Gary and the custody battle onscreen with Heather and MTV's producers. If the camera crew is in her home filming, that means that they are working, and being paid by MTV to do this labor, at a day and time Amber agreed to in advance. Like an actress being called to set, Amber owes it to Heather and the crew to do her job.

As with *An American Family*, this production process muddies the waters when someone's job is to perform the emotional labor of her personal life onscreen. Amber knows she must be the At-Risk Girl, and she resents having to do so on cue. As Amber becomes increasingly enraged, Heather feigns surprise at her reaction. But Amber does not buy it; after seven years of filming a reality TV series, Amber knows Heather as well as Heather knows Amber: "Don't try the ignorant director bullshit with me!" Here the camera cuts to Heather looking confused and denying that she is goading Amber into talking onscreen. "Don't look confused!" Amber shrieks. This tense scene is truly unprecedented in an MTV reality series. It's not simply that the characters and crew have broken through the fourth wall to interact together onscreen; it's also remarkable that the previously unseen work of producers like Heather is laid bare. This episode clearly demonstrates how

Teen Mom's narrative is built on the pain and drama of its cast and the emotional labor of its producers.

Another remarkable example of *Teen Mom*'s destruction of the fourth wall is in season 5's handling of Farrah. Her absence from the series is not addressed until roughly halfway through the premiere, when Catelynn Lowell and Tyler Baltierra head to Los Angeles for VH1's *Couples' Therapy* reunion show, a reality series they participated in, alongside Farrah, during the interim between seasons 4 and 5 of *Teen Mom*. This, in itself, is remarkable in that it is the first time MTV has revealed the publicity machine behind the *Teen Mom* girls. Reunion shows typically function as a way to recuperate the sins of the Bad Mother in order to clear the way for her return in the next season of *Teen Mom*. Once again, as discussed in chapter 2, structures of melodrama are what enable audiences to view and comprehend Farrah, not as an immoral woman who will do anything for money, but rather as the ultimate sacrificing mother. Farrah must perform her victimhood before a studio audience—by weeping, accepting critique, and apologizing—in order for her morality to be legible and for forgiveness to be granted. During this particular reunion show, Farrah and her castmates, Catelynn and Tyler, exchange barbs. Farrah chastises the couple for getting pregnant (a second time) and derailing the goals they had made for themselves, namely, getting their college degrees and getting married. Catelynn replies, "We're disappointed in the choices *you* make. At least admit you're a porn star and not be in denial." When Farrah objects to this pejorative label, Catelynn mocks the excuses Farrah has used to explain away her participation in *Backdoor Teen Mom*: "It was a leaked sex tape? You sold your vagina!" At this, the live audience goes wild, clapping and hooting. When Catelynn asks, "Would you ever want your daughter to do that?" Farrah tearily replies, "I hope that I work hard [so] that she doesn't have to." After this statement, sentimental nondiegetic music plays and the room goes silent. It is clear Catelynn regrets her attack because she quickly adds, "You are an awesome mom. That little girl looks up to you for everything and you do everything possible that you can for her." This leads Farrah to finally make the important statement "I regret it," as she gingerly wipes away her tears. Catelynn assures her, "It's good that you regret it." The audience bursts into applause. It is significant that Farrah must admit, before a live studio audience, that she regrets performing in pornographic movies before she can return to being a Teen Mom. On *The Hills* "coming clean" entails allowing yourself to be filmed, but only with perfect makeup and scripted scenarios. Everything is controlled. By contrast, for the Teen Mom, "coming clean" means admitting to her mistakes, apologizing for them, and *meaning* it.

It's true that the Teen Moms already occupy a tenuous position as role models, given that their celebrity is built on an unintentional teen pregnancy, a "mistake." But for the series to work, the Teen Moms must be on a clear path to redemption. They must be At-Risk Girls who transform themselves. With her admission of guilt and regret before a live studio audience, who bear witness to her confessions, the series is free to reinsert Farrah into the *Teen Mom* narrative, which occurs in episode 5 of the season. The scene of her return, in the final minutes of the episode, opens with Heather, Farrah's producer, busily directing her camerapersons, who are assembled on the front lawn of a large suburban home. Then a slow panning shot across the front of the house is paired with Heather's instructions: "Let's just get us walking, so we get that shot." The next shot is a close-up of a clapperboard, used to mark the beginning and end of scenes on both the video and audio tracks of the footage. Again, none of these elements—the producers, their equipment, the clapperboard—had ever been seen within the frames of *Teen Mom* prior to this season. As the production team marches toward the front door of the home, Heather cheers them on, "You roll, baby, you roll!" A shaky handheld camera follows Heather's steps, focusing on her feet and then her back, as she rings the doorbell. All of this suspense paves the way for the next shot, the opening of the door (in the TV broadcast, this was the moment when the episode cut to a commercial).

After the door opens, Farrah is finally revealed with full makeup and a big smile. "Hello," she says, pleasantly. A beat later her name appears onscreen, written in the characteristic Teen Mom font. The appearance of the chyron is a formal acknowledgment that Farrah's identity as a Teen Mom has been returned to her. Heather and Farrah embrace, and upbeat music plays on the soundtrack. A series of quick cuts reveal Farrah's daughter, Sophia, the first look the audience has had of the girl in two years. Heather once again directs the cameras where to go, with shots going in and out of focus as they are moved around, casual cinematographic mistakes that would, in previous seasons of the series, be the first to hit the cutting-room floor. But in season 5 such authenticating moments are now integral to the series' purpose and effect. Heather begins, "Since you're coming back to *Teen Mom*, we need some sort of scene where you're explaining that you're back on *Teen Mom*." Here the camera cuts back to Farrah, who looks tense. This question clearly makes her angry: "So, like, ummm, I was dropped a year ago. . . . *Then*, apparently, I'm not so crazy, and it's okay that I'm back on TV." There is a temporal ellipsis here, cutting to a long shot of Farrah and Sophia interacting, their backs to the camera. "I'm just over being judged, and I guess I don't wanna talk about that." Another temporal ellipsis occurs, followed by a quick cut from Farrah and Sophia to the back of a cameraperson who is following Farrah from room to room.

The camera finally catches up with Farrah as she is looking in the mirror, putting on makeup. Farrah is already wearing makeup, as a matter of course, but the frantic act of primping and reapplying lipstick gives her an excuse to look away from Heather. Heather, who has drawn back, aware that Farrah is on the edge and will, perhaps, not agree to provide any more footage for the crew, backs down from her original ask, telling Farrah she can shoot the scene any way she likes. Heather explains that the scene just needs to establish, for the (future) audience, that Farrah is now back on the series; it must be documented for the narrative to make sense and move forward. Both Heather and Farrah understand this but Farrah ignores Heather's entreaties, announcing, just after her oven timer rings, "The pizza's done," before leaving the room and hurrying downstairs again.

Downstairs is Farrah's mother, Debra, who is dolled up for the return of MTV's crew. Debra and Heather embrace, and then Debra turns to the camera and beams, saying, "You guys are like family, and, yes, hi Jon . . . good to see you." She waves at something just beyond the frame, and a hand appears from behind the frame and waves in return. Jon is shooting the scene. As Debra catches Heather up on her life over the past two years (she lost part of her intestine; she divorced her husband, Michael; she moved from Omaha to Seattle), Farrah stomps around angrily in the background. The camera catches her in the frame as she storms into the kitchen, chastising her mother: "I just really don't even like that you're having a fake, wannabe happy conversation." Debra's overt kindness to Heather and the crew stands as a rebuke to Farrah, who expects her parents (and boyfriends) to adapt to her mercurial mood swings. But, even in her act of rejecting the production, Farrah nevertheless contributes to the production; her noncompliance is an entertaining spectacle. Farrah is playing Farrah very well. Heather tries again to get the footage she needs to establish Farrah's return to the series: "How do you feel about being back? Are you excited to film, or no?" Farrah bends over the oven and answers with her back to the camera: "I don't care if you guys are here or not."

The way Farrah stages her body here is a key moment of resistance: seven years of reality TV labor have trained her to know how to perform on camera. She knows the producers need her to face the camera when she speaks, to allow her face to be open to the probing of the lens. By moving quickly through the frame or turning her back to the camera when she speaks, Farrah is registering her defiance against the cast and crew of *Teen Mom*. Heather heads outside and consults with Larry, another producer on the show. Larry assures his coworker, "[Farrah's] not going to yell at me. She can't yell at me," to which Heather responds, "She's gonna shut down production is what she's gonna do." It is remarkable to watch a scene like this unfold because, while it is about Farrah's drama and her life, for the first time the audience is seeing how Farrah's drama impacts how *Teen Mom* is made. The labor behind the seemingly authentic identity Farrah and the other moms have been performing for seven years is finally recoupled with its other half: the emotional labor of the series' producers:

LARRY   Farrah, you're having an issue about your entry to the show?
FARRAH   I mean, why are we worried about an "entry"? Why don't we just, like, be *real* about that?
LARRY   I'm all about being real, but at the same time, we have to be mindful about how we introduce you. . . . How is it that, one day, your fans all of a sudden see you when they tune into the show? How does that start?
FARRAH   Whatever. We all agree on the same thing. It's weird that I wasn't a part of it and now I'm a part of it. The End.
LARRY   If I was all of a sudden left out of a project I was a part of . . . there's a feeling of rejection . . .
FARRAH   [cutting him off] I already went to counseling about it. I'm not gonna talk about it anymore. . . .
LARRY   Everybody else that's kind of been part of . . . this show, we felt that there was something missing. It just didn't feel right not having you.

There is a pregnant pause after this statement and the camera cuts to Farrah's face in medium close-up. It's a money shot, reality TV–wise, because it is the moment just before Farrah's face crumples, her mouth twisting as she starts to cry.[30] She leaves the room in tears while a plangent guitar plays and her young daughter calls after her. Farrah's battles with the *Teen Mom*'s producers serve to highlight the tenuous barrier between work and life for a reality identity TV show and its cast and crew.

The tension of this scene is generated by the fact that Farrah is angry and hurt by MTV's initial decision not to recast her for season 5 of the series she helped to make a success. She clearly wants to be on the show, as evidenced by the fact that this footage has been recorded and broadcast to audiences, but she resents having to replay and perform the trauma of that rejection. It hurts that MTV—the channel that made her fame and her identity—has rejected what she has become (an outcast, a punchline), an identity for which the channel is, in many ways, responsible. Heather wants Farrah to rehearse the rejection on camera, for continuity, but Farrah is an unruly subject.[31] She will not perform the labor demanded of her, not because she feels the labor is unfairly compensated or because she feels the labor is unethical, but because her feelings are hurt. This difference is key. Traditionally, a refusal to perform the labor you are paid to do is based on an abuse: low wages, poor working conditions, or unfair workloads. But for Farrah the refusal is rooted in pain, specifically the pain of being rejected by her own reality series. This should not be surprising, given that Farrah's labor is this emotional labor. To be sure, Farrah's acknowledgment of the crew, even a begrudging one, becomes exactly the footage Heather and Larry need to build the narrative of Farrah's return to the series. Even as she resists the production, Farrah still gives the crew what they need.

One of Farrah's major character arcs in season 5 is the way her real life—including her past in pornography and her initial ouster from *Teen Mom*—keeps disrupting her attempts to self-brand as a super "mompreneur" in front of MTV's cameras. The taboo nature of her identity is best displayed in season 5, episode 13, when Farrah is planning to attend an "exclusive white party" in the Hamptons, hosted by Lisa Vanderpump, star of the hit Bravo reality TV series *Vanderpump Rules*. While riding in her car, Farrah receives a phone call from Heather (not her producer, but her business partner), informing her that she may no longer attend the event. "The organizers of the white party have asked me not to bring you as a guest," Heather explains over the phone. Heather reads an email she received that explains Farrah is not "the right fit" for the party because the guest list is limited to "noncontroversial celebrities," and that the hosts "would like to keep [the party] as upscale as possible." After Farrah hangs up on Heather, she complains to her mother, "I don't understand people acting or treating me like this because of my association with *Teen Mom*. . . . A lot of people treat me as trashy, low class, whatever. Because of *Teen Mom*." Blaming Vanderpump's shunning on her role in *Teen Mom* is a more comforting explanation for Farrah, because she views her labor on the MTV show as "sharing her story" and "helping other girls." Sex work is rarely described in such lofty terms, which is why Farrah avoids it (attributing her rejection to her association with teen motherhood, rather than pornography). As with her earlier denials on the *Couples Therapy* reunion, Farrah attempts to disavow her past labor.

Ultimately, Farrah decides to attend Vanderpump's party anyway, in order to make a statement about her pride in herself and her status as someone who keeps it "top notch." Farrah triumphantly exits the car in a fuchsia fascinator and a white lace dress, and heads into the party. Four minutes later, according to the onscreen chyron, she is kicked out. After this public humiliation, Debra tries to reassure her daughter: "We've been kicked out of much better places than that!" But Farrah will not even acknowledge the humiliation, converting the experience, once again, into evidence of her superiority: "I'm happy that I'm so damn fabulous that no one knows what to do. . . . I actually feel like I'm so much more important now because they did that." In the labor economy of identity, Farrah takes her ejection from Lisa Vanderpump's white party as evidence of her dominant position in the celebrity pecking order; she is important enough to be kicked out of something. Or at least, that is what she says on camera. This positive attitude disappears in the next scene, when Farrah locks herself in her hotel bathroom to cry in private, beyond the reach of MTV's cameras. Heather (the producer) stands outside the door, apologizing, though it is unclear what Heather has done wrong. As the scene continues, Farrah is filmed from the inside of the room as she reapplies her makeup (after crying). Throughout the episode, Farrah is in a perpetual state of makeup reapplication; it is a mask that threatens to slide away with every set back, every negative tweet, and every tear. As she gazes in the mirror, she tells a nodding Heather, "I keep it classy . . . I keep it top notch."

Farrah is anxious to reshape her identity on the show. She wants to be identified as a businesswoman and a role model for young girls.[32] Her perfect posture, her perpetually glossed lips, and her flawless appearance (the result of numerous, highly publicized, plastic surgeries) are all methods Farrah employs to convert her celebrity narrative from that of the At-Risk Girl to the Can-Do Girl (see *Us Weekly* 2018). Anita Harris argues that Can-Do Girls "seize the opportunities made available within the new economy and make projects of their work selves from an early age" (2004a, 17–18). Farrah believes strongly in this postfeminist narrative and her do-it-yourself project of the self. If only she can attend the right parties, wear the right dress, or start the right business, she can finally succeed and gain respect. Farrah has fallen under the spell of postfeminism, believing that conspicuous consumption and self-surveillance are enough to lift her out of a scandal of her own making. While early examples of MTV's reality identity series highlight choice and agency, this move to break the fourth wall actually highlights how the postfeminist subject is controlled by her surroundings, rather than the reverse. She controls her body (through plastic surgery and makeup), wears the right clothing, and styles herself the way a sexy young starlet should. Yet, she still fails. She is still a single mother who is disinvited to upscale white parties in the Hamptons. No matter how hard she tries, Farrah has no control over her destiny.

Conclusions

The professionally and physically successful white femininity at the heart of MTV series like *Laguna Beach, The Hills,* and *The City* is itself a product sold to and consumed by MTV's female audiences in a neoliberal, postfeminist economy (Harris 2004a, 20). Lauren and Whitney both successfully built (respected, nonscandalous) careers based on their MTV-generated stardom, such as Lauren's fashion and retail businesses and Whitney's clothing line, Whitney Eve. These products promised a direct link between Can-Do qualities and success, thereby eliding the fact that Lauren and Whitney have successful lives because they are wealthy, white, heterosexual, cisgendered women. Lauren was an ideal Can-Do Girl before a single frame of *Laguna Beach* was shot: she was well coiffed, fashionable, slim, confident, and, most important, wealthy and white. When placed side by side, the lessons of these series are clear. Maintaining a Can-Do status is simply a matter of avoiding all of the pitfalls that At-Risk Girls like *Teen Mom*'s Amber and Farrah experience. They struggle to build careers based on their celebrity identities since they are associated with their At-Risk status, that is, their overall failure to live up to gendered expectations of postponing motherhood until after love and a career have been secured. Their celebrity identities are tied to shame. In the next chapter I discuss how MTV reality identity series packaged the identities of working-class white people (*Buckwild*) and symbolically nonwhite people (*Jersey Shore*). Instead of being offered up as models for emulation (the Can-Do Girls of *The Hills*) or avoidance (the At-Risk Girls of *Teen Mom*), these identities (the Guidos of *Jersey Shore* and the Rednecks of *Buckwild*) are offered up for the viewer to ridicule.

"If You Don't Tan, You're Pale"
The Regional and Ethnic Other on MTV (2009–2013)

I n 2009, a hot-dog restaurant in the college town of Greenville, North Carolina (home to East Carolina University, aka ECU), named Sup Dogs, hosted the first of what would become an annual spring concert called Doggie Jams. Doggie Jams is held in the asphalt parking lot that Sup Dogs shares with Shop 'n' Go, a convenience store that primarily sells cigarettes to local bar patrons and kegs to fraternities and sororities. Having resided in this college town since 2007, I never thought to attend Doggie Jams since its primary clientele are highly intoxicated, eighteen- to twenty-two-year-old students enrolled at the university where I teach. But, in the spring of 2016, the *East Carolinian*, ECU's student newspaper, announced that the Doggie Jams headliner was DJ Pauly D, aka Paul DelVecchio, star of MTV's *Jersey Shore*; I immediately purchased a ticket for the show and successfully convinced several friends to go with me so that I would not be the only Doggie Jammer over twenty-two at the event. On the day of the big event, my colleagues and I put on hats and sunglasses (a disguise that did not prevent three of my students from recognizing me) and received our neon wristbands (which would allow us to legally purchase Sup Dogs' signature cocktail, the Orange Sup Crush). After a long stretch in which various fist-pumping hits blared over the parking lot loudspeakers, DJ Pauly D finally walked onstage and behind a set of turntables. Pauly D was looking, as he might say, "fresh to death" (a frequently invoked phrase on *Jersey Shore*) in shorts and a black T-shirt, with a large gold chain around his neck. After hyping up the crowd with the usual exaltations to "party" and "get hype," Pauly D commenced his DJ-ing.

During his performance, Pauly D was often on his phone, though it was unclear whether he was consuming content, making content, or both. At one point during the set, Pauly D conspicuously popped the cork on a bottle of Dom Perignon and drank it, exultantly, straight from the bottle. After drinking his fill, he shook up the bottle and *appeared to* spray the expensive champagne onto the crowd in a show of devil-may-care financial abandon. I say "appeared," because one of my colleagues, who had snaked her way toward the front of the drunken throng of coeds, reported back that Pauly D had *actually* sprayed the sweaty multitude with a cheap bottle of sparkling wine; he only *pretended* to spray the Dom. If we were not the only ones who noticed, we were certainly the only ones who cared, because right here, in our quiet college town, was an MTV reality star.[1]

The Pauly D performance at Doggie Jams was not the first time I attended an event aimed at my students because it featured a star of an MTV reality series. In 2015, *Teen Mom* star Maci Bookout was invited to speak at ECU as part of a designated Wellness Passport event. These events are mandatory for any ECU students enrolled in either a required health class or a bridge class that teaches new students skills related to public speaking, time management, and test taking. According to ECU's website, Wellness Passport events provide students with "an added opportunity to experience a variety of health and wellness activities, services, and programs at ECU relative to the 8 Dimensions of Wellness."[2] All Wellness Passport events must be free and, most important, must be educational. Unsurprisingly, the crowd who showed up to see Maci Bookout was different in form and behavior from the one who attended Doggie Jams. They remained seated for the entire event, and some of the audience members, who were almost entirely white, cisgendered women with long sleek ponytails, XXL T-shirts emblazoned with Greek letters, and Nike zoom shorts, even took notes.[3] Everyone at the Wellness Passport event was sober (or acted sober) because no one had attended the event in the hopes of "partying," as they had at Doggie Jams. Although these identically attired women were probably at the Maci Bookout event for a course, or perhaps even a sorority requirement, the fact that these young women chose *this* particular event to get their Wellness Passports stamped

4.1 When Pauly D performed at the 2016 Doggie Jams in Greenville, North Carolina, his identity as a hard-partying Guido from *Jersey Shore* was on display.

(ECU offers many opportunities each semester) is a good indication that they, like me, were excited to see the *Teen Mom* star in real life. While students attended Pauly D's event to party, they attended Maci's event to *learn* from her many struggles as a Teen Mom. Their interactions with Pauly D were mostly physical (to drink, dance, sing, and snap selfies), while their interactions with Maci were more educational (to listen and learn). No one was fist pumping, dancing, or getting sprayed with cheap sparkling wine as Maci signed copies of her autobiography, *Bulletproof* (2015), in the lobby of the auditorium.

I open this chapter with these two anecdotes about two longtime stars of two of MTV's most successful reality series, *Jersey Shore* and *Teen Mom*, because their appearances at my university, and the behavior of the audiences they drew, highlight how MTV's reality identity cycle offers up different identities to its youth audience for very different rhetorical purposes. Pauly D's purpose was to drink and party with college students, while Maci was tasked with educating them; one was brought to Greenville by a local bar and hot-dog joint, while another's stay was sanctioned by the university's curriculum. Pauly D's identity as a hard-partying Guido from *Jersey Shore* manifested itself in the wild ecstasies of the crowd, who screamed, sweated, and even vomited during his performance. Maci's identity as a girl who made a mistake, and then rehabilitated was meant to be illustrative for the primarily white, sorority-girl audience who attended her talk. The discourses of these two different MTV reality identity series are clear in both instances: being a Guido is about partying and having fun, and being a (white) Teen Mom is about learning and growing from your past mistakes so that you, one day, might serve as a role model for other young women: to be a productive citizen.

Indeed, MTV reality identity series perform different functions depending on the subjects they feature. As Laura Grindstaff and Susan Murray argue, "some reality television stars exist not only as the concrete embodiment of heightened emotion on-screen but also as *brands* in relation to the spectacular emotion or affect they produce/evoke" (2015, 111). Some, like *The Hills* and *Teen Mom*, present both aspirational and cautionary identities, respectively, for young, white, cisgendered girls. These series can also serve a pedagogical role. To name one prominent example, *Catfish* (discussed in the conclusion to this book) offers lessons on how to not get "Catfished" (i.e., deceived) by an online lover. But a significant function of MTV's reality identity series is, of course, to entertain audiences through the spectacularization of certain identities, turning them into displays of beautiful wealth (as is the case with *The Hills*) or into outlandish, comic figures. The series I discuss in this chapter, *Jersey Shore* and *Buckwild*, fit firmly into the latter category. As I discussed in chapter 3, the classed (wealthy) and raced (white) identities of *The Hills* cast were never explicitly discussed or engaged (they just *were*). The concealment of artifice (the set-up shots, the telephoto lenses) further normalized the show's vision of aspirational whiteness. However, the classed (working or lower) and/or ethnic (Italian American) identities of the *Jersey Shore* and *Buckwild* casts are central to each series' appeal, and therefore made highly visible. The *Jersey Shore* cast members have built their careers on their performance of their so-called Guido identity, and the series is peppered with catchphrases that codify and prop up this branded self, like "Gym. Tan. Laundry" (GTL) and "the shirt before the shirt." *Buckwild*, like *Jersey Shore*, also transformed a previously derogatory label—Redneck—into something clearly defined (e.g., thick West Virginia accents, a love of dangerous outdoor activities, and an aversion to cultural snobbery) *and* as a badge of honor. This chapter explores how each series exploited these broad stereotypes, and why this imagery resonated so strongly with MTV's primarily white youth audiences.

The Ethnic Identities of *Jersey Shore*

By the fall of 2009, the focus on the privileged, navel-gazing, white women of *Laguna Beach*, *The Hills*, and *The City* was no longer resonating with MTV's target audience of twelve- to thirty-four-year-olds. The Great Recession (2008–2012), when many Americans lost their savings, jobs, and homes, is a likely explanation for the precipitous drop in *The Hills'* (and *The City's*) ratings (Klein 2014, 149). MTV's president of programming and development in 2009, Tony DiSanto, believed the network's audiences wanted "their reality more 'real'" (qtd. in Seidman 2010), which led to the creation of *Teen Mom*. *Teen Mom's* At-Risk Girls offered a possible antidote to *The Hills'* Can-Do Girls since the former were not worried about landing high-status internships or wearing outfits the viewers might want to purchase after the show. In the same year *Teen Mom* premiered, MTV embarked on another "more real" reality show tentatively titled *Bridge and Tunnel*. Camille Dodero (2011), who profiled the never-aired series for the *Village Voice*, called *Bridge and Tunnel* "the anti-*Hills*, a blue-collar rebuttal to the grossly loaded California clan that begat plastic-surgery monster Heidi Montag." While *The Hills* and *The City* presented the easy success of wealthy, white Americans living in Los Angeles and New York City, respectively, *Bridge and Tunnel* was created to focus on working-class kids striving toward a better life in the ethnically circumscribed neighborhoods of Staten Island, New York. In other words, the series wanted the class status of the cast emphasized. During the preproduction process, MTV suggested putting *Bridge and Tunnel's* cast into a house, *Real World*–style (i.e., providing cast members with a hot tub and a steady stream of alcohol), and renaming the series *Staten Island* (thus keeping in the MTV tradition of naming reality identity shows after the location in which they are set). But the independent production company behind *Bridge and Tunnel*, Ish Entertainment, refused, arguing that its show was about "kids with stories, not kids whose only stories [a]re the show" (qtd. in Dodero 2011). Ish Entertainment felt strongly that taking cast members out of context, that is, out of their neighborhood, would jeopardize the authenticity of their stories.

As with so many of MTV's reality identity series, including *The Real World* and *Teen Mom*, there is a tension between control and authenticity, stereotypes and nuanced portrayals. Soon after this dispute, *Bridge and Tunnel* was permanently shelved, and, in its place, MTV aired a new reality series featuring cast members, Italian Americans in their twenties, remarkably similar to those of *Bridge and Tunnel*. Only, instead of filming these young Italian Americans in their own neighborhoods and homes (as Ish Entertainment wanted to do with *Bridge and Tunnel*), MTV placed its cast members in a beach house along the New Jersey shoreline.[4] But perhaps the biggest difference between *Bridge and Tunnel* and the series that would come to be known as *Jersey Shore* was the latter's foregrounding and fetishization of a derogatory term for a certain type of Italian American: the Guido. Indeed, the very first promotional trailer for *Jersey Shore* promised to showcase the lifestyles of the "hottest, tannest, craziest Guidos," that is, Italian American youth who enjoy grooming, showing off, and partying.

Although the exact origin of the word "Guido" is unclear, it likely dates back to turn-of-the-century America, when it was an epithet used by established Italian Americans to insult newly arrived Italian immigrants (Brooks 2009). The term implies an ignorance that is profoundly tied to Italian identity: Italians who had not yet learned to conceal their Italianness were labeled Guidos. Consequently, some factions of the Italian American population see the use of "Guido" as offensive and view *Jersey Shore*'s cast members as ethnic caricatures (Hyman 2009b). Andre DiMino, president of UNICO, the largest Italian American service organization in the United States, told the *New Jersey Star-Ledger* in 2009, just before the premiere of the series, "It's a derogatory comment. It's a pejorative word to depict an uncool Italian who tries to act cool" (qtd. in Hyman 2009a). The National Italian American Federation (NIAF) (2013) released an official statement on its website as the first season of *Jersey Shore* came to a close in 2010, arguing that the series "tapped into a sore spot for many Italian Americans, who have a long history of negative stereotyping in media and are often portrayed as gangsters and buffoons." The NIAF's outrage is directed at MTV, rather than the cast of the series, for portraying "the program's characters as representative of the Italian American community. This is simply not accurate and its prevalence in the media is damaging to Italian American identity." In recent decades, however, some Italian American youth have reclaimed and reappropriated the term "Guido" as a source of ethnic pride. *Jersey Shore* star Nicole "Snooki" Polizzi, to name one example, views the term as a neutral label for the subculture she embraces. "I don't take offense to it," she told reporters in 2009. "I feel we are representing Italian Americans. We look good. We have a good time. We're nice people. We get along with everybody. I don't understand why [Guido] would be offensive" (qtd. in Hyman 2009a). Certainly, the cast members of *Jersey Shore* embraced the term when they responded to MTV's original casting call for "Guidos." This was their first moment of identity confession.

So what is a Guido? Sociologist Donald Tricarico argues that the term denotes a specific subcultural identity signified by a series of distinctive clothing styles, music preferences, behavioral patterns, and choices in language and peer groups (2007, 38). This label provides coherence and a solid ethnic character to a set of otherwise unmarked stylistic choices, including the acquisition of expensive clothing, footwear, jewelry, and cars. Embedded in this chosen identity is a predilection for display that goes beyond conspicuous consumption. Dancing and mingling at nightclubs, which forms the crux of Guido subculture depicted on *Jersey Shore*, is about visibility and performance, seeing and being seen.[5] A *Washington Post* article on Guidos highlights the to-be-looked-at-ness of this identity: "The guido ethos is showy, it bumps shoulders and yells. It is a hey-baby culture, in which the men are macho and the women wear spandex. When cruising in cars—a popular pastime—guidos like loud dance music and loud-looking girls. When they walk, they thrust their shoulders back and take over sidewalks" (Copeland 2003). Guidos are "unruly" because they identify as Italian American, flaunt the "wrong" image of Italian Americans, and then demand that this transgressive image be witnessed and admired. In dressing to be noticed, not to assimilate, Guidos reject the white, Protestant work ethic. Their focus on consumption over the acquisition of cultural capital subverts the classic immigrant trajectory in American society. Concerns within the Italian American community over Guido identities are therefore rooted in its ties to youth culture and in its perceived lack of cultural capital (Cappelli 2011, 12).

The subculture's lack of cultural capital is most evident in the perceived opposition between "hip" Manhattan clubgoers and those who live in New Jersey, Staten Island, or New York's outer boroughs: the much-maligned "bridge and tunnel" (B&T) crowd. The animosity for the B&T crowd, that irrelevant "monstrous urban limbo" of Bronx-Brooklyn-Queens, extends beyond the city native's typical distaste for tourists, and instead it highlights both a class- and ethnicity-based bias (Cohn 1976). For example, in March 2011, street artists Jeff Greenspan and Hunter Fine began setting B&T traps (including hair gel, cheap cologne, and self-tanning spray) outside of hip New York City clubs like Mason & Dixon (Coscarelli 2011). These art installations, while intended to be whimsical and humorous, nevertheless relegate a working-class, Italian American identity to an outsider status. Guidos are something to trap and quarantine in order to preserve the hipness of the nearby club. Although Italian Americans are an entrenched part of

New York City's multiethnic identities, the Guido is subjected to a culturally sanctioned xenophobia.

Because Italian Americans have the ability to pass for a range of ethnic identities in America, including Jewish, Latinx, or Greek, self-identified Guidos must make their identity visible and unambiguous to those outside of the subculture in order to be read as a Guido.[6] In this way, Guidos are different from many other ethnic subcultures in that style is used to highlight and emphasize ethnic differences, rather than to escape from their presumed constraints (Thornton 1997). As discussed in the introduction to this book, only certain ethnic groups have the freedom to choose their identities. In particular, Mary Waters notes, "white ethnics have a lot more choice and room for maneuver than they themselves think they do" (1996, 449). The cast members of *Jersey Shore* are, by contemporary understandings of the term, "white," and yet their identities on the show mark them as nonwhite. Hunter Hargraves notes that *Jersey Shore*'s fetishization of the tan, a key feature marking the cast members as part of the Guido identity group, "is at once part of and detached from whiteness" (2014, 294). The cast members enjoy many of the privileges of whiteness (such as averting police surveillance) but are also subject to critique based on their distance from whiteness and white taste cultures. The Guido identity functions as an "ethnic pull" rather than as a "racial push" (Gans 1979).[7]

Codifying the Guido on MTV

Whereas on *The Hills* and *Teen Mom* the women are defined by their job aspirations or their poor decisions, the cast members of *Jersey Shore* are defined, first and foremost, by their Guido identities. Adopting the Guido identity has provided *Jersey Shore*'s cast members with fame, money, and lucrative business opportunities.[8] Several *Jersey Shore* personalities have published books, started clothing lines, and agreed to endorse products that range from weight-loss supplements and bronzer to muscle-enhancing vodka. Interestingly, their financial success and fame are built on a Guido identity, despite the fact that it is nevertheless associated with unrefined tastes. For example, in 2010, one of Gucci's competitors sent *Jersey Shore* star Snooki a free Gucci handbag in the mail. The competitors sent the expensive bag to Snooki in the hopes that it would discourage her from donning one of *their* products in public. *Observer* columnist Simon Doonan (2010) calls this "preemptive product placement," or "unbranding": "As much as one might adore Miss Snickerdoodle, her ability to inspire dress-alikes among her fans is questionable. The bottom line? Nobody in fashion wants to co-brand with Snooki." As discussed in chapter 3, not all reality TV celebrity functions in the same way. While Lauren Conrad was able to convert her MTV fame into a clothing line at Kohl's department stores (among many other commercial deals), Farrah Abraham's brand of MTV fame, pornography, got her kicked out of Lisa Vanderpump's party. By performing in a pornographic film, Farrah squandered the opportunity to rehabilitate her At-Risk image. Farrah's violations of taste are clear, but what did The Situation and Snooki do to earn their toxic celebrity identities? The answer, of course, is their status as Guidos. To wit, in 2011 the Abercrombie & Fitch clothing line reportedly offered to pay another *Jersey Shore* star, The Situation, to *stop* wearing their clothing, stating, "We understand that the show is for entertainment purposes, but believe this association is *contrary to the aspirational nature of our brand*, and may be distressing to many of our fans" (qtd. in Holmes 2011; emphasis mine). Guidos, at least according to Abercrombie & Fitch, are not aspirational. As much as The Situation, Snooki, and the rest of the *Jersey Shore* cast embrace being Guidos and celebrate their ancestry, this identity is always-already coded as something nonaspirational. Brands that depend on cultural capital for their existence, like Abercrombie & Fitch or Lisa Vanderpump, must dissociate themselves from these tainted identities. This is just one of the ways in which gender, class, and racial norms structure the way MTV reality stars are marketed and treated.

Hargraves argues that *Jersey Shore* marks a shift in the way MTV reality programming addressed issues of diversity and multiculturalism because it "depict[s] racial and ethnic identity, in contrast to the multiculturalist approach of the early *Real World*" (2014, 293). Jonathan Murray and Mary-Ellis Bunim initially structured *The Real World* seasons as "liberal utopias free of racism" as a way to bring together different ethnicities and cultures with the hopes that they would learn from each other over the course of a season. As Kraszewski argues, "multiracialism allowed *The Real World* to portray race as a project of self-management where individuals would rely upon themselves, not the government and the welfare state, to succeed in society" (2010, 140). By contrast, a series like *Jersey Shore* aims to isolate a single homogeneous identity and amplify it, creating another page for MTV's identity workbook. It is also important to note that *Jersey Shore* isolates this ethnic identity, not to honor it but to mock it. *Jersey Shore* therefore sits somewhere in the middle of the shame/aspiration spectrum occupied previously by the contrast between *Teen Mom*'s cast and *The Hills'* cast. *Jersey Shore*'s cast of

4.2 The original cast of *Jersey Shore* self-identified as Guidos.

Guidos have not violated or transgressed any moral codes (like the women of *Teen Mom*). If anything, they "live up" to the stereotypes circulating about Italian American identities, and, consequently, they do not need to perform their absolution onscreen, like Amber or Farrah, in order to profit from their celebrity identities, "low class" though they may be. However, as working-class bodies codified as "nonwhite," the cast of *Jersey Shore* is still subject to shaming and ridicule, as evidenced by Abercrombie & Fitch's desire to distance its brand from the casts' adoration of the clothing and a handbag company allegedly tricking Snooki into carrying a competitor's bag.

The more the cast members inflate their ethnic identity, making it clear and unambiguous to viewers, the more successful they are on *Jersey Shore* as well as in ancillary markets (but only when selling products that emphasize partying or grooming for a party). As discussed in the introduction to this book, identity confession is a necessary prerequisite for these MTV reality series to make sense. From their first moments of screen time, the *Jersey Shore* cast embraces being a Guido, whether by explicitly using the term or by engaging in the behaviors the series implicitly aligns with Guidoness, such as grooming, tanning, exercising, or eating Italian food. Catchphrases and codified behaviors help MTV cast members to self-brand and make the messy signifiers of real-life ethnicity more legible onscreen. Perhaps the most salient signifier of the Guido subculture is the daily grooming ritual, known as "Gym. Tan. Laundry," or "GTL." In season 1, episode 6, The

Situation explains the ritual: "If I didn't do my GTL or take care of myself, I don't know what I'd look like. If you don't go to the gym, you don't look good. If you don't tan, you're pale. If you don't do laundry, you ain't got no clothes." The Situation's description of his ritual is paired with a montage of his GTL routine: lifting weights at the gym, getting into a tanning bed at the salon, and picking up freshly laundered clothes from the laundromat. The amount of time, energy, and money required to perform these tasks is considerable, and the fact that they need to be performed before any socializing can take place highlights the price The Situation and his roommates pay to look "fresh to death." The Situation is familiar with the conventions of reality television and understands that extreme personalities and catchphrases play well with audiences, yet his insistence on GTL as a ritual, by its very utterance on camera, has become a compulsory ritual for The Situation (and eventually for his roommates).[9] By proclaiming GTL as his daily ritual on TV, The Situation has placed himself in a situation (no pun intended) where he must abide by these (self-imposed) grooming habits to maintain his Guido identity (Klein 2014, 162–164).

Of course, The Situation's interpretation of what it means to be a Guido was not embraced initially by all of his castmates. For example, the introduction of cast member Vinny Guadagnino in the pilot episode (entitled "A New Family") finds him seated at a large table covered with homemade Italian dishes and surrounded by a dozen family members. His mother is leaning over his plate, cutting his meat for him. As she does this, Vinny's voice-over explains: "She cooks for me, cleans for me, she loves me to death." For Vinny, being an Italian American man means being with family, having a doting mother, and eating authentic Italian food. Later in his introductory segment, Vinny, who calls himself a "mama's boy" and a "generational Italian," explicitly distances himself from the stylistic trappings of the Guido subculture practiced by his roommates: "The guys with the blow outs, the fake tans, that wear lip gloss and make up . . . those aren't Guidos, those are fucking retards!" Vinny is a Guido, just not *that kind of Guido*. As Vinny expresses his disdain for this particular iteration of Italian American identity, the camera cuts to his future roommate (and future best friend), Paul DelVecchio, blow-drying his hair and applying lip gloss. It is clear that Vinny sees these subcultural behaviors as feminine and, therefore, incompatible with his understanding of Italian masculinity. He also claims to prefer activities with masculine gender attributions, like playing pool and basketball, over GTL, and accuses his roommates of being "robots" for strictly adhering to the regimen. But by season 3, Vinny's hair, physique, and clothing are nearly identical to those donned by The Situation and Pauly D. In other words, the branding of the catchphrase "GTL" codified the Guido identity so strongly that Vinny had to adapt in order to continue to think of himself as a Guido (and remain on the series).

GTL is a salient example of how the series creates and codifies, rather than simply reports or documents, identity. This becomes clear in season 4 of *Jersey Shore*, when MTV sent the cast to live in Italy for just over a month. The ostensible reason behind the European trip was to give the cast members a chance to experience their homeland, the country of their Italian ancestors. In reality, the trip provides various opportunities for MTV's production crew to point out how *different* the cast members are from their country of origin and their ancestors. The cast members spend much of their time in Italy attempting to replicate their lifestyles from America, and thus the season 5 premiere focuses on the cast's joy over returning to the United States. What did the *Jersey Shore* men miss most about America while in Italy? Their GTL ritual. When they are away in Italy, the men are unable to partake in this ritual with the frequency and quality to which they are accustomed in the States, forcing The Situation to declare an emergency: "We're losing weight and we're getting pale!" After a tanning session, a good workout, and a fresh cut from the barber shop, cast member Ronnie Ortiz-Magaro explains, "I feel like I'm in heaven because I get to GTL again." Although the crew was only gone for forty days, and Italy boasts some of the world's most beautiful beaches (perfect for tanning pale American skin), the crew cannot be truly "fresh to death" unless they are in America. While their identities as Guidos are tied to a presumed Italian ancestry, it is, ironically, only America that can shore up the borders of their Guido identities.

The women also have codified identities. In "Boardwalk Blowups" (season 1, episode 6), Snooki describes Vinny's mother as "a true Italian woman" because she wants to "please everyone else at the table. And then when everyone's done eating, you clean up and then you eat by yourself."[10] Here, Italian American femininity is defined by hard work, self-denial, and sacrifice. The Italian American woman is most feminine when she makes her desires secondary to those of everyone else, particularly male relatives. Snooki explains in the pilot episode that her "ultimate dream" is to "move to Jersey, find a nice, juiced, hot, tan guy, and live my life." To get the hot, tan guy, the Italian American woman must also groom herself properly, adopting conventional models of femininity in her dress and hair styles. The *Jersey Shore* women wear their hair long and usually dye it a shade darker than their natural color, in accordance with their Italian heritage. Makeup must be bright and noticeable, with an emphasis on the eyes, lips, and nails. And, like their male roommates, Snooki, J Woww, Samantha, Deena, and "Sammi" Giancola invest a lot of time in creating and maintaining their appearance. Most *Jersey Shore* episodes include a montage of the women preparing for a night at the club.

The codified nature of the women's grooming practices reached an unsettling peak in 2017, when the cast of *Jersey Shore* returned to the reality TV camera's gaze after five years away, for an E! television special titled *Reunion Road Trip: Return to the Jersey Shore*. The success of this special led to MTV's announcement, two months later, that it was rebooting *Jersey Shore* as a new series called *Jersey Shore: Family Vacation*. The series includes the original cast (minus Sammi Giancola) and is set in Miami, Florida, where the group is reuniting for a month-long vacation. The 2017 series included numerous flashbacks to the original 2012 series, featuring footage of the various *Jersey Shore* women—Snooki, J Woww, Deena, and Angelina Pivarnick—from the years 2009 to 2012. There is a striking contrast between the women of *Jersey Shore*'s past and present, due almost entirely to the amount of plastic surgery each woman has had in the intervening years. The fact of the plastic surgery is not remarkable in itself; as discussed in chapter 3, the former *Hills* star Heidi Montag rendered her face virtually unrecognizable in 2010, using her MTV money to convert her appearance into a semblance of what she believed was her best self, as did *Teen Mom*'s Farrah (Serpe 2012). What is remarkable is that Snooki, J Woww, Angelina, and Deena have all undergone similar cosmetic procedures—lip injections, rhinoplasty, Botox injections, brow lifts, and cheek implants—generating an eerie similarity among their faces when they appear onscreen together (see, e.g., Schnurr 2018). Of course, even though all four women look very different from the stars of the original *Jersey Shore*, their new look aligns with, rather than disrupts, the Guido identities the women have publicly fashioned for themselves since 2009. The procedures are both to align the women with current beauty standards (full lips, high cheek bones) and also, more important, to signal their newfound wealth. Instead of conspicuously consuming jewelry and cars to showcase their capital, the women are showcasing their very expensive faces and bodies. As Vinny notes in the premiere of *Jersey Shore: Family Vacation*, "Nicole's face has the price tag hanging off of it." The "showiness" of the Guido identity is here embodied by who can spend the most money to alter their appearances.

While the white, female identities presented on series like *The Hills* and *Teen Mom* present both aspirational and cautionary identities, respectively, the female Guido identities on *Jersey Shore* are marked by abject displays of their bodies and bodily processes. In *Powers of Horror: An Essay on Abjection*, Julia Kristeva defines the abject as that which threatens to violate the boundary between self and other "as body fluids, this defilement, this shit are what life withstands, hardly and with difficulty, on the part of death" (1982, 3). In many episodes, the female cast members threaten these tenuous boundaries by belching loudly, urinating outside, discussing their breast size, falling down due to extreme intoxication, vomiting on camera, and discussing the relative pain of their periods. Since women historically have been associated with out-of-control menstruating bodies, they are expected to conceal the intimate functions of their bodies if they wish to be viewed *as* feminine (Brumberg 1997, 30). But the women of *Jersey Shore* take pleasure in the conspicuous display of these normally hidden functions. J Woww has urinated in bars and alleys while on camera, admitting that this activity is a favorite indulgence, and on several occasions Snooki has inadvertently (or advertently?) exposed her genitals to MTV's cameras. This behavior stands in contrast to the so-called old-school Italian image of femininity that asks women to be clean, demure, and quiet. On *Jersey Shore*, femininity is loud, messy, lusty, gluttonous, and self-serving. It is primary, abject, and visible. The women of *Jersey Shore* take what is usually "thrust aside"—or, at least, obscured from the reality TV camera's gaze—and place it in the center of the frame. Shit, urine, and vomit, all that which is expelled by the body, become the primary display. As a result, these bodies cannot be aspirational. The class politics of *Jersey Shore* are explicit in these moments: wealthy white women are role models and working-class Italian Americans are entertainment.

Other features of *Jersey Shore*'s aesthetics position both viewer and cast as lower order. For example, the earliest reality series on MTV, like *The Real World*, maintain a consistent "realist" aesthetic: long takes and mobile cameras in order to maintain a realistic temporality and spatiality as well as direct sound and "talking head"–style interviews or confessionals. These techniques appeal to a viewer's ideas, primarily gathered from exposure to the filmic documentary, about what "authenticity" looks like. However, as discussed in chapter 3, in most of MTV's reality series the aesthetics of each show condition the viewer's reception, inviting them to see each program's performance of identity as being tied to specific notions of taste and cultural capital. If *Laguna Beach*, *The Hills*, or *The City* connote glossy Hollywood spectacle, *Jersey Shore*'s aesthetic resembles an old home video. Establishing shots of the shoreline, as well as the castmates' house, are filmed with shaky, handheld cameras that go in and out of focus. These shots are frequently interrupted with jump cuts, as if pieces of the footage have been lost or damaged. There are scratches and imperfections on the surface of the image, as if the film has run through the projector one too many times. Occasionally, the entire frame will appear to jump or shake, again creating the impression of watching a film through a rickety projector. Further adding to the feeling of watching a grindhouse film is *Jersey Shore*'s use of leaders, a length of film inserted at the beginning or end of a piece of film, containing technical information for the projectionist. In *Jersey Shore*, "faux leaders" are used to provide information to the audience about the narrative contained in the episode to follow. For instance, the season 2 episode "The Letter" opens with blurry establishing shots of Miami, followed by a leader with the words "The Plan." This leader prepares the audience for an episode revolving around Snooki's and Jenny's decision (after weeks of deliberation) to write Sammi an anonymous note, detailing her boyfriend's indiscretions. Later in the episode, after Sammi discovers the note and confronts Ronnie, the leader contains the words "Lies." In both cases the leader serves as a chapter heading of sorts, highlighting the key plot points or themes of the narrative segment that follows. The aesthetics of the program remind the viewer that the show she is watching is trash. While the artifice of *The Hills* highlighted the unattainable nature of the lifestyles it chronicles, the artifice of *Jersey Shore* served a different purpose: to ghettoize its stars and its viewers, reminding them that their interests are prurient and low-brow. Therefore, it is not surprising that college students attending Pauly D's concert felt that drinking to excess and partying were expected behaviors.

Jersey Shore provided MTV audiences with an opportunity to laugh at onscreen identities rather than long for their wealth and way of life (as in *The Hills*). The strategy worked; *Jersey Shore* became the highest-rated series in both cable and broadcast television in the summer of 2010 (Seidman 2010). The series was extremely profitable for MTV, running for six seasons and leading to (less successful) spin-offs like *Snooki & J Woww*, *The Pauly D Project*, and *The Show with Vinny*. By 2012, *Jersey Shore* stood as MTV's highest-rated show of all time, pulling in more viewers in the coveted twelve- to thirty-four-year-old demographic than *American Idol*, the former ratings juggernaut. Recall that when MTV first thought about offering its post-Recession audience less aspirational and more realistic youth identities, it turned to the Italian American youth of Staten Island depicted in *Bridge and Tunnel*. But the never-aired series' interest in class struggles and "kids with stories" was replaced by *Jersey Shore*, a show about "kids whose only stories [a]re the show." The former would have offered context and nuance for the ethnic identities onscreen, whereas the latter trafficked in broad ethnic stereotypes. This approach to filming the youth Other is taken up again with the creation of *Buckwild*, which succeeded by converting its cast into derisive stereotypes that the cast nevertheless embraced.

Regional Identities in *Buckwild*

Nonwhite, non-middle-to-upper-middle-class characters in reality television are required to be representatives for their race, ethnicity, or class. A Black person who appears on a reality series, for example, is frequently saddled with the expectation to "speak" for his or her race. By contrast, representations of white characters on reality television run the gamut from rich to poor, old to young, criminal to saint, all without any assumption that one of these character traits is definitive of the white race. Richard Dyer calls this the white person's "right to be various" (1997, 49). Dyer further explains that "the uncertainties of whiteness as a hue, a color and yet not a colour, make it possible to see the bearers of white skin as nonspecific, ordinary and mere, and it just so happens the only people whose color permits this perception" (60). Two of the most disliked characters on MTV's popular reality series *The Hills*, Spencer Pratt and Heidi Montag, are white (Arthur 2008). But their bad behaviors are never explicitly linked to their status *as* white people; neither cast member ever invokes their race as a source of identity, as a hurdle to overcome, or as impacting their behavior. This aspect of Heidi and Spencer's identity—their whiteness—remains invisible, secondary to their status as villains or foils to Lauren Conrad. They are the exception, rather than the rule, for whiteness and white people on *The Hills*, therefore they are never critiqued for making white people on TV "look bad."

As Dyer notes, whiteness has largely escaped analysis and critique within Western culture because it is generally recognized not as a raced identity but as the *absence of race or identity* (1997, 4). But whiteness has steadily lost its dominant demographic hold on the United States over the last few decades; by 2044, people who identify as white in America will be a minority, behind those who identify as Latinx (El Nasser 2014). Interestingly, the less hegemonic power that white people hold in the United States, the *more visible* whiteness has become in the American popular imagination. In the wake of the Great Recession of 2008, poor, white Americans became the focus of a number of sociological tomes and hand-wringing profiles exploring the financial and political sea changes of this demographic.[11] There has also been a rising interest in films, television series, novels, music, and political ideologies that examine whiteness as an explicit racial category. It is now possible to speak of whiteness and white privilege, and with that possibility comes the need on the part of white people to rebrand whiteness and take ownership of its meaning. MTV provided a scratch for that itch.

This interest in whiteness as something that was both fragile *and* proud reached an apex with Donald Trump's successful bid for president of the United States in 2016. Trump's anti-immigrant and antiminority rhetoric mobilized this white, working-class voting base by capitalizing on white Americans' fears about a loss of racial hegemony. The countless investigative articles and polarizing think pieces published after the historic 2016 election attributed this demographic's Trumpism to an amorphous "economic anxiety." Even when many Trump supporters publicly proclaimed their white supremacist and neo-Nazi rhetoric—on the internet and on live television—it was difficult for American media outlets to accuse white America of racial bias. Instead, news outlets adopted euphemisms for "racism," including "racially tinged" or "racially inflammatory."[12] In the last decade, dozens of reality shows have portrayed working-class, white subjects who have made a choice to appear on television and have their lives documented through the particular lens of the hillbilly or Redneck, a production cycle that Andrew Scahill (2012) calls "white trash spectacle."[13] Scahill argues that this cycle rhetorically mirrors the Victorian freakshow because these series encourage a derisive gaze on the part of the spectator, making a spectacle of "bad whiteness" for the viewer to mock. He posits that a series like *Here Comes Honey Boo Boo*, which focuses on the life of the titular child and her "Redneck" family, makes the cast members complicit in their own humiliation in exchange for the opportunity to earn a living in a post-Recession economy.

It is in this environment of a newly visible whiteness that MTV turned its cameras to West Virginia. MTV's programming head, David Janollari, explained, "We'll give our viewers a singular and fun glimpse at this generation's experience as we go into Appalachia to capture the lives of a lovable group of dynamic young people" (qtd. in Alzayat 2011). Helen Wood and Bev Skeggs argue that performance and performativity are central to reality television because, within this medium, "'real life' is broken down and commodified into forms of spectacle, encoding certain ways of seeing ourselves and seeing others which is constitutive (not just representative) of social hierarchies and distinctions" (2011b, 8). Thus while reality TV does indeed draw on "real life," its necessarily selective nature (i.e., only so much footage can be screened in a forty-two-minute time slot) means that what the audience sees sampled onscreen will in turn come to shape the audience's understanding of the identity performed onscreen. Therefore, it is not surprising that many West Virginians were unhappy about MTV filming their community. Joe Manchin III, a West Virginia Democratic senator, wrote an angry letter to MTV president Stephen K. Friedman about the series, claiming, "You preyed on young people, coaxed them into displaying shameful behavior—and now you are profiting from it" (qtd. in Schillaci 2012). He was right, though the cast hardly needed coaxing into displaying these behaviors. The West Virginia film office turned down the show's application for tax incentives for filming in and around Charleston and Sissonville. Much as former New Jersey governor Chris Christie denied tax credits to the *Jersey Shore* production, the West Virginia film office stated that *Buckwild* painted an unflattering portrait of their community and as such, MTV did not qualify for the 31 percent in tax incentives (Schillaci 2012). Certainly *all* MTV series paint young people in the same unflattering light, as endlessly horny, restless, and looking for a good time. But there is a reason why shows like *Buckwild* and *Jersey Shore* are protested and denied tax incentives while shows like *Laguna Beach* merely had to avoid shooting on school grounds.[14] The latter depicted their settings—the hills of Los Angeles and the beaches around Orange County—as high-status and aspirational. By contrast, *Jersey Shore* and *Buckwild* made their regions (New Jersey and West Virginia), and the people who live there, into objects of ridicule. In an interview with the *American Conservative*, J. D. Vance, author of the best-selling memoir *Hillbilly Elegy* (2016), discussed his upbringing in rural Ohio and the way "white trash" has been understood in the American imagination. Vance quoted his grandmother, Mamaw, who once told him, "We [hillbillies/Rednecks] are the only group of people you don't have to be ashamed to look down upon" (qtd. in Dreher 2016). That is, all people feel a need to look down upon another social group as a way to shore up their own superiority; for wealthy, educated whites, looking down on other white people, so-called hillbillies/Rednecks, fulfilled that need without the nasty baggage of feeling like a racist or a xenophobe. Much as New York City residents do not feel shame for ostracizing the B&T Guidos, white people can guiltlessly mock Rednecks.

So what is a Redneck? Kristen Hatch (2013) argues that the term has become shorthand for rebelliousness against restrictive norms of modern capitalism. Much as the LGBT community has reclaimed "queer" and the Italian Americans of *Jersey Shore* reclaimed "Guido," the rural whites of West Virginia have reclaimed the slur, making being a "Redneck" a point of pride. Redneckness is "celebrated as self-acceptance" and an unwilling-ness to "succumb to the dictates of neoliberal citizenship" (Hatch 2013). In the context of *Buckwild*, being a West Virginia Redneck is about embracing freedom and living life in the moment and to its fullest. *Buckwild* establishes this theme of freedom and liberation during the series opening credits with the following voice-over: "West Virginia is a place founded on freedom. For me and my friends, that means the freedom to do whatever the fuck we want!"[15] This voice-over is paired with a montage of youthful hijinx: bridge diving, muddin' (driving off-road vehicles through the mud), drinking, and shooting firearms. These activities are a summary of the cast's freedom, as neoliberal citizenry, to make the most of their limited means. As one cast member cheerfully points out during the opening-credits montage of dangerous behaviors, "When you ain't got much, you gotta get creative." Like so many working-class Americans living in a post-Recession climate, the cast of *Buckwild* was trying to find ways to do more with less.

This idea of freedom is most frequently conveyed through the cast's choice in leisure activities, which revolve around *Jackass*-style antics. In episode 11, Shain Gandee and Tyler Boulet take Katie Saria, the new girl in town, for her first muddin' experience. The object of muddin', according to the show's cast, is to drive a pickup truck directly into mud holes, which creates a doubled effect: the bump and crash of the truck going into and out of a hole, and the splash of mud generated by the impact. As Shain's truck backs out of the driveway, Katie asks, fear creeping into her voice, "Why are there no seatbelts?" They drive her out to the middle of the woods, where deep sinkholes can accumulate puddles of mud without disturbance. The cinematography alternates from long shots outside of the truck and medium close-ups taken inside the truck's cabin. The diegetic sounds of the trucks' revving engines are amplified, thus enhancing the impression of their mechanical largess, and by extension, the masculinity of the men operating the vehicles. Engaging in dangerous activities serves as a form of capital among *Buckwild*'s Rednecks, and it works as well for the women as it does for the men.

During nearly every scene in which the crew engages in dangerous behaviors—diving off bridges, lighting things on fire, shooting homemade potato guns—aggressive rock or rap music plays in the background. It is important that this is not diegetic music (i.e., music that the cast members have chosen to listen to), but rather nondiegetic music that MTV producers have selected to shape the mood of the scene. In the muddin' scene described above, the song used is "Mud Slingers," by the group Mud Digger.

4.3 *Buckwild*, which aired for just one season, focused on the antics of West Virginia youth who called themselves Rednecks.

The lyrics, which are in the form of a rap, include, "Get like you? / No, get like me / We don't rock them / Gangster clothes we be / Wearin' Wrangler jeans / People rollin' with them ATVs / We be muddin', jumpin', stuntin', / hummin' with the mud kings MDS." This song, like *Buckwild* itself, celebrates emblems of Redneck culture, including Wrangler jeans and ATVs, while partaking in the MTV tradition of appropriating Black popular culture. More radically, the song makes a case for the value and desirability of these emblems, chastising listeners to adopt Redneck culture as well. The song acknowledges what Vance's Mamaw told him many years ago—that Redneck culture is derided and devalued—but then rejects this idea ("Get like you? / No, get like me").

The *Buckwild* women love danger as much as the men do, a fact that the series plays for laughs much in the same way that *Jersey Shore* highlighted the abject femininity of characters like Snooki and J Woww, because it appears to contradict gender stereotypes. Episode 6 opens with establishing shots of rural Sissonville and cuts to footage of a middle-aged woman washing laundry in the river, an idyllic image of stereotypical Appalachian gender roles. In the next scene, the *Buckwild* women are relaxing in their living room when one exclaims, "Someone's shootin' guns!" In a reversal of popular stereotypes regarding women and guns, they run outside, not out of fear, but because they wish to shoot, too, explaining, "How else we gonna get frustration out?" Shae Bradley, who is trying to get over her ex-boyfriend, shoots in high heels, implying that she can remain traditionally feminine, even while shooting a gun.[16] Later in the episode, the girls pay for matching tattoos that read "NPS," which stands for "No Pussy Shit." Since all of these women have "pussies" of their own, it is unclear why they would denounce a fundamental body part as a way to assert their strength. Shae decides to get her NPS tattoo on the inside of her lip, while her girlfriends cheer her on. The moment is reminiscent of a *Jersey Shore* episode in which Vinny gets his ears pierced to affirm his manhood among his identity group (Klein 2014, 163–165). The NPS tattoo is likewise meant to be a moment of same-sex bonding, creating solidarity among the women *as* Rednecks. For example, in episode 6, the gang celebrates Joey's birthday by making potato guns, which involves sawing large PVC pipes in half and sealing them on one end. One must then place a fire inside the tube, load it with a potato, place the contraption on their shoulders like a rocket launcher, and wait for the heat and pressure to eject the spud from the pipe. As music blares on the soundtrack, Shae announces to no one in particular, "This is how you make 'tater salad in West Virginia!" Joey watches as Shae shoots the potato gun and remarks that she looks sexy in the act; he is turned on by Shae's willingness to engage in dangerous activities. In a later episode, the gang goes bull riding and several of the girls take on the challenge, with Ashley getting tossed off the bull onto her head, damaging her T7 vertebrae. The women of *Buckwild* also engage in dangerous or "extreme" activities, risking injury and pain, as a way to assert their allegiance with their region.

Buckwild's portrayal of whiteness is bound to region, to West Virginia, and to the Redneck (or "hillbilly" or "white trash") culture. However, one of the series' cast members, Salwa Amin, identifies as South Asian. Her nickname, "Bengali in Boots," highlights the incongruity of her ethnic heritage with the region in which she lives. In episode 2, Salwa tells the camera, "I may look exotic but I'm as country as it comes." This particular moment of identity confession is illuminating because Salwa Others herself ("I may look exotic") only to reassert her membership in the group ("but I'm as country as it comes"). While Salwa's *presence* in the otherwise all-white *Buckwild* cast might signal the fact that ethnicity is not a barrier to entry into Sissonville's Redneck community, her *representation* on the series indicates otherwise. Salwa barely appears in the series' 2013 promotional trailers and is not even given her own introduction in the pilot's opening-credits sequence.

Salwa appears in multiple episodes as a secondary character who comments on the main plot arcs (she engages in behaviors similar to those of the other women in the cast, like drinking, partying, and firing a shotgun in high heels), but she is almost never in the spotlight herself. The only episode in which Salwa has a central role is episode 3, when she informs Shae that her current boyfriend, Jesse J., propositioned her when they were both intoxicated. Previous episodes have established that Jesse J. is, in Ashley's words, "a loser" and a liar, but Shae chooses to believe her boyfriend over Salwa. Salwa is dumbstruck but Shae simply tells her, "You're a shady person." Shae eventually dumps Jesse J. (for other reasons, namely, he lies), but the series never reengages with this bit of drama or addresses whether or not the women have reconciled. Despite Salwa's claims that she is "as country as it comes," her marginalized status in the series narrative indicates otherwise.

The cast members of *Buckwild* may have the freedom to do what they want, but the cast is also careful to police the borders of its group. Muddin' and shooting guns may be indicative of West Virginian Rednecks, but sleeping with men in your roommate's bed, as Cara Parish did to Anna in episode 2, represents a violation of that same code. After this transgression, Cara is ejected from the house and, for all intents and purposes, the *Buckwild* narrative, until she formally apologizes to Anna at work. Another example of this policing occurs in episode 5, when the gang is invited to drink at the home of a friend of a friend, known as Jesse B. Jesse B.'s rundown living conditions disgust them: there is garbage everywhere, the bathroom door does not fully close, and, as Tyler laments, even the porch was "depressing." After Ashley informs Jesse B. that the gang will be leaving to party elsewhere, he sighs, "I guess it was too country for them." In episode 5, Jesse B. further demonstrates his inappropriate behavior by showing up to the girls' party covered in vomit and then, later, repeatedly hitting on Salwa. "Your boyfriend's not gonna stop me," he slurs at her. Though the *Buckwild* cast engages in violent and misogynist behavior toward women, Jesse B. has once again crossed a line and must be ejected. Tyler beats Jesse B. in front of the group until he is restrained and Shain kicks out Jesse B. for good. The girls are aroused by Tyler's masculine display, squealing "Damn Tyler! That was hot!" Joey embraces Tyler and tells him, "I'm proud of you, son." With the borders to the group firmly sealed once again—no Rednecks shall enter unless they are approved—the gang can celebrate with a round of "naked lap time," which is how the episode ends.

Buckwild suggests that its young cast are having a great time, just like the girls on *The Hills*. Lacking money, Birkin bags, or a spot on Les Deux's guest list does not matter; rather than clubbing at Los Angeles's hottest bars, these twentysomethings find their fun in nature and the raw materials of their environment. Their inventiveness was charming, but it also obscured the financial differences between the *Buckwild* cast and the cast of *The Hills*, *The City*, and *Laguna Beach*. Their leisure-time activities are, just like Lauren Conrad's activities in *The Hills*, positioned as choices and as *freedom* rather than any necessity of their economic situation. Rather than complaining about their limited options, the *Buckwild* cast position their lifestyles as the ultimate freedom and the ultimate fun. In this way, *Buckwild* offered the same neoliberal narrative of self-sufficiency as *The Hills*, albeit in different wrapping. On *The Hills*, success is the result of having made the correct consumption choices—the right hair color for fall, the perfect boot for spring—without acknowledging that those choices are only possible in the context of a life that is always already successful. On *Buckwild*, success is about doing more with less—without acknowledging that this status quo coexists in the same economic system as the status quo of *The Hills*. Likewise, while behaviors on *The Hills* are never coded as indicative of whiteness, most activities on *Buckwild* are explicitly associated with West Virginia and frequently serve as a moment of identity confession for the cast members. Cast members preface their behaviors with the phrase "Round here we . . . ," as if every activity featured on the series is a West Virginia tradition.

Although the behaviors on display in *Buckwild* are often dangerous and reckless, the product of boredom combined with a lack of money, audiences are never supposed to see the cast's behaviors as pitiable or in need of reformation. In another context, the binge drinking, fistfights, and dangerous, ad hoc sports practiced by the cast would be something to discourage, especially in young people. But these behaviors are not framed as problems in need of a solution, like Farrah's foray into pornography or Amber's drug addiction in *Teen Mom*. For the cast of *Buckwild*, the "problems" associated with living in rural West Virginia, including a lack of entertainment or gainful employment, are solved with the appearance of MTV's cameras. The group's reaction to their life circumstances—to go muddin' or make a swimming pool out of an abandoned dump truck—are ways not only to make lemonade out of lemons, but also to monetize that lemonade via MTV. *Buckwild* cast member Ashley Whitt recalls the night that she and her friends met the MTV casting crew: "It was a bunch of creepy old men in the corner. . . . Everyone started drinking. They said, 'Mind if we bring out our cameras?' We signed forms. I mud wrestled my best friend. It went from there" (qtd. in Wallace 2013). Ashley is surprised to discover that her life and her friends are worthy material for a TV show, an arrangement that makes "the borders between the time and space of life and those of so-called 'productive' labor seem to disappear, in order to account for the phenomenon of 'setting affect to work' or 'setting life to work'" (Corsani 2007, 124). In an economically depressed, post-Recession Sissonville, working for MTV—by playing themselves—is an appealing vocation. After all, how many jobs pay you to have fun and be yourself?

When cast members on reality identity series are featured in an MTV-curated home, as in *The Real World* or *Jersey Shore*, they are removed from their established lives (and jobs). But in series like *Teen Mom*, *The Hills*, and *Buckwild*, in which cast members remain in their own homes, the audience can catch a glimpse of what youth employment looks like in a variety of socioeconomic environments. The cast of *The Hills* and *The City* have high-paying, exciting jobs in their fields of interest, but the employment status of the *Buckwild* cast is precarious. Employment, if it exists, is not aspirational and does not lead into promotions at *Teen Vogue* or internships in Paris. Instead, as Joey Mulcahy helpfully explains in episode 6, "I'm out of money. And I don't have any gas for my truck." Employment in the series served short-term needs but never offered stability or upward mobility. Anna and Ashley worked at a tanning salon, Cara was a club promoter, and Shain worked in a factory. Joey and Tyler briefly took jobs mowing lawns but quit when they discover that the woman who hired them just wanted to ogle them as they worked. Joey does not again mention how he will get money or how he will put gas in his truck because the viewer is not intended to ponder such a concept.

As the show began to take off in the ratings—*Buckwild* had an average of three million viewers per episode and ranked eighth among all the cable series in fiscal year 2013—many of the cast members were hopeful about making more money. When asked about how he planned to spend his future earnings, Joey said he would use his money to purchase vehicles and to make "our own place, and just making our own tracks and trails" (qtd in Wallace 2013). In other words, Joey would use the money he made performing his Redneck identities to purchase more ways to perform his Redneck identity. In the same interview with *Vulture*, Joey discussed the cast's optimism about the show's future: "I was, like, man, we could actually make something out of this, and be big stars, and it was looking pretty cool." The cast's salaries were reportedly increased by 400 percent for season 2 (Wallace 2013). But these hopes for season 2 raises were cut abruptly short in April of 2013, when Shain, arguably *Buckwild*'s breakout star and main draw, died unexpectedly. Shain was the ideal West Virginian Redneck: danger-loving, laconic, frightened of the big city, and filled with amusing insights about what it means to be a West Virginian. Interviews with and profile pieces published about Shain reveal that he had never stepped foot on an airplane until MTV flew him to New York City to promote the show and that MTV also required him to use his first cell phone. Shain's identity was that of the isolated rural woodsman who shuns modern technology and has a great time doing it. In episode 4, when Cara invites Shain to a club in Charleston and asks if he's ever been to a club before, he quips, "I've *hit* someone *with* a club!" Shain was highly invested in the performance of dangerous tasks, and he explicitly ties danger with masculinity.

In April 2013, the *Buckwild* cast and crew were given the weekend off for Easter. To celebrate the holiday weekend, Shain and two friends drove off in Shain's truck for some muddin' and other off-roading activities. They disappeared for thirty-one hours. After an exhaustive search, Shain's family eventually found his Bronco on its side in a mudhole, with the tailpipe stuck in the mud. The three men inside, including Shain, had died of carbon monoxide poisoning. As the show's central figure—the most West Virginian, the most Redneck, the most *Buckwild*—it's significant that Shain died while muddin', one of the cast's favorite activities and one that is showcased in much of the series' press materials and trailers. At the time of Shain's death, four episodes of season 2 were shot and in the can. But MTV ultimately decided to cancel the series, a move that angered and disappointed the cast. Susanne Daniels, MTV's head of programming, explained the decision: "This is a show that for me is about *joie de vivre*, about youth and having fun and throwing caution to the wind and taking chances and playfulness and partying. . . . So how do you continue with the show when you've lost the heart of that show?" Shain's unexpected death had poisoned the series' brand. The dangerous activities performed by Shain and his friends were now tainted with the reality of tragedy.

The *Buckwild* cast labored to redefine their identities from that of poor, disenfranchised, white West Virginians to a group of individuals who are free to endanger their bodies and to earn money and fame in the process. Instead of a source of shame, their Redneck identities became something to celebrate and monetize. But the symbolic value of the West Virginian Redneck identity—a person who is unfettered by the regulations and rules that the rest of society must follow—ultimately collided with the material reality of this identity in April 2013. For while it is true that Shain and his friends would have gone muddin' on that fateful Easter morning with or without the presence of MTV's cameras, their deaths—*a result of performing West Virginia*—highlighted the danger in building a career out of one's identity, especially an identity that is at odds with one's physical safety. When your job is to play yourself, you are never not working. And when being yourself means endangering your body, then both work and being yourself generates a never-ending state of precarity.

Conclusions

If MTV's core audience is the allegedly "culture-less" white suburban teen, it is not surprising that series like *Jersey Shore* and *Buckwild* could offer these audiences the opportunity to see their own identities not as whiteness itself but as a constellation of highly specific and, thus, meaningful identities. The young people cast on these two series are interesting enough for MTV's cameras due to identities that stem from whiteness but that are never explicitly discussed in such terms (because to do so would be unnerving to MTV's primarily white, suburban demographic). This neoliberal effacement of race and class and promotion of the idea of "choice" also dovetails with the distinctly postfeminist ideologies that underpin contemporary reality television, and MTV's reality programming throughout the 2010s in particular. As discussed in chapter 2, during the 1993 season of *The Real World*, Cory Murphy, a straight, white, cisgendered woman, found herself surrounded by a diverse group of roommates who seemed to take great pride in their identities; she then despaired over her status as a "boring" white person. Cory, like so many members of Generation X who were reared under the colorblind ideologies of the 1980s and 1990s, was ignorant of white cultural hegemony. Blind to her own racial privilege, Cory believed that her whiteness was empty of meaning. But by the time that series like *Jersey Shore* and *Buckwild* aired on the same network, nearly twenty years later, ideas about identity had shifted, and white people, who were symbolically threatened and denigrated in a broad way for the first time in American history, wanted to feel that *their* identities were *also* interesting and unique and worthy of MTV's cameras. In this way, MTV's programming provided a venue for whiteness to be something other than invisible. *Jersey Shore* allowed otherwise-assimilated Italian Americans the opportunity to convert a label that denigrates their taste and class into an identity that they can celebrate and from which they can profit. Similarly, *Buckwild* provided a model of whiteness for youth audiences that celebrates rural living, the value of American machinery, and post-Recession resilience, while also implying that that this identity is productive and income-generating. *Buckwild* suggests that being a Redneck is not all that bad as long as you can still have fun, and once you start having fun, MTV might come to your town and film you and your friends.

This shift to visible whiteness is not simply harmless fun in the form of diverting reality television. Rather, the making-visible of whiteness as an identity over the last decade has also had the unfortunate side effect of emboldening the ideologies of white supremacy. In August 2017, white American identity—the need to define it, embody it, and defend it—became painfully literal when Jason Kessler, a white, cisgendered, heterosexual, alt-right activist, organized a protest march to be held in Charlottesville, Virginia. The purpose of this "Unite the Right" rally on August 11 and 12, 2017, was to protest the removal of a statue of Confederate General Robert E. Lee from Charlottesville's Emancipation Park. The rally brought together a variety of identity groups: supporters of the newly elected president of the United States, Donald Trump; white nationalists; white supremacists; neo-Nazis; neo-Confederates; and numerous right-wing, armed militias (with much overlap among these identity groups). The idea behind the march, beyond the claim that it was protesting the removal of a Confederate statue, was to bring together groups that had previously communicated with one another only online via political opinion sites like *Breitbart*, *The Daily Stormer*, and *The Daily Caller*, as well as social media platforms like 4chan, Reddit, Twitter, and Gab. Prior to the Unite the Right rally, these various groups existed in primarily virtual space, gathering in public only for Donald Trump's campaign rallies in 2016 and at the public speeches of "celebrity" alt-right figures like Richard Spencer and Milo Yiannopoulos. However, a common refrain about this group of individuals was their formlessness, the belief that they were cowards hiding behind their computer monitors, unwilling to align their bodies with their politics. The Unite the Right rally in 2017 presented these identity groups with an opportunity to become flesh.

In a *Vice* news documentary that went viral after the march, reporter Elle Reeve (white, cisgendered) interviewed both leaders of and participants in the Unite the Right rally to find out what exactly they were hoping to achieve with the event. When asked about how the alt right was beginning to adopt some of the strategies of the left, Christopher Cantwell, a white supremacist YouTube personality, explained: "We don't have the level of trust that our rivals do. And that camaraderie and trust is built up through activism, and that is one of the tactics that we're adopting." In other words, while the Unite the Right rally was explicitly about Confederate statues, it was implicitly about building a sense of community among disparate identity groups who shared the same political goals. Another participant in the march, Robert Ray, a self-proclaimed neo-Nazi who writes for *The Daily Stormer*, told Reeve, "I believe, as you can see, we are stepping off the internet in a big way. . . . People realized that they are not itemized individuals, they are part of a larger whole because we have been spreading our memes, we have been organizing on the internet, and so now they're coming out" (*Vice News* 2017). Called into being, this new white identity, composed of differing factions but stitched together by a shared sense of oppression and loss, needed to make its presence seen and felt (which it did). The rally ended with the death of a white woman named Heather Heyer, who was in Charlottesville as part of a counterprotest.

It is important to keep in mind here that these various online groups formed specifically in reaction to the rise of so-called identity politics and the increasing visibility of whiteness as an identity group and the perceived attacks on whiteness. Social media has, like Dr. Frankenstein, helped to piece together various dead limbs of white identity: the neo-Nazis, the white supremacists, the men's rights activists, and the neo-Confederates (Scheff 2017). As much as new technologies, like the internet and social media, have worked to spread information and democratize the range of voices that get to speak and be heard, it has also contributed to the fragmentation of discourse into various slices of like-minded individuals, into specific identities. In the last few years white supremacist groups have claimed that "Black Lives Matter" is an attack on white identity, leading them to create the inflammatory counter slogan "All Lives Matter." Similarly, men's rights activists have developed in reaction to what is seen as a coordinated attack on (white, cisgendered) men by "angry" feminists. Ironically, the tools and tactics that oppressed minority groups have been using to break out of the prison of white, heterosexist patriarchal American culture are now being wielded against them.

The premiere, as well as the untimely cancellation, of *Buckwild* highlights the importance of whiteness, here coded as Redneck, as a performative identity in contemporary America. Much like "economic anxiety," in the context of *Buckwild*, Redneck becomes a term for pride in white identity and resilience against a perceived loss in white hegemony, as well as a resistance to the perceived "threat" of the imminent majority status of Americans of color. Similarly, the Italian Americans of *Jersey Shore*, whose grandparents most likely wanted nothing more than to assimilate and appear as white people, are now re-asserting their difference, as Guidos, allowing them to reap the benefits of white privilege while simultaneously making claims to an ethnic heritage. In addition to grappling with whiteness as an identity, both *Jersey Shore* and *Buckwild* are shows that highlight working-class or poor facets of white America. MTV freely indulges in audience contempt for poverty, blue-collar work, or a perceived lack of cultural capital. The Italian American Guidos and the West Virginia Rednecks featured in these series are differentiated from white people due to their class status, which is what engenders laughter at their behavior. They are white people who don't know how to be bourgeois. In the final chapter of this book, I examine two other MTV reality programs that take a different approach to their depictions of nonwhite, homosexual, and/or working-class identities. Comparing these series, and their later cancellations, with the great success of *Jersey Shore* and *Buckwild* (until Shain Gandee's untimely death) demonstrates MTV's contribution to discourses on youth identities in the twenty-first century.

"That Moment Is Here, Whether I Like It or Not"
When MTV's Programming Fails

(2013–2014)

W hen I interviewed Jonathan Murray, one of *The Real World*'s cocreators, about his experiences producing one of the most influential and long-running reality series of all time, I asked him about the role of casting in making a compelling TV series. As outlined in chapter 2, one of the main criteria used for making casting decisions on *The Real World* was "diversity." That is, to ensure that something interesting (i.e., worthy of MTV's cameras) occurs onscreen, it is necessary to bring together people who are very different from one another. Murray told me, "You can't always know what's gonna happen. It's not always that specific— we just knew at the beginning that if a cast was diverse, that there would be conflict and growth."[1] This model of "seven strangers" who are selected to live together in close quarters for several months was the bedrock of *The Real World* and its appeal. It was a social experiment, one in which mostly white, cisgendered, heterosexual cast members learned big and important lessons about prejudice and tolerance from roommates who were not like them. As Jon Kraszewski argues, in *The Real World* intolerance is depicted as stemming directly from identity (2009, 179). However, as discussed in chapters 3 and 4, once MTV began transitioning from mostly music videos to reality TV in the 2000s, they adopted a different model of casting. Instead of putting together a diverse cast, these reality series focused on homogeneous groups: the white, cisgendered, upper-class women of *Laguna Beach* and *The Hills*; the Italian American, mostly blue-collar Guidos of *Jersey Shore*; and the white (with the exception of Salwa), mostly blue-collar Rednecks of *Buckwild*. The high ratings and pop-culture buzz surrounding these series might indicate that MTV's reality programming can also work if the featured casts are similar to one another. But, as this chapter will demonstrate, that is only the case when this homogeneous group is composed of white cast members (*The Hills*) or individuals whose nonwhite status is used as a running joke in the series (*Jersey Shore*) or whose particular brand of whiteness *is* the joke (*Buckwild*). When nonwhite cast members appear in MTV reality series as separate from prominent stereotypes tied to their identities, they prove to be "uninteresting" to MTV's mostly white, mostly middle-class audience.

To illustrate this theory, this chapter discusses two far-less-successful iterations of MTV's reality identity cycle: *Washington Heights* and *Virgin Territory*. I argue that these series failed because they did not perform any of the aforementioned functions of previously successful MTV reality identity series: being aspirational (dress like Lauren Conrad!), instructional (don't be a Teen Mom like Farrah Abraham!), and/or comical (look how silly Pauly D is!). Like *Jersey Shore*, *Washington Heights* is about nonwhite youth who strongly identify with their ethnic, historical, and cultural identities and who take pride in their heritage (Dominican American). So why was *Washington Heights* canceled after just one season, while *Jersey Shore* was a hit? Because, unlike *Jersey Shore*'s Guidos, the young Dominican Americans profiled in *Washington Heights* were difficult to categorize or stereotype. They did not dress, talk, or speak like one another. They lacked catchphrases and could not clearly define (and/or commodify) what it is to be Dominican American in the way that *Jersey Shore* defined (and commodified) what it is to be a Guido. This chapter also discusses *Virgin Territory*, which, like *Washington Heights*, received low ratings and has yet to produce a second season. The cast members featured on *Virgin Territory* don't share a living space (like *The Real World*), an area code (like *The Hills*), or a strict tanning regimen (like *Jersey Shore*). What they share, instead, is a status that is both symbolic and corporeal—their virginity. The reasons behind each cast member's decision to wait varies—religious beliefs, medical complications, fear of coming out, fear of pregnancy, fear of diseases, fear of rejection—

but being a Virgin remains each cast member's defining trait, over and above the expected markers of identity that are typically highlighted in MTV identity series. This chapter explores the specific conditions under which MTV can showcase nonwhite, nonheterosexual identities in its reality identity programming, and when those depictions succeed with audiences, as well as when they fail.

Ethnic Identities in *Washington Heights*

In 2013, *Washington Heights*, a series about primarily working-class Dominican American youth living in the Washington Heights neighborhood of New York City, premiered on MTV. Like other entries in MTV's reality identity cycle (*Laguna Beach, The Hills, The City, Jersey Shore*), *Washington Heights* is named for its setting. However, the pilot episode's opening narration creates distance between *Washington Heights* and *The Hills*: "This ain't the Hollywood Hills, this is the Heights, one of the last true neighborhoods left in Manhattan." According to Keara Goin's study of Dominican American identities in the media, *Washington Heights* was "the first mainstream Dominican-centric media text" on television as well as "an inroad to active negotiations concerning the nature of *dominicanidad*" (2015, 118). In *Washington Heights*, this *dominicanidad* is primarily defined and represented as a shared heritage stemming from the Dominican Republic and the fact that the cast often refers to themselves as "family." This shared heritage is also expressed through each character's attempt to find success in their chosen careers as actors, singers, rappers, poets, painters, and clothing designers, with much of their artistic expression focusing on their neighborhood and sense of *dominicanidad*. Although the series combines the ethnic identities celebrated and lampooned by *Jersey Shore*, the hip New York City career aspiration vibe of *The City*, and the aesthetics of *The Hills*, *Washington Heights* was a flop, with just over 756,000 viewers (Cantor 2013). On paper, the series appeared to fit the formula of past successful MTV reality identity series, so why did *Washington Heights* fail where others succeeded?

Other than the musical *In the Heights* (1999), helmed by a pre-*Hamilton* Lin-Manuel Miranda, the neighborhood of Washington Heights lacks a strong stereotypical image that can be easily conveyed on a television series. As *Grantland*'s Amos Barshad (2013) wrote after the series premiered, *Washington Heights* was an odd entry in the MTV canon of reality programming in that it was set in a neighborhood that is not well known to those living outside its borders: "Most New Yorkers probably haven't been, and

5.1 *Washington Heights* focused on the lives of Dominican American youth.

certainly couldn't tell you much about [Washington Heights]. It's its own entity, isolated and preserved." In previous decades the neighborhood was primarily known as a bustling drug exchange, the country's largest wholesale drug market to be exact, but a crackdown in the 1990s led to the end of this neighborhood economy (Halbfinger 1998). According to Jorge Duany, the neighborhood is appropriately described as a "transnational space" in that its inhabitants have transformed an American neighborhood to reflect Dominican culture (qtd. in Goin 2015, 169). This means that local businesses sell products imported from the Dominican Republic and residences display flags and folk art (Goin 2015, 156–157). But one aspect of Dominican culture missing from *Washington Heights* is the presence of Spanish. In Goin's interviews with Dominican viewers of *Washington Heights*, one of the biggest complaints was the absence of Spanish. Goin concludes, "To not see the type of linguistic code switching—which also includes a frequent use of 'Spanglish'—was a clear indication to Dominican audiences that the show did not have the intention of depicting a more 'authentic' *dominicanidad*" (168–169). Of course, the glaring absence of Spanish is not surprising, given MTV's track record with depicting nonwhite communities; even when the subject is nonwhite, MTV is always catering to a white, non-Spanish-speaking audience.

Perhaps another reason why the *Washington Heights* cast was difficult to define in a series of bounded traits is because the series was pitched to MTV by the cast itself, specifically the show's narrator, J.P. Perez. J.P. pitched his series as a midpoint between *The Hills* and *Jersey Shore*—that is, J.P. consumed these reality TV programs, looked at his own life, and realized that his friends in the Heights could perform a similar living labor for MTV. J.P. saw *Washington Heights* as a way to document his community's culture before it disappeared. In an interview with *Grantland* he explained it this way: "People of Washington Heights are really proud of our town. . . . They don't wanna be misrepresented or represented at all. It's like, 'This the last bit that we have — damn, y'all exposing it?' But it has to be exposed. 'Cause the world is dying. There's no culture no more" (qtd. in Barshad 2013). *Washington Heights* is the first (and only) MTV reality identity series to provide a view of an identity from the inside, rather than from the outside. The *Washington Heights* cast was also more difficult to stereotype than the casts of previous MTV series because the ethnic profiles of the cast members are ambiguous: "Not appropriately hailed by either category [of *latinidad* or Blackness], those who are of both Latino and African heritage when in the U.S. must attempt to negotiate and position themselves within a racialized system that fundamentally has no room for them" (Goin 2015, 5). For example, J.P. presents as African American until he speaks with his Dominican accent. The cast also includes a white resident, Taylor Howell, who is accepted as part of the group because she was born and raised in the Heights. Goin calls Taylor's presence in the cast an example of "reverse tokenism," an attempt to inject a white face into the otherwise nonwhite cityscape (141). Despite her whiteness, it is clear that Taylor is a key member of the group, and, as J.P. explains in the pilot, "Even though she was raised around a lot of Dominicans, she's still white." In other words, Taylor is a member of the neighborhood, but not the ethnic group; she does not try to claim *dominicanidad* for herself. This nuanced understanding of neighborhood and how it is both connected to and separate from ethnic identity likely impacted the series' success.

Washington Heights' opening credits emphasize the isolation and pride of this New York City neighborhood. Against the backdrop of the Washington Heights skyline, names of different cast members appear onscreen, with lines pointing to their location in the neighborhood. The credits' narrator, J.P., explains that his fellow cast members were "born here, grew up here, survive here." The conflict between location and ethnic heritage as a source of conflict comes early in the series when the tight-knit group of friends clashes with Jimmy Carceres's girlfriend of nearly two years, Eliza Jefferson. When Eliza is introduced in the pilot episode, J.P. describes her as "somewhat of an outsider, she's from New Jersey and is kinda new to the group." Eliza is Dominican and speaks Spanish but is considered an out-sider because she was not born and raised in the Heights, like everyone else featured on the series (including Taylor). The group also marginalizes Eliza because Reyna Saldana, another cast member, once dated Jimmy. In the pi-lot episode, Reyna and Eliza mention, in separate conversations, that there has been tension between them, which sets them up for a face-to-face alter-cation at a music and poetry showcase organized by J.P. As with *The Hills*, *Washington Heights* uses editing and cinematography to create tension/conflict without relying on explicit statements or actions by cast members. When Jimmy enters the bar, he embraces Reyna and tells her, "I love you, too." After Jimmy walks away, the camera stays on Reyna, in order to catch her reaction as Eliza walks by, saying nothing. A reverse angle on the same brief, but dramatic, moment serves to expand screen time, stretching out this morsel of tension. As with *The Hills*, tension is conveyed through shot/reverse-shot exchanges, rather than yelling. This does not last long because eventually the women engage in a physical altercation that drops them both to the sidewalk. They pull hair, scream, and curse, and the police show up. J.P. is disappointed in his friends, confessing, "I thought we were better than this." The fight, and the police's arrival, implies a class distinction not pres-ent in *The Hills*, where most public fights have far more mild conclusions, mainly tears or a slammed door.

Another major difference between *Washington Heights* and other MTV reality identity series is the way in which ethnic identity is presented and contextualized. In *Jersey Shore*, the Guido identity is either isolated in the MTV-owned beach house where the cast members live during filming, or it is displayed in public, where it becomes a source of spectacle and Otherness (hence the many fistfights that take place when cast members head out to bars followed by their camera crew). But, on *Washington Heights*, *domini-canidad* is the default identity. The faces in the streets, in the bars, and at the bus stops are all brown, tan, and Black. White people, when they ap-pear onscreen, seem out of place (with the exception of Taylor), like they stepped into the frame from another series. Episodes are also peppered with signifiers of *dominicanidad*: old men playing dominoes on a fold-out card table on the sidewalk, spray-painted bridges, chain-link fences, fruit carts and flavor-ice vendors, check-cashing businesses, and taquerias. Dominican flags peek out of windows and shop displays. These neighborhood-specific details are not presented to be aspirational in the way that the beachfront homes on *The Hills* are, nor are they intended as something to ridicule, like the dump-truck-turned-swimming-pool in *Buckwild*. Instead, these details are intended to convey both a collective *dominicanidad* in the neighborhood and the specificity of J.P.'s friend group.[2]

When J.P. and his friends leave the Heights, their ethnicity becomes more visible. This is demonstrated when Reyna gets an interview to work at a wine bar that is located "uptown" (i.e., not in the Heights). When Reyna interviews with the bar's owner, a white man, her ethnic and class differences are, for the first time in the series, placed on display as the Other. The employer asks her what she likes to drink and she answers with "Luscious," a brand of inexpensive wine, and Jarritos, a soda produced in Mexico that is frequently used as a mixer in cocktails. These inexpensive and ethnically marked choices act to Other Reyna, who remarks, after the white man looks at her blankly, "I think the wine here in uptown is different." Later in the episode, Reyna returns for training with the bar sommelier. He instructs on how to swirl the glass, inhale the bouquet, and then taste and spit. After sampling a Bordeaux, Reyna makes a face. "Do you not like heavy wines?" he asks, bemused. Reyna, aware that her taste levels are being judged, replies, "Oh, no, I love heavy wines." But her expression indicates otherwise. This is one of the few moments in the series where Reyna's identity as both working class and nonwhite is played for laughs (as it is in series like *Jersey Shore* and *Buckwild*). Her lack of access to wine culture puts her at a distinct disadvantage in this interview, whereas Lauren's and Heidi's inexperience in their fields was never addressed or acknowledged in workplace scenes in *The Hills*. Although Reyna is a fish out of water uptown, she nevertheless is able to apply this cultural capital back in the Heights when she and Manny (her boyfriend) go out to dinner. At dinner she opens the wine list and causally makes suggestions, before telling her boyfriend that she needs to move out. In other words, the series aligns Reyna's burgeoning independence with her ability to navigate the social and cultural spaces that exist outside of the Heights.

Unlike the brothel-house chic aesthetic of *Jersey Shore* or the *verité*-style cinematography of *Teen Mom*, *Washington Heights* employs the aesthetics of *The Hills* and *The City*: telephoto lenses, widescreen compositions, and a consistent color palette (browns and grays, to match the concrete backdrop of the series' setting, connoting a sense of the "urban"). Similar to the women of *The Hills*, *Washington Heights*' cast members are also filmed going out to clubs and to brunch, or sitting in picturesque New York settings as they discuss their personal lives and recap key plot points for viewers. The bumpers between scenes mimic the aesthetics of *The Hills* and *The City* by offering aerial shots of the city skylines, followed by long shots of specific locations in that milieu. But whereas *The Hills* and *The City* focused on high-end storefronts, well-dressed residents, and other icons of wealth, taken as the default, *Washington Heights* is filled with more modest imagery. The cast members lounge on rooftops in folding chairs, sit on concrete stoops, or cluster next to graffiti-covered walls in the park. The *Washington Heights* cast members appear to be primarily working class, as evidenced by their small, cramped apartments, but they also have the cultural capital to pursue careers in art, music, and literature.

Each character on *Washington Heights* is pursuing a different dream of "making it" in their chosen career, but with art that is profoundly grounded in their own local Dominican American identities. Frankie Reese, an aspiring poet, organizes a talent night in a local venue, featuring performances and art installations by members of the community. She explains, "I wanna show people what a whole bunch of kids from the Heights can do." While cast members on *Jersey Shore* and *Buckwild* lampooned their ethnic and regional identities as a way to earn a living, the *Washington Heights* cast amplifies their ethnic and regional identities by channeling what their neighborhood and their culture means into their chosen medium: Frankie's spoken-word poetry is focused on the physical location of Washington Heights as well as the people who inhabit it, including the refrain "you molded me and I will forever be indebted to you"; J.P.'s stage name is Audubon, a street in the Heights; and Ludwin Federo's silkscreens are renderings of his younger brother, Alexis, a former Washington Heights resident who was serving jail time for selling drugs when the series was filming. This portrayal of *dominicanidad* as bohemian artists contradicts the narratives constructed around urban artists and might also account for the series' low ratings.

By focusing the series on each cast member's attempt to launch a career, *Washington Heights* could be categorized with series like *The Hills* and *The City*, which also feature twentysomethings pursuing their dreams in a big city. But whereas those shows were aspirational (something audiences could *desire*), *Washington Heights* is presented as inspirational (something audiences could *do*). The path to success is less obvious (and therefore more realistic) for these characters, more plagued with setbacks and frustrations. In *The Hills* and *The City*, jobs are plentiful, and simply showing up at work in a nice outfit is enough to be viewed as competent or even an asset. But in *Washington Heights*, characters work harder for less payoff. J.P. books gigs in the hopes of helping his mother to pay her electricity bills, only to discover that the gig does not pay anything. Later in the season he travels across the borough for a job that ends up being next to an airport hotel. J.P. balks at the venue until he realizes he needs the money. Similarly, Jimmy, who wants to play professional baseball, is stymied by his own financial needs. He cannot attend practice with his local league because he has to work. But if he quits work to focus on baseball, he will starve. In *Washington Heights*, labor and economics are clearly foregrounded, instead of ignored or glossed over, as it is in other reality identity series on MTV. This, too, may account for why the series was canceled.

In the season/series finale, each character's narrative arc is brought to closure. After "grinding it out all summer," J.P. finally bends the ear of a producer who ultimately gives J.P. a spot on his tour, based not on his music, but on his drive and spirit. When J.P. shares the good news with his mother, she chants, in ever-louder refrains, "It's happening! It's hap-pen-ing!" Their excitement and relief are palpable. Fred Rasuk gets an acceptance letter to the Fashion Institute of Technology, and his brother, Rico, lands his first acting gig. It is significant that we see Rico's initial hesitance toward acting classes, followed by a lackluster first take on set. But after taking direction, his second take is perfect, and the director goes wild. The finale also depicts the breakup of Jimmy and his girlfriend because Jimmy decides he needs to go to Florida to embrace his final chance to train for a career in baseball. Their closing conversation is rational and touching, with both agreeing that their relationship made them better people. And although Ludwin successfully held his own art show, displaying his work and his artistic vision, he ultimately decides to leave Washington Heights because, as he tearfully tells Frankie, "I feel like I'm not doing enough—you and me, we hang out every day . . ." Then he trails off. It's important that the series showcases both moments of success and moments of failure, moments of idealism and moments of realism, and the rise and fall of expectations. Unlike *The Hills*, which offered an unrealistic picture of twentysomethings working and succeeding (such as when Lauren chooses her boyfriend over a fashion internship in Paris), *Washington Heights* is more grounded in the realities of work and life.

So why did this series fail when series like *The Hills*, *Jersey Shore*, and *Buckwild* were so successful? As Keara Goin discovered in her interviews with Dominican viewers of the series, in its attempts to appeal to its mostly white audience, MTV alienated viewers who were tuning in to *Washington Heights* for a slice of authentic *dominicanidad*. For example, one interview subject, Diego, a US resident of Dominican birth, told Goin, "It is not authentic and I had hoped that the show would have turned out to be a bigger deal. But it lacked narrative conflict and the show's producers fundamentally misunderstood Dominican culture. In the end the show was a big let-down. Being Dominican is more than our music. It depicted the characters as dream chasers and was not a true reflection of Washington Heights" (2015, 167–168).

Other viewers complained about the lack of Spanish, as mentioned previously, as well as the fact that the cultural specificity of the neighborhood was obscured in all but the establishing and transitional shots. When the series focused on cast members, their status as Dominican was often white-washed and Americanized, making these figures interchangeable with other working-class, immigrant communities living in New York City.[3] Some fans of the series blame MTV's mishandling of publicity and promotion for the show's failure. One blogger noted that *Buckwild*, which premiered the same week as *Washington Heights*, was more heavily promoted by the channel, with appearances on *Access Hollywood* and the *Today Show*, as well as MTV's Tumblr page: "It was obvious from the beginning that *Buckwild* was the show MTV was pushing, and *Washington Heights* just happened to be premiering the same week" (Akosua 2013). And once the series launched, MTV did not run weekend marathons (a key method for hooking new viewers) as it did with other entries in the identity cycle. When they feared the show's low ratings might lead to cancellation, *Washington Heights* fans began a Change.org petition to convince MTV to renew the series. The petition fell short of its goal of five thousand signatures, and MTV did not make another season (Change.org 2012).

Ultimately, *Washington Heights* failed because it did not fit into MTV's previous models of successful reality programming and because the identities it offered were too specific, too niche, but also too nonwhite. *Jersey Shore* was a success because it made identity legible by converting Italian Americanness into a clear list of traits: gelled hair, big jewelry, and heavy makeup. *Buckwild* was a success because it translated Redneck identities into a different, though equally rigid brand: a love of danger, a distaste for the city and its technologies, and an overall embrace of activities associated with rural regions, like hunting, muddin', and dirt bikes. But *Washington Heights*' depiction of the Dominican American community and its culture did not line up with the spectacularized, Othered identities—of Guidos and Rednecks and Teen Moms—that MTV was disseminating at the time. Kristen Warner (2017) argues that what stands in for "diversity" in much of contemporary media texts, namely colorblind casting, is a kind of "plastic representation." She continues, "There is no great depth in plastic, nor is there anything organic." *Washington Heights* attempted to straddle this divide between plastic representations of *dominicanidad* (i.e., *The Hills* in the Heights!) and what Warner calls "meaningful, resonant diversity" rooted in the lives of these characters, and it failed to do both. The cast of *Washington Heights* lacked the "breakout" personalities that would have transferred the tone of *Jersey Shore* to a Dominican American cast. Yet the specificity offered by the show was not resonant enough to win over the demographic that wanted it the most. The Dominican American cast's fairly normal lives—which were neither glamorous and aspirational nor something to laugh at—proved to be uninteresting to MTV's audiences.

Sexual Identities in *Virgin Territory*

Virgin Territory, which premiered in 2014 and aired on MTV for just a single season of eleven episodes, is also about the ways in which identity can be both embodied and symbolic, permanent and ephemeral, on reality TV. For *Virgin Territory* to cohere as a series, MTV had to find a way to make virginity legible. After all, a Virgin does not have a particular accent, like *Buckwild*'s Redneck; a particular look, like *Jersey Shore*'s Guido; or a shared location and/or ethnicity, like the cast of *Washington Heights* or *The Hills*. And unlike the cast of *Teen Mom*, the cast of *Virgin Territory* cannot provide tangible, physical evidence of their identity status; a Teen Mom can present her offspring as proof of her identity, but a Virgin cannot provide proof of an absence. Lacking a clear method for establishing their identities, each cast member therefore declared their status onscreen, via webcam confessional, and recited an identical script: "Hi, my name is X, I'm X years old, and I'm a Virgin." This incantation renders each new Virgin a member of the TV series, and it stands as the most explicit example of identity confession in MTV's reality series.

The reasons for being a Virgin vary from cast member to cast member. For some, it is religious; Luke (episodes 2–5), a white man, admits, "If I wasn't a Christian, there's no way I'd be a Virgin." Alec (episodes 8–11), a white man, is a Virgin because he is still figuring out his sexual orientation. Keiyara (episodes 8–10), a Black woman, is a Virgin for a very practical reason—she does not wish to become pregnant. Still others maintain their virginity as a point of pride: Dominique (episodes 1–3), a Black woman, describes her virginity as her "most prized possession," while Shelby (episodes 4–6), a white woman, refers to herself as a "unicorn," a title that MTV endorses by flashing it onscreen when Shelby is introduced to the viewer for the first time. And Emily (episode 11), a white woman, is a Virgin due to

5.2 The cast of *Virgin Territory* shared an invisible identity: the Virgin.

a rare medical condition. All of the cast members on *Virgin Territory* are cisgendered.

Because each cast member's Virgin identity is initially invisible, it must be clearly articulated before new relationships can proceed. For example, both Keiyara and John (episodes 9–11), a white cisgendered man, feel the need to announce to their dates their status as Virgins, treating the status with the same weight and stigma that first dates treat divorce, children, or STDs. Announcing one's Virgin status helps the cast members explain not only the presence of MTV's cameras, but also, preemptively, their lack of sexual experience. When Kyle (episodes 2–4), a white man, kisses his crush, Amanda, for the first time, she remarks, "You kiss good for a Virgin." What if Kyle had not offered the warning first? Would he then be categorized as a "bad" kisser? Even when the cast members don't overtly mention their Virgin status, the presence of MTV's cameras certainly does. Nearly every onscreen conversation in the series, even when parents and employers are around, is about sex: if they should have it, when they should have it, how they should have it, and with whom they should have it. Mark Andrejevic writes that "in the era of comprehensive [reality TV] surveillance, even the mythical is rendered transparent" (2004, 74). Each Virgin is literally surrounded by bright lights, microphones, and camera crews who are only there, documenting their lives, because they are Virgins.

In the right environment and with the right framing, even virginity can be made legible on the two-dimensional TV body. For example, eighteen-year-old Abby (episodes 10–11), a white woman, is introduced via a montage of her socializing with friends, hanging out with her boyfriend, and serving trays of food at her waitressing job. When her coworker at the diner asks, "What's up with you? You look so excited," Abby confides, "I'm, like, freakin' out. I can't work. I can't focus." This conversation is intercut with Abby's first-person confessional, where she explains, "Tomorrow is Valentine's Day. [My boyfriend and I] got a hotel room and we are going to have sex." When the episode cuts back to Abby's workplace conversation about losing her virginity on Valentine's Day, the onscreen chyron reveals that the coworker with whom Abby has been discussing her virginity is, in fact, her boss. This type of workplace intimacy would seem out of place in nearly any other context. But Abby's boss knows why she is on camera—her willingness to discuss Abby's virginity. In some cases, the highlighting of the Virgin's identity works against their mission, as is the case with Anike (episodes 5–7), a Black woman, who plans to lose her virginity to her boyfriend on their first anniversary. When the eager couple return to Anike's house following a romantic dinner out, they are disappointed to see Anike's mom awake and alert in the living room, along with a full production crew. Her mother tells them, "No hanky panky." With the series' unrelenting focus on teen sexuality, its cast appears to be in a perpetual state of anxiety, horniness, or frigidity. Whether seeking out sex or rejecting it, cast members are always already defined in relation to sexual activity.

To offer another example, Anna (episodes 3–6), a white woman, is first introduced as she is heading to a local bar after work with some coworkers, still wearing their uniforms of short plaid skirts and midriff-revealing blouses (which are unbuttoned to reveal black bras underneath). After securing drinks, the women climb on top of the bar and dance seductively (this is replayed in slow motion to further emphasize the seductiveness). These images are intended to contrast with Anna's voice-over narration: "People think they have me figured out, and then, if I tell them I'm a Virgin, then they're, like, mind's blown." In the same episode, Anna hosts what she calls a "CEOs and Office Hos" party. The men attending the party dress up as "CEOs," in button-down shirts and ties, and the women dress as "Office Hos," in button-down shirts, tight skirts, and, sometimes, glasses. Though MTV does not overtly explore the politics of a cast member holding a party in which the men get to dress up as rich, powerful professionals and the women dress up as either women who sleep with a lot of men or women who sleep with men for money (depending on your definition of the word "ho"), the party theme implies a direct relationship between dressing seductively and snagging a financially stable mate. Anna has orchestrated this result and takes her crush upstairs partway through her party.

Unlike the participants in MTV's other reality identity cycle series, the four cast members featured each week on *Virgin Territory* are all looking to "lose" the very label that has made them interesting enough to appear on camera. Once a cast member has sex, they disappear from the series' opening credits and are replaced with a new Virgin in the next episode. Lisa, a white cisgendered woman introduced in episode 1, marries her boyfriend of three years, Nick, without ever having masturbated, and she treats the loss of her virginity as a somber ritual. Her final episode features her wedding ceremony and reception, including cake and dancing. This montage is intercut with Lisa's first-person camera address where she admits, "You almost get used to saying, 'Yeah, we've been dating for three and a half years, we haven't slept together, you know we're waiting till marriage.'" After years of defining herself as a Virgin by choice, Lisa will be losing that identity. Here the nondiegetic music shifts from an upbeat pop song to a more somber one to signify the seriousness of the identity shift Lisa is about to begin. Nick and Lisa's car, decked out in the traditional "Just Married" decorations, leaves the reception as Lisa explains in a voice-over, "That moment is here, whether I like it or not." This does not sound like someone who is excited to consummate her marriage. Indeed, the next shot features Lisa and Nick walking down the hallway of their hotel in slow motion, as if they are walking to their own execution.

In the next scene, the title card reads "The morning after," which is followed by a series of shots connoting the after-ness of sex: Lisa brushing her teeth, the wedding band on her finger, and the crumpled wedding dress tossed on the couch. In the next shot, Lisa is sitting on her bed, facing the camera: "Well, umm, we *did* end up having sex?" She says this less as a statement and more like a question. This first-person address is intercut with Lisa talking with Nick. "It's my official first day of not being a Virgin," she tells him with a sigh. "It wasn't anything breathtaking, I guess." During this voice-over, the camera returns to shots of Lisa and Nick packing up their honeymoon suite. Lisa looks frazzled, placing her hands over her face and sighing, as Nick looks on. "I don't know," she tells him. "Do you think [sex is] one of those things that, like, you just have to adjust? And, like, learn?" Nick looks down and says, "Yeah. Yeah." Despite this rather grim review of her first sexual experience with the love of her life, Lisa's first-person address to the camera ends on an upbeat note. In these final shots, Nick and Lisa sit together in an overstuffed chair, seeming far more connected and in love than in the earlier scenes where they discussed their wedding night. The final shot belongs to Lisa, though. She looks at the camera, smiles, and declares, "I am no longer a Virgin." She reaches up to turn off the camera.

Similarly, in the *Virgin Territory* finale, after Abby finally loses her virginity to Kyle, she tells the camera, "I feel like I have a new identity." As with Lisa, the newly deflowered Abby does not appear particularly happy or blissful, likely because of her heteronormative expectations for romance. She schedules her virginity loss for the most commodified day of the romance calendar, Valentine's Day, and decorates her hotel room with rose petals, pink balloons, and sparkling juice. She is thus highly disappointed when, moments before taking a necessary pre-virginity-losing shower, her boyfriend goes into the bathroom for twenty minutes to defecate. Abby's image of how her first time should go, free of the stink of her boyfriend's abject bodily waste, is thus destroyed. Her virginity is preserved for one more episode. Abby's postcoital disappointment is linked to the way she understood her virginity's social capital. Abby tells her boyfriend that being a Virgin shielded her from being labeled in negative terms: "When people called me a slut, I could say, 'What do you mean? I'm a Virgin.'" Abby is worried family and friends who once respected her for her resolve will be all the more disappointed in her after she has sex. Nineteen-year-old Anna explains in her introductory confessional, "Even though I was raised religiously and I went to a private Christian school, I still do everything besides sex, which, in my definition? Is when a man's penis goes into a woman's vagina." Anna looks uncomfortable as she states this definition, but the details are needed for Anna to declare and affirm her Virgin status. She may fool around but she is absolutely a Virgin. The women's attachment to their virginity explains why, out of the six cast members who lost their virginity during the filming of *Virgin Territory*, it was only the men—Kyle and John—who had sex with partners outside of a long-term, committed relationship. For these men, their Virgin status was a source of shame and anxiety, and so its loss is a necessary ordeal both had to muddle through. The men describe their loss of virginity with a visible sense of relief. By contrast, the women who lose their virginity are either married to their partner or have been in a long-term monogamous relationship with their partners, which implies that self-proclaimed Virgin women cannot have sex for fun or enjoyment, just as an expression of commitment.

Of course, not everyone on *Virgin Territory* loses the identity that got them on the series. Episode 10 closed with Keiyara telling the webcam, "So for right now, I'm gonna try to take the time out and find a guy that's right for me. . . . But until the right guy comes along I'm *so* happy remaining a Virgin." She turns off the camera and in the next episode she is replaced with a new Virgin named Emily (episode 11). Just as Abby and Lisa leave the series once they proclaim their virginity loss on camera, Keiyara must leave the series because she has announced that she will *not* (for now) lose her virginity. Like Lisa and Abby, Keiyara must make this announcement into the webcam, the first-person confessional aesthetics promising a holy blessing of authenticity onto the cast member's identity. When the screen goes dark, it signals that this cast member is permanently a Virgin, a Virgin for eternity, unless they reappear on another season of *Virgin Territory* to once again make the pivotal decision: "Am I a Virgin or not?" Dominique, who is first introduced in the pilot episode, explains that she wishes to remain a Virgin until marriage, with her oft-repeated mantra "No ringy, no dingy." Dominique, like Anna, enjoys wearing form-fitting clothing, drinking, and dancing with men at bars. She explains, "People say to me, 'Dominique, you don't act like a Virgin,' and I always say, 'Well what do a Virgin act like?'" Like Anna, Dominique appreciates the security of her Virgin status, which shields her from accusations of being promiscuous. In episode 3 Dominique also reveals, during a heartfelt talk with her estranged mother, that her "pickiness" about men is due to the trauma of her parents' divorce. During the conversation, Dominique cries openly. The episode concludes with Dominique enjoying a family barbecue and bonding with her mother and extended family. In her final confessional Dominique explains that she has learned to be more open "in order to succeed in relationships." She also reaffirms her commitment to remaining a Virgin until marriage and then turns off her webcam. In episode 4, Dominique is replaced by Shelby, a sorority girl.

Another example of a cast member who decides to retain his Virgin status, and thus exit the series, is David (episodes 6–8), a white man. David's status as a Virgin ties strongly to his wholesale ignorance about the rules and limits of heterosexual courtship. His introductory montage includes David playing foosball and laser tag and then falling down while skiing, images that juvenilize him. David believes he is still a Virgin at nineteen because he is "permanently in the friend zone" due to his "gentle nature." As his episode opens, David admits to never having been on a date and that he was bullied throughout his childhood. He eventually works up the nerve to ask a young woman in his friend group, Cairo, on a series of dates. These dates, which are filmed in excruciating detail by MTV's cameras, reveal that David's cues for romance hail mainly from rom-coms and supermarket paperback covers. At various points in their nascent relationship he hand-feeds Cairo chocolate-covered strawberries, buys her a single red rose, and offers contrived pick-up lines. Given that these tactics have worked for legions of fictional screen lovers, David is perplexed when his interactions with Cairo remain awkward and stilted. The rules of heterosexual courtship are more complicated than he originally thought, and so David informs Cairo that they should remain friends. At the end of the episode, David decides to stay a Virgin for the time being. He is replaced with John in episode 9.

Virgin Territory features just one nonheterosexual cast member, twenty-year-old Alec, whose identity as a closeted gay man overshadows his identity as a Virgin, for most of his screen time. In his opening webcam confessional he states, "I'm gay. Nobody knows it. I'm still in the closet. Growing up you see people make fun of gay people, and how they're looked down upon, and you realize that's who you are and you don't want to be looked down upon. You don't want to be made fun of, you don't want to be bullied, and you don't want to be left out." Alec explains that he struggled to come to terms with his sexual identity for many years ("I would do anything I could not to be gay"), but he recently became comfortable with his sexuality. Obviously, the fact that he is discussing his sexual identity openly on camera, knowing it will be broadcast to millions of MTV viewers, indicates that Alec is ready to come out. Alec seeks advice on how to come out from a local support group for gay and lesbian people. A circle of gay men discuss what it is like to come out to family and friends, framed by rainbow flags. "When it comes to coming out," one of the men notes, "it's not just our journey, it's everyone around us." Another man urges Alec to be "patient with folks who may not really be keen to it at first." Yet another tells him that coming out is going to be "a huge relief," and that no matter what happens, he will never be alone.

Armed with this knowledge, Alec comes out to his family at the end of episode 8. His family is supportive and the scene culminates in a group hug. In episode 9, Alec comes out to his friends by putting the words "Hey, I'm gay" on a cake and serving it to them. Some of Alec's friends look shocked, while one declares with glee, "I knew it! I knew it!" Later Alec tells the webcam about the "after" of coming out: "I haven't felt this much love for a long time. . . . It feels really good to finally be open and tell my friends that this is who I am." Alec seeks and receives advice, takes action, and then explains how it all went. It is only after Alec has completed this process that he is able to pursue his true purpose on the series: the loss of his virginity. His gay identity is now in the background, and his status as a Virgin is firmly in the

5.3 "Hey, I'm gay":
Virgin Territory's
Alec comes out to his
friends with a cake.

foreground. In episode 11, Alec has his first kiss ever, while finally out of the closet. He is so excited that he is unsure how to mark the occasion. He turns to the camera: "Do I tell people? Do I tweet it?" At the end of this episode, Alec also decides to remain a Virgin for the time being.

The final episode of the series features Emily (episode 11), who is a Virgin due not to religious beliefs or sexual repression or fear or trauma, but to an actual physical condition—a "septate hymen." This rather obscure medical issue is explained to Emily with charts by her sex therapist. Emily has surgery and goes on to have sex therapy in order to help her disassociate her own vagina from the words "pain" and "closed"; she models the slow, and often frustrating, road to recovery. Emily's narrative demonstrates how talking to teens and college students about sex, not simply the morality or ethics of choice but the actual physical act of sex attached to bodies, can be uncomfortable, such as when Emily tells her girlfriends that the therapist gave her "vagina homework" to do. Unlike every other cast member who became an un-Virgin over the course of the series, Emily, whose story begins and ends in the series finale, the shortest of the series as well, declines to announce her virginity loss via webcam. Instead, her story ends with a long shot of the apartment she shares with her boyfriend, followed by a black screen explaining that Emily and her boyfriend had sex and that she stopped filming afterward to protect her privacy. MTV still declares her an un-Virgin by proxy; whether she dismisses the cameras from her home or not, Emily is branded, her identity delimited, for MTV's profit.

Virgin Territory differs from MTV's other reality identity programming because it is one of the few series that features a range of racial, ethnic, and sexual identities under the same identity label: Virgin. In this way, the series parallels *The Real World*, which also brings together a diverse range of identities. The key difference between these two series is that *Virgin Territory*'s cast members do not interact with one another; they are filmed separately in their own living spaces. Race, class, and ethnic differences all appear on the series, but these identities do not have an impact on the cast members' identities as Virgins. Keiyara, Dominique, and Anike are all Black women, but this aspect of their identity is not central to their stories (in fact, Blackness is not mentioned at all during their episodes). Eighteen-year-old Marjorie (episodes 7–9) is Brazilian, and being Brazilian is clearly important to her; all of her friends are Brazilian, and she and her family speak Portuguese. Still, her identity as Latinx has very little to do with Marjorie's Virgin status. *Virgin Territory* claims that these identities (Black, Brazilian), which would have formed the key focus of a cast member's narrative in a different kind of MTV reality series, are secondary to the shared trait of virginity. The only exceptions to this are Alec, whose virginity is tied to his ability to accept his gay identity, and episode 11's Emily, who is a Virgin because of her septate hymen. But other than these two cast members, MTV attempts to melt away identity difference under the shared label of Virgin.

This is, perhaps, why *Virgin Territory*, despite its rather scandalous and intimate subject matter, was not a hit for MTV and has yet to be renewed for a second season. The series offers none of the pleasures produced by hits like *The Hills* and *Jersey Shore*. MTV's reality identity series are generally hits only if they model certain identity-based behaviors, such as the Can-Do and At-Risk identities depicted in *The Hills* and *Teen Mom*; if they teach identity-based lessons, as in *The Real World*; or if they lampoon an identity, as was seen in *Jersey Shore* and *Buckwild*. Unlike a show like *Teen Mom* or *16 and Pregnant*, there is no universal position to take on the shared Virgin identity. *Teen Mom* and *16 and Pregnant* are premised on the assumption, to quote the series' creator, Dia Sokol Savage, again, that these are girls "who have made a mistake." But *Virgin Territory*'s central identity offers too many possible readings, for there are innumerable reasons for why a person may or may not be a Virgin (and for why they may or may not be proud of this identity).

Conclusions

Both *Washington Heights* and *Virgin Territory* offer useful insights into prominent discourses about Millennial youth in the 2010s, namely the grounding nature of a shared identity and of knowing one's self. In *Washington Heights*, cast members frequently reference the name of their neighborhood ("In the Heights, you only get one chance") and use it as a way to define behaviors ("You can't do that [in the Heights]") and to brand themselves. The cast members' shared status as residents of this neighborhood literally defines their livelihoods in that their artistic aspirations are firmly rooted in the Heights. Season 1 concludes with each cast member finding their way toward a future they desire, primarily because they acknowledge and pay homage to their identities as residents of Washington Heights. The greenlighting of *Washington Heights* signaled MTV's desire to depict more nonwhite youth in its reality series; however, in the channel's desire to make the cast into ethnic Others while also watering down their Otherness, it ended up dissatisfying *all* viewers. Similarly, *Virgin Territory* depicted a range of youth identities (white, Black, Latinx, gay, religious, etc.), but unlike other MTV series featuring a "diverse" cast (i.e., *The Real World*), this diversity was not deployed to generate conflict or plot points. For the most part, white Virgins spent time with white Virgins and religious Virgins spent time with other religious Virgins. These scenes of homogeneity, which, for the most part, never leaned toward stereotypes or hyperbole (as with other homogeneous identity programming on MTV like *Jersey Shore*), lacked the conflict and excitement promised by its reality predecessors. The failed series discussed in this chapter are further proof of the narrow parameters in which MTV can depict nonwhite or nonheterosexual identities.

In the conclusion, I examine the current state of MTV reality programming, starting with an in-depth look at *Catfish*, one of MTV's most successful reality identity programs. The series premiered in 2012, at a time when MTV's ratings for its target demographic of twelve- to thirty-four-year-olds had dropped by 29 percent. Barry Lowenthal, president of Media Kitchen, explains, "MTV has been the voice of a generation—one that was connected through music and celebrities. . . . But today young people are connected through their devices, which is driving down ratings across cable and broadcast" (qtd. in Zara 2015). *Catfish* highlights a highly specific, but ever-growing, form of intimacy in the twenty-first century: the bodiless, online romance. It was the next logical step for MTV TO create a reality show that focused on internet-enabled devices and the relationships they generate. The conclusion also includes a brief look at current reality programming on MTV, including *Siesta Key*, *Floribama Shore*, and *Young + Pregnant*, all of which represent an attempt to recapture the success of previous MTV hits like *The Hills*, *Jersey Shore*, and *Teen Mom*. If the latter were created for a Millennial audience fixated on the performance of identity, then what do the former indicate about MTV's newest demographic, Generation Z? What messages about identity and the self are conveyed in this programming?

Catfish and the Future of MTV's Reality Programming

(2012–)

Whon I interviewed Max Joseph, cohost of MTV's then wildly popular reality series *Catfish*, in November 2015, he had just wrapped up a shoot in Rochester, New York. Since it was fresh on his mind, I asked him to walk me through the basic structure of the episode he just shot. He explained that, after Skyping with someone from their previous shoot in Wyoming (footage that would then appear just before the credits in that episode), Max and his cohost, Nev Shulman, are alerted that they have received a new email. The email asks for their help: "because they had been talking to *X* person for *X* amount of time and something seems fishy, but their hopes and dreams are attached to meeting this person and we call that person the Hopeful. There's the Hopeful and there's the Catfish. If there's a glossary, this will be an important glossary term." When I interviewed Joseph, the term "catfish" had already been added to the *Merriam-Webster Dictionary* (in 2014), a move reflective of MTV's power to effectively label youth identities as they form and then to shape their contours via its powerful multiplatform approach to viewership. The Catfish and the Hopeful, by appearing on *Catfish*, are articulating their desires to be named as such, to, unconsciously or not, be deemed a fool, or a liar, in other words, a person we all have been in some way, at some time, while navigating the internet. By the time *Catfish*'s second season aired on MTV in 2013, it was the number one telecast of the day and one of the top, most-watched series of the fall television season (Nielsen 2013).[1]

In this concluding chapter, I analyze *Catfish*, and how it contradicts earlier incarnations of MTV's reality identity cycle, which presented identity as bounded and definable (the Guido, the Can-Do Girl, the Redneck). In this way, *Catfish*, at least in its early seasons, might be the most "authentic" representation of youth identities to appear on MTV during the peak of this production cycle; it demonstrates how challenging it is to pin down identity in the ineffable free-floating, virtual landscape where so many of us communicate, conduct business, and fall in love: the internet. *Catfish* is also one of the few MTV reality identity series (along with *The Real World* and *Teen Mom*) to run continuously across the transition from Millennials to Generation Z (aka the iGeneration, Homelanders, or post-Millennials). In 2018, the Pew Research Center designated the year 1996 as the official cutoff point for Millennials and as the beginning point of Generation Z (Dimock 2019). If baby boomers grew up alongside the television, Generation X coincided with the personal computer, and Millennials came of age during the spread of the internet and social media, then what technology defines Generation Z? *More* internet and *more* social media (Dimock 2019). A 2018 study of this young generation finds that 95 percent of American Generation Z teens own a smartphone and 45 percent "say they are online on a near-constant basis" (Anderson and Jiang 2018). There have also been massive social and cultural shifts in the United States (and globally) since MTV first began making these reality identity series in the early 2000s: the start and end of the presidency of the first Black president, a sharp uptick in fatal mass shootings, an increase in extreme weather events and natural disasters, broad-based protests against social inequalities like #BlackLivesMatter and #MeToo, and the election of former reality TV host Donald Trump as the forty-fifth president of the United States in 2016.[2]

Generation Z, which experienced all of these foundational events as teens or young adults, is also on track to be both the most diverse and the most educated generation of American youth, a title formerly held by Millennials (Fry and Parker 2018). This audience, not Millennials, is the demographic that MTV was targeting in 2017 when it began to recycle previously successful reality identity series: *Siesta Key* is like *Laguna Beach* in Florida; *Floribama Shore* is a *Buckwild* / *Jersey Shore* hybrid, also set in Florida; and *Young + Pregnant* is an updated *Teen Mom*. Around this time, MTV also embarked on overt reboots of past hits, such as *Jersey Shore: Family Reunion*, which brought (most of) the original cast back together, and *The Hills: New Beginnings*, which featured all of the original cast members with the exception of Lauren Conrad and Kristin Cavallari (who had headlined and narrated the series from 2006 to 2009 and 2009 to 2010, respectively). A reboot is a text that retells the same story with the same characters, but which "attempts to disassociate itself textually from previous iterations while at the same time having to concede that it does not replace—but adds new associations to—an existing (serial) property" (Verevis 2016). Thus, these rebooted series, along with new seasons of *Teen Mom* and *The Real World*, seem to be appealing to Millennial audiences who grew up watching MTV and are on the trail of some easy nostalgia as they make their way into, and through, their thirties, as well as to the audience who followed them, Generation Z.

Catfish

MTV's *Catfish* is a spin-off of the popular film documentary *Catfish* (2010, Ariel Schulman and Henry Joost), starring Nev Schulman. The documentary focuses on Nev's online relationship with a young, attractive dancer named Megan, as well as a revolving cast of characters in Megan's life (including her sister, Abby, an eight-year-old painting prodigy, and Abby's mother, Angela). Halfway through the film's narrative, Nev discovers that all of these people are one woman, Angela, a middle-aged housewife and mother. Angela's role as caretaker to a set of teenaged sons with severe mental and physical disabilities requires the expenditure of physical and emotional labor. But in her romance/friendship/bond with Nev, Angela gets to escape her challenging daily routine. Posing as Nev's lover, friend, and artistic protégée, roles she did not (currently) play in real life, gives Angela a sense of being desired sexually, platonically, and creatively. The documentary's title comes in its final scene, in which Vince Pierce, Angela's good-natured husband, explains why he values his wife, using an unlikely metaphor:

> They used to tank cod from Alaska all the way to China. They'd keep them in vats in the ship. By the time the codfish reached China, the flesh was mush and tasteless. So this guy came up with the idea that if you put these cods in these big vats, put some catfish in with them and the catfish will keep the cod agile. And there are those people who are catfish in life. And they keep you on your toes. They keep you guessing, they keep you

thinking, they keep you fresh. And I thank god for the catfish because we would be droll, boring, and dull if we didn't have somebody nipping at our fin.

Angela, presumably, is the catfish to Vince's cod, nipping at his fin to keep him from going mushy. Although the Catfish is deceiving the Hopeful, pretending to be prettier or younger or of a different gender, they nevertheless provide the Hopeful with a little nip of excitement in what might otherwise be a mundane existence. Though Vince could not have known it at the time, this metaphor would come to define the pervasive phenomenon of deceptive online dating.

Once Nev and Angela's story migrated to MTV, it had to be told from the perspective of younger Catfish and Hopefuls, to appeal to MTV's twelve- to thirty-four-year-old demographic. As Nev states in the opening credits to every episode of *Catfish*, "*Catfish* the movie was my story; *Catfish* the TV show is *yours*." But whose stories get told? Max Joseph told me that some of the most interesting catfish stories occur "when some middle-aged man is talking to a woman in Sweden or Russia, and there's some scam involved." But these Hopefuls will never be cast on the series because the stories of men in their forties, fifties, and sixties are not of interest to MTV's audience. The circumstances surrounding the choice of who appears onscreen and what can be shown about their real lives are circumscribed in these specific ways. MTV's charge to appeal to a youth audience has presented some unique filming challenges for the series, such as where and who they can film. For example, the age of the individuals who are cast for the show limits the production's ability to show all the factors that impact and shape their lives, and by extension, the explanations behind why they were catfished. Joseph told me that sometimes a Catfish's or Hopeful's family and friends do not wish to appear on camera: "And I'm saying 'how the fuck do we not meet their parents? These are kids!' Their whole psyche is somewhat based on their relationship with their parents."

Joseph also describes how the nature of reality TV production impacts the sample size of who appears on the series, what he calls the "self-selecting" problem. "The people who do elect to come on the show are generally people who . . . need the show to pay for the [plane] ticket. . . . So there are socioeconomic factors that determine who is on the show. And I think that may be true of a lot of reality shows." Hopefuls who earn enough money to buy a bus ticket to the next town, or a cross-country flight, may have less motivation to contact the series in order to meet their Catfish in real life (IRL).

Despite these limitations imposed by the production, Joseph maintains that the stories, emotions, and reactions of the Hopeful and the Catfish that are captured on the series are "authentic." Indeed, Joseph felt, quite strongly, that the series was more authentic than most reality series on the air, especially those on MTV: "I think *Catfish* is one of the most honest shows. . . . What is different about our show is that we let things unfold; we let the characters and people on the show do what they do, and if they don't want to do something we can't make them do it." He cited *The Hills* as an example of a scripted reality series that asked its cast members to reenact certain moments for the camera and how, as a result, many reality TV audiences have become cynical about the possibility that what they are watching is real or authentic (see also Corner 2002).

As *Catfish* the TV series demonstrates, stories of online deception are prevalent among Millennials, who were adolescents during the launch of Web 2.0, the internet, social media, and other telecommunication technologies.[3] A Kaiser Family Foundation study from 2010 revealed that eight- to eighteen-year-old Millennials spent an average of seven hours and thirty-eight minutes on "entertainment media" in one day. These numbers do not account for the fact that many of these media consumers are "media multitasking," tweeting while watching a TV series, for example. In *It's Complicated*, danah boyd studies the fraught relationship between youth and social media technologies: "As the internet started gaining traction among youth, the same fears and anxieties that surrounded other publics and media genres reemerged in relation to networked publics and social media" (2014, 105). It was a logical next step for MTV to create a reality show that focused on internet-enabled devices and the relationships they generate and cultivate.

In addition to concerns over the impact of too much "screen time" on the impressionable minds of youth audiences, parents, researchers, and legislators were concerned about the physical safety of youth engaged with these technologies. Programs like *To Catch a Predator* convinced the US Attorney General to research technical interventions to stop sexual predators from preying on unsuspecting, networked youth. These fears were rooted in the anonymity of the internet and the slipperiness of identity in these spaces. As Adrien Chen (2013) argues, "*Catfish* has struck such a nerve because it combines old fears of Internet strangers with newer anxieties about the authenticity of online friendship." But while middle-aged white men tend to get caught with their pants down—pun intended—on "gotcha" shows like *To Catch a Predator*, the deceivers represented in MTV's *Catfish*

C.1 Nev and Max, the hosts of *Catfish*, investigate their subjects onscreen.

often have *no* desire to meet their Hopefuls in person. Their transgression is not the intent to abuse these Hopefuls "in real life"; instead, the intensity of the lie, of the fabricated romance, of the feeling of intense emotional connections can be fostered and nurtured for years merely through voices and words.

Like MTV's previous reality identity programs, *Catfish* offers a neoliberal solution (reality TV will be your private investigator!) to the problems and anxieties generated by modern society (is my online lover really a liar?). Joseph described the relationship between the series and its subjects as a quid pro quo: "The Catfish may not want to be on the show. And sometimes the Hopeful doesn't even want to be on the show, but it's their best chance to meet this person. And . . . we are providing a service. In return for the service we are providing, we get to tell the story on TV. In that case, it's a win-win." Joseph tells me that the identities of the Catfish are researched and then selected by MTV's casting department *before* the show's hosts are filmed doing their own research. The two men then (re)perform the research on camera because, as Joseph tells me, "we're not good actors. . . . We want reactions in real time, on camera. We go very carefully through the Facebook pages. And the Instagram accounts. We look at the URLs of the handle, which is very often a tell. . . . So, yeah, Spokeo, People Search, White Pages, My Life is another one that's good. Not rocket science." It sure isn't rocket science! Googling the name of the Catfish, looking them up on Facebook, and/or reaching out to the friends who appear on the Catfish's page, as well as a handful of reverse image searches can uncover enough evidence to call the Catfish's identity claims into question. The only tools most Hopefuls need in order to determine whether or not their lover is real is a laptop with a Wi-Fi connection and a working phone. The fact that the Hopeful has not done this seemingly simple background research reflects how denial is central to the tropes of the series.[4] Implicit in every episode of *Catfish* is a critique of the seemingly willful ignorance of the Hopeful.

When *Catfish* premiered, more than forty million people were using online dating services (and that number has only increased since). The series' success lies in the way it highlights the risks in disembodied intimacy and the betrayals that result from asynchronous computer-mediated communication and its reliance on "ambient intimacy." Leisa Reichelt (2007) defines ambient intimacy as "being able to keep in touch with people with a level of regularity and intimacy that you wouldn't usually have access to, because time and space conspire to make it impossible." Social media has made it simple and comfortable, almost reflexive, to communicate with people who are not physically near, which removes proximity from the intimacy equation altogether. Ian Curry compares ambient intimacy and its tactile presence in terms of Mikhail Bakhtin's "phatic" utterances: "Like saying 'what's up?' as you pass someone in the hall when you have no intention of finding out what is actually up, the phatic function is communication simply to indicate that communication can occur" (qtd. in Reichelt 2007). During the duration of the relationships depicted on the series, which can last anywhere from a few months to eight years, the Catfish and Hopeful exist in a symbiotic relationship, always available to soothe, coax, and adore one another. It might be tempting to think of these light exchanges as poor substitutes for IRL kisses and caresses because they lack the bodies we claim to need for sexual satisfaction. But as sociologist Nathan Jurgenson (2012) explains, "We're coming to terms with there being just one reality and digital is part of it, not any less real or true." When I interviewed Joseph about his experiences filming the series, he described the appeal of online romance in a similar way: "Most people are just looking for someone to listen to them and to give them daily affirmation. It's the ritual of calling and having someone, somewhere else—and it *has* to be somewhere else—it's because you're telling your secrets to a hole in the wall that it works." *Catfish* demonstrates that it is precisely *the absence of the body* that makes these relationships so titillating. Often accessed through smartphones clutched close to the body, texts and messaging form the media of intimacy on the series. Lovers bring their phones to bed, with the Catfish's glowing avatar standing in for the absent, beloved body.

Catfish is fascinating because it provides a window into the intimacy of the online romances that surround youth audiences as they post photos to Facebook or check out the headlines on Twitter. The discourse between the Catfish and the Hopeful is the most stripped-down version of language. It is free of capital letters and punctuation, grammatically incorrect and riddled with purposeful misspellings. In a medium in which the human voice effectively disappears, words and images rule. The cloak of capital letters and the formality of periods and complete sentences are needed for professional relationships, but the Catfish and Hopeful require little in the way of formality. "Digital punctuation can carry more weight than traditional writing because it ends up conveying tone, rhythm and attitude rather than grammatical structure," explains linguist Ben Zimmer. "It can make even a lowly period become freighted with special significance" (qtd. in Bennett 2015). The repeated close-ups of texted sentiments like "no one understands me like you do" and "I would do anything for you" indicate that there is little variety in online lovemaking, as if they all speak in the language of the Catfish, the language of ambient intimacy. When discussing *Badlands*, his 1970s classic about an affectless teenage girl who abets a murderer, Terence Malick explained, "When people express what is most important to them, it often comes out in clichés. That doesn't make them laughable; it's something tender about them. As though in struggling to reach what's most personal about them they could only come up with what's most public" (qtd. in Barshad 2011). The very mundanity of the messages exchanged between the Hopeful and the Catfish, and their assumption of particularity, is what makes them so personal. The Hopeful falls for the same clichéd words, ordered and reordered on the screen like an incantation. In the Catfish, the Hopeful is presented with an idealized mirror to their own best self. The beloved, the Catfish, is the perfect lover: supportive, complimentary, and nurturing.

In *Catfish* the documentary, Angela, the original Catfish, describes the numerous online profiles she used to communicate with Nev, the original Hopeful, over several months as "fragments of the things I used to be, wanted to be, never could be." Similarly, on the MTV reality series almost all of the Catfish generate their profiles using photographs of highly attractive people, many of whom turn out to be models or dancers in real life, and with careers and lifestyles more exciting or fulfilling than their own. This is because "social networking sites make it easy for people to pick and choose what aspects of themselves they want to highlight and what they want to hide. And in extreme cases, it allows people to create completely new versions of themselves, something they cannot do in the tangible world" (Hoover, Teklits, and Eshbach 2019). To list just one example from the TV series, Michael, a Hopeful involved with Caroline, a slim redhead, for eighteen months, was surprised to discover he had been noodled by Heather, an overweight woman he had scorned previously in real life. Heather initially invented Caroline as a way to hurt Michael, but she quickly found herself falling in love during the process of her deception. Upon the moment of revelation, Michael asks what *is* real about Heather and she tellingly replies, "Other than my name and picture and being a teacher and having cancer, it was all real." This statement gets to the heart of *Catfish*'s value in understanding the stakes of online identity; the internet offers users a way to detach from their bodies and connect with their minds, feelings, ethics, or intelligence. Those who don't like their profile page in real life can place a face over their own, a mask, the Catfish, in order to navigate the often-hostile online waters.[5] When the lovers finally meet face to face, and the meeting almost always takes place outside, in the daylight, their embarrassment is palpable.[6] Their intimacy was real, their connection was real, but in real life, the metaphorical last call of online mingling, it appears bland or tawdry.

Some episodes of MTV's *Catfish* position the Catfish as a villain, but many create a sympathetic view of the deceiver as someone who used the anonymity of the internet to invent a persona that would allow them to feel better loved by the world. Joseph told me that "the version of the story is so biased, it's the story they've been telling themselves, it's their victim's narrative." The stories told by the Catfish are not always objectively true, but they are reflective of a *kind of truth*—the story that the Catfish tells themselves about themselves and what they choose to reveal. For example, Hopeful Keyonnah, a young Black woman, believed she was chatting with the famous rapper and TV host Bow Wow, only to discover (by being cast on *Catfish*) that her lover was actually Dee, a woman who courts heterosexual

C.2 The first meeting between the Catfish and the Hopeful is often awkward or anticlimactic.

women online. In her small city, Dee, a Black, butch lesbian who likes rapping in baggy jeans and white T-shirts, has a difficult time meeting other lesbians. But social media has offered Dee a possibility for forming intimate, romantic relationships with women (by pretending to be a famous man). Though her deception is unethical, the series also paints Dee's behavior as a survival mechanism.

Like other entries in MTV's reality identity cycle, *Catfish* maintains a consistent aesthetics that replicates the aesthetics of the screen and of social media in particular. Much screen time is devoted to the various digital images the Catfish and the Hopeful have exchanged. Sometimes the Catfish, who has usually stolen their profile pictures from the home pages of obscure musicians and models, provides only a handful of photos, forcing the episode producer to endlessly cycle through the same images. As a result, the audience is also placed in the role of the Hopeful, gazing at the same image of the Catfish over and over. Because of this relentless focus on the screen, the aesthetics of the program are often of pixels and glowing computer screens. The footage replays the traces the Catfish has left behind on Facebook profile pages, both real and fabricated, abandoned MySpace pages, Instagram accounts, or any site that traffics in personal photos. There are close-ups of text messages and the opaque bubbles of Facebook Messenger conversations. There are blinking cursors and words being typed and erased. Likewise, whenever a new individual is introduced to the viewer onscreen they are labeled with a rectangular onscreen tag, similar to the tags employed by the Facebook user interface. Here, the audience is positioned as the social media user, her mouse suspended over the image to make a tag visible. *Catfish*, like all reality identity series, also uses signature sound effects to transition from scene to scene and from show to commercial break. *Catfish*'s soundscape is stitched together by the rhythms and beats of online courtship and the aural residue of digital society: the tapping of fingers on the phone, the clicking of the mouse, the beeps and zings of push notifications.

Ratings for *Catfish* dropped in its later seasons for a variety of reasons: the world may be running out of Catfish and Hopefuls, Joseph announced he would be leaving the series (Nakamura 2018), and Nev Schulman has been dogged by accusations of sexual misconduct, leading MTV to "pause" production of season 7 in 2018 and not release the episodes in the fall of 2019 (season 8 aired in 2020). *Catfish* was a programming anomaly on MTV in that its success coincided with the end of MTV reality identity powerhouses like *Jersey Shore* and the failure of new series like *Virgin Territory*. The series was a phenomenon because it relentlessly worked to pin the Catfish to a *real* face, a *real* identity, in an effort to breach the gap between signifier and signified, to right the wrong, and to fill in the blank. Once the Catfish and Hopeful meet in real life (and on camera), there is a *feeling* (but not the reality) of mastering the ineffability of the internet. And while Nev and Max invariably discover the Catfish behind the fabricated online identity—Bow Wow is really Dee, Caroline is really Heather—they never truly find out who the Catfish *really* is, since trying to pin down an individual's "true" identity has never been possible, whether online or in real life.

M TV did not start these conversations about youth identity, and it is not solely responsible for their continuation and dispersal. When *The Real World* premiered in 1992, it featured white, cisgendered, heterosexual cast members like season 3's Cory Murphy, who, when faced with a diverse (by Jonathan Murray's definition) group of roommates, found herself feeling, for the first time, like a white person.[7] Having been raised by popular culture's colorblind approach to the representation of youth, in which race was never discussed but was always present nevertheless, Cory finds her whiteness an unwelcome surprise. It is unwelcome because, as she explained in 1993, "I have no major cause, no really close connection to my culture and my history and my race." Cory's lack of racial awareness is possible only *because* she is white, and her confrontation with her own racial status is possible only because she was cast on *The Real World*. This was the main goal, the main driver of narrative in *The Real World*, in a landmark TV show about youth identity.

As Jonathan Murray told me when I asked him to explain how the series was, at least in its initial incarnations, capable of producing dialogue about identity, "We're gonna be surprised, we're gonna find out new things about them, we're going to discover new aspects of their personality as they are challenged by the situation of living with people different from themselves." The assumption here is that the only way to force young people to think critically about identity is to place them into a diverse environment. However, this assumption is premised on whiteness and white identities, which are the only identities with the privilege to ignore these issues. Youth of color do not need to be cast on a reality series to be reminded of their identity status, and the conflicts it generates; this happens when they walk to school, go to the mall, or watch television. Thus, the legacy of *The Real World* has less to do with helping American youth, to use Jonathan Murray's terms, learn and grow from exposure to one another's differences, than it has with helping *white* American youth to learn these important life lessons. This racial myopia makes financial sense, given that MTV's target audience both then and now has always been white middle-class youth. With the exception of a few key programs, like *Yo! MTV Raps*, MTV has generally been concerned only with capturing the hearts and minds of white youth.[8]

Likewise, when MTV shifted its programming from primarily music videos to primarily reality television in the early 2000s, the reality series chronicling the life of American youth stuck close to MTV's overall project of catering to and shoring up whiteness. Early examples of MTV's reality identity series, like *Laguna Beach: The Real Orange County* and *The Hills*, escape the constraints of casting for diversity by instead casting by region. Set in the wealthy, primarily white neighborhoods of Southern California, those shows depicted a world filled with wealthy white people. The casts' perfectly lit complexions and expensive outfits were aspirational for the primarily white, middle-class viewers MTV was courting. At the same time as these viewers were provided with aspirational models of consumption in the form of the Can-Do Girl, the channel released *16 and Pregnant* and *Teen Mom*, which also served as warning to would-be Can-Do Girls. The At-Risk Girls featured on these series were cautionary tales about what happens when an individual fails in the care of the self. Mirroring the neoliberal discourse of so much reality TV of the era, like *Extreme Home Makeover* and *The Biggest Loser*, *Teen Mom* promised to help its viewers be the best version of themselves they could be and still be entertained in the process. As with MTV's California-based series, MTV's teen pregnancy series focused almost entirely on white people, with this racial category effaced by the presence of another identity: motherhood.

Unlike Cory's experience on season 3 of *The Real World*, the white youth cast on MTV's reality identity cycle of the 2000s were not confounded by their own whiteness. Instead, the channel offered a way for its primary audience, white suburban youth, to feel as if they, too, had a culture, a history, and an identity, something Cory longed for but never got (at least while she was on TV). As I discussed in chapter 4, series like *Jersey Shore* and *Buckwild* offered a different approach to whiteness. *Jersey Shore* offered MTV's audiences the opportunity to openly ridicule working-class, Italian American identities. Rather than inspire or instruct, these series serve to lampoon certain white identities, namely the Guido and the Redneck, precisely because they fail to live up to the aspirational depictions of whiteness in shows like *The Hills*. Italian Americans are now considered "white," but the Guidos of *Jersey Shore*, by lampooning their ethnic identities, allow a space to laugh at whiteness and also depict whiteness as multifaceted. Similarly, *Buckwild* celebrates a certain kind of whiteness, one that is rural and working class, at the same time that it mocks this identity. While neither series is responsible for the surge of emboldened white nationalism in America in recent years, both series are part of the larger public discourse about identity and a perceived loss in white, cisgendered, heterosexual male hegemony as people of color, women, and gender nonconforming Americans have become more visible.

As I discussed in chapter 5, there were outliers to MTV's reality TV formula, like *Virgin Territory* and *Washington Heights*, both of which made a pass at inclusivity by focusing on Dominican youth and a handful of nonwhite Virgins. But both series failed to generate ratings because these nonwhite identities were distilled to the point that they became generic and useless as markers of difference. *Catfish* might offer the most authentic portrait of youth identities, namely their ability to be manipulated. Though it is too soon to speculate on how more recent programming like *Floribama Shore*, *Siesta Key*, *Young + Pregnant*, and recent reboots of *Jersey Shore* and *The Hills* will function in the lives of youth audiences, they demonstrate that MTV is still incapable of addressing issues of race and ethnicity, even as it at-

C.3 *Young + Pregnant* is one of several recent reboots of previously successful MTV reality series.

tempts to diversify its casting strategies in *Young + Pregnant* (which features interracial couples as well as a transgender cast member).

Throughout this book I have shown that MTV's reality identity cycle is a crucial part of the dominant discourse on the subject of identity and youth in the twenty-first century, and that this programming has contributed to the contemporary, sometimes liberating, sometimes contentious conversations that Americans, and American youth in particular, are having about identity. Misha Kavka argues that contemporary reality television "intervenes in a range of social discourses about the self, the family and the community" by "making manifest the tender spots on the American body politic" (2012, ch. 4). The most recent examples of MTV's reality identity programming seem to signal a new tender spot—a nostalgia to return to a more recent past—the early 2000s, before the Great Recession, before an increasing wave of school shootings, before the rise of the alt-right movement, before the election of Donald J. Trump to the office of president, and before brigades of Russian bots turned us all into victims of political Catfishing.[9] As Henry Jenkins puts it, "Reality television does not do things to us, but it can represent to us some of the things we are doing to ourselves" (2006, 41). I believe that the trajectory of MTV's programming since 1981 is revealing of what American youth have been "doing to themselves." Whether they are chasing the radio star, the video star, or the reality TV star, MTV's shifting youth audiences are forever struggling to articulate the ongoing divides over issues of race, gender, sexual orientation, and difference in American culture. MTV's shift in programming does not highlight how different the MTV of 2019 is from the MTV of 1981. Rather I have demonstrated that the channel has never really changed; it will always be courting whoever is young.

MTV Reality Series since 1981

Precursors to MTV's Reality Identity Cycle

The Real World (1992–) (this series both predates and, eventually, makes up part of MTV's reality identity cycle)
Road Rules (1995–2007)
True Life (1998–)
Made (2002–2014)
Sorority Life (2002–2004)
Fraternity Life (2003–2005)
Rich Girls (2003)
I Want a Famous Face (2004)
Pimp My Ride (2004–2007)
Room Raiders (2004–)
MTV's The 70s House (2005)
My Super Sweet Sixteen (2005–)
PoweR Girls (2005)

All Seasons of *The Real World*

Season 1: *The Real World: New York* (1992)
Season 2: *The Real World: Los Angeles* (1993)
Season 3: *The Real World: San Francisco* (1994)
Season 4: *The Real World: London* (1995)
Season 5: *The Real World: Miami* (1996)

Season 6: *The Real World: Boston* (1997)
Season 7: *The Real World: Seattle* (1998)
Season 8: *The Real World: Honolulu* (1999)
Season 9: *The Real World: New Orleans* (2000)
Season 10: *The Real World: New York* (2001)
Season 11: *The Real World: Chicago* (2002)
Season 12: *The Real World: Las Vegas* (2002–2003)
Season 13: *The Real World: Paris* (2003)
Season 14: *The Real World: San Diego* (2004)
Season 15: *The Real World: Philadelphia* (2004–2005)
Season 16: *The Real World: Austin* (2005)
Season 17: *The Real World: Key West* (2006)
Season 18: *The Real World: Denver* (2006–2007)
Season 19: *The Real World: Sydney* (2007–2008)
Season 20: *The Real World: Hollywood* (2008)
Season 21: *The Real World: Brooklyn* (2009)
Season 22: *The Real World: Cancun* (2009)
Season 23: *The Real World: Washington, D.C.* (2009–2010)
Season 24: *The Real World: New Orleans* (2010)
Season 25: *The Real World: Las Vegas* (2011)
Season 26: *The Real World: San Diego* (2011)
Season 27: *The Real World: Charlotte Amalie* (2012)
Season 28: *The Real World: Portland* (2013)
Season 29: *The Real World: Ex-plosion* (2014)
Season 30: *The Real World: Skeletons* (2014–2015)
Season 31: *The Real World: Go Big or Go Home* (2016)
Season 32: *The Real World: Seattle* (2016–1017)
Season 33: *The Real World: Atlanta* (2019)

MTV's Reality Identity Cycle (U.S.)

The Real World (1992–)
Laguna Beach: The Real Orange County (2004–2006)
8th & Ocean (2006)
The Hills (2006–2010)
Engaged & Underaged (2007–2008)
The City (2008–2010)
From Gs to Gents (2008–2009)
The Girls of Hedsor Hall (2009)
Jersey Shore (2009–2012)
16 & Pregnant (2009–2014)
Teen Mom (2009–)
Teen Mom 2 (2011–)
Catfish (2012–)

The Pauly D Project (2012)
Snooki & JWoww (2012–2015)
Buckwild (2013)
Generation Cryo (2013)
The Show with Vinny (2013)
Teen Mom 3 (2013)
Washington Heights (2013)
Slednecks (2014)
Virgin Territory (2014)
Floribama Shore (2017–)
MTV's The 90s House (2017)
Siesta Key (2017–)
Teen Mom: Young + Pregnant (2017–)
Jersey Shore: Family Vacation (2018–)
How Far Is Tattoo Far? (2018)
Pretty Little Mamas (2018)
Winter Break: Hunter Mountain (2018)
The Hills: New Beginnings (2019)

EXCLUDED NEWS/AWARDS SHOWS

This Week in Rock (1987–1997)
House of Style (1989–2012)
Like We Care (1992)
MTV Sports (1992–1997)
MTV News (1998–2004)
How's Your News (2009)

EXCLUDED: STUNT/PRANK SHOWS

Kevin Seal: Sporting Fool (1990–1991)
The Tom Green Show (1999–2000)
Jackass (2000–2002)
Punk'd (2003–2011)
Viva la Bam (2003–2005)
Ridiculousnsess (2011–)

EXCLUDED: GAME SHOWS/DATING SHOWS

Remote Control (1987–1990)
Singled Out (1995–1997)
The Challenge (1998–)
Making the Band (2000–)
MTV Cribs (2000–)

Date My Mom (2004–2006)
Parental Control (2006–2010)
A Shot at Love with Tila Tequila (2007–2008)
America's Best Dance Crew (2008–2015)
Disaster Date (2009–2011)
Friendzone (2011–2014)
Nick Cannon Presents: Wild 'n Out (2013–2016)
Are You the One? (2014)
Ex on the Beach (2018)

EXCLUDED: CELEBREALITY

MTV Cribs (2000–)
The Osbournes (2002–2005)
Newlyweds: Nick and Jessica (2003–2005)
The Ashlee Simpson Show (2004–2005)
Run's House (2005–2009)
Rob & Big (2006–2008)
There & Back (2006)
Paris Hilton's My New BFF (2008–2009)
Follow the Rules (2015)
The Life of Ryan (2017)

Other Television Series Discussed in This Book

The Adventures of Ozzie & Harriet (ABC, 1952–1966)
Ally McBeal (Fox, 1997–2002)
American Bandstand (WFIL-TV, 1952–1957; ABC, 1957–1987; syndicated, 1987–1988; USA Network, 1989)
An American Family (PBS, 1971)
American Idol (Fox, 2002–2016; ABC, 2018–)
America's Most Wanted (Fox, 1988–2012)
America's Next Top Model (UPN, 2003–2006; CW, 2006–2015; VH1, 2016–)
The Apprentice (NBC, 2004–2018)
Arrested Development (Fox, 2003–2006)
As the World Turns (CBS, 1956–2010)
Backyard Oil (Discovery Channel, 2013)
Baldwin Hills (BET, 2007–2009)
The Ben Stiller Show (MTV, 1992–1993)
Beverly Hills 90210 (Fox, 1990–2000)
Big Brother (CBS, 2000–)
The Biggest Loser (NBC, 2004–2016)
The Big Record (ABC, 1957–1958)
Cajun Pawn Stars (History Channel, 2012–)
Candid Camera (ABC, 1948–1949, 1974; NBC, 1954–1959, 1959–1967)
Club MTV (MTV, 1987–1992)
The Contender (NBC, 2005; ESPN, 2006–2007; Versus, 2008–2009; Epix, 2018)
Cops (Fox, 1989–2013; Spike, 2013–2017; Paramount, 2018–2020)
A Current Affair (syndicated, 1986–1996)

The Cut (CBS, 2005)

Dancing with the Stars (ABC, 2005–)

Dark Shadows (ABC, 1966–1971)

The Ed Sullivan Show (ABC, 1948–1971)

Extreme Makeover (ABC, 2003–2012)

Fight for Fame (E!, 2005)

Gidget (ABC, 1965–1966)

Happy Days (ABC, 1974–1984)

Hard Copy (syndicated, 1989–1999)

Headbanger's Ball (MTV, 1987–2007)

Hear It Now (CBS, 1950–1951)

Hell's Kitchen (Fox, 2005–)

Here Comes Honey Boo Boo (TLC, 2012–2017)

Hillbilly Handfishing (Animal Planet, 2011–2012)

Honey We're Killing the Kids (TLC, 2006–)

Hullabaloo (NBC, 1965–1966)

I've Got a Secret (CBS, 1952–1964)

Just Say Julie (MTV, 1989–1992)

Keeping Up with the Kardashians (E!, 2007–)

Kell on Earth (Bravo, 2010)

The Legend of Shelby the Swamp Man (History Channel, 2013–2015)

Liquid Television (MTV, 1991–1994)

Lizard Lick Towing (truTV, 2011–2014)

The Many Loves of Dobie Gillis (CBS, 1959–1963)

The Mary Tyler Moore Show (CBS, 1970–1977)

Moonshiners (Discovery Channel, 2011–)

My Big Redneck Wedding (CMT, 2008–2011)

Nashville Star (USA Network, 2003–2007; NBC, 2008)

The O.C. (Fox, 2003–2007)

The Office (NBC, 2005–2013)

Oprah (syndicated, 1986–2011)

The Perry Como Show (NBC, 1955–1959)

Phil Donahue (syndicated, 1967–1996)

Pit Bulls and Parolees (Animal Planet, 2009–)

Princes of Malibu (Fox, 2005)

Project Greenlight (HBO, 2001–2003; Bravo, 2005)

Project Runway (Bravo, 2004–2008; Lifetime, 2009–2017; Bravo, 2019–)

Redneck Intervention (CMT, 2012–)

Redneck Island (CMT, 2012–)

River Monsters (Animal Planet, 2009–2017)

Rocket City Rednecks (National Geographic, 2011–2013)

Rock Star: INXS (CBS, 2005)

Santa Barbara (NBC, 1984–1993)

The Secret Life of the American Teenager (ABC Family, 2008–2013)

See It Now (CBS, 1951–1958)
Sesame Street (NET, 1969–1970; PBS, 1970–2016; HBO, 2016–2020;
　　HBO Max, 2020–)
Sex and the City (HBO, 1998–2004)
Shindig! (CBS, 1964–1966)
The Simple Life (Fox, 2003–2007)
Soul Train (syndicated, 1971–2006)
So You Think You Can Dance (Fox, 2005–)
The Starlet (WB, 2005)
Surf Girls (MTV, 2003)
The Surreal Life (VH1, 2003–2006)
Survivor (CBS, 2000–)
Swamp People (History Channel, 2010–)
The Swan (Fox, 2004–2005)
To Catch a Predator (MSNBC, 2004–2007)
Top Chef (Bravo, 2006–)
Total Request Live (MTV, 1998–2008, 2017–)
To Tell the Truth (CBS, 1956–1958)
Truth or Consequences (CBS, 1950–1954; NBC, 1954–1965)
Vanderpump Rules (Bravo, 2013–)
What's My Line (CBS, 1950–1957)
Yo! MTV Raps (MTV, 1988–1995)

NOTES

Introduction

1 Trevor Horn, lead singer of the Buggles, explains the lyrics this way: "It came from this idea that technology was on the verge of changing everything. Video recorders had just come along, which changed people's lives. We'd seen people starting to make videos as well, and we were excited by that. It felt like radio was the past and video was the future. There was a shift coming" (qtd. in Tannenbaum and Marks 2011, 41).

2 The term "Generation X" did not gain widespread use until Douglas Coupland published *Generation X: Tales for an Accelerated Culture* (1991). His novel helped to define the ethos of the generation as explicitly cynical, disillusioned, deeply invested in popular culture, and implicitly white and middle class. For more on the depiction of Generation X in popular culture, see Oake 2004.

3 The term "Millennials" was first used by William Strauss and Neil Howe in 1987 (Schonfeld 2018).

4 See, for example, the discourses surrounding the gun-control activists from Stoneman Douglas High School (Miller 2018), the climate activist Greta Thunberg (Gessen 2018), and the water-safety activist Mari Copeny, aka "Little Miss Flint" (Burton 2019), all of whom belong to Generation Z.

5 See Jones 2005 on the importance of MTV as an object of study.

6 To name just a few prominent examples of works that have focused on specific series, see Grindstaff 2011a; Hargraves 2014; Hearn 2010; and Ouellette 2014b.

7 For more on the neoliberal utility of reality TV, see Kraidy and Sender 2011; Kraszewski 2010; Ouellette 2018; Ouellette and Hay 2008; and Weber 2009.

8 As Annette Hill's (2005) research has demonstrated, one of the main draws of reality television is the ability to "learn" from the practice of people watching.

9 Both of these terms originated as slurs. "Guido" is an epithet used in turn-of-the-century America by established Italian Americans to insult newly arrived Italian immigrants (Brooks 2009). "Redneck" is a derogatory term for economically disadvantaged white Americans (Huber 1995). Despite their origins as insults, both identities—Guido and Redneck—are embraced and used by the cast members on *Jersey Shore* and *Buckwild*, respectively. I deploy both terms as a way to reference the identities that are showcased and celebrated but also derided on each series.

10 Sokol Savage explained that "TV friendly" is a "network way of saying 'attractive enough to be on TV.'"

11 Misha Kavka introduced the term "flaunting" as a way to discuss the specifically gendered performances that occur on reality television and to highlight the ways in which these gendered performances are like showing off and "displaying something that one expects to be desired by the audience" (2014, 57–58). Therí A. Pickens offers the term "ratchet imaginary" as a way to talk specifically about how Black women's performance of race in reality TV is not engaged "in narratives of racial progression or social uplift" because it pits the individual against the needs of the collective (2015, 44). Kristen Warner (2013) has also discussed the concept of "ratchet" in relation to reality TV performances as excessive, hypervisible, and reflexive, and as a component of Black identity politics. Adding to the above gendered and raced concepts for the ways in which performance is linked to identity within the space of reality television, Jon Kraszewski contributes the term "amplifying." Amplifying is a useful delimitator in this context because "like flaunting and ratcheting, amplifying exaggerates a few identity traits," but it is not limited to describing just raced or gendered performance (2017, 111). This book's concept of reality TV identities is shaped by these scholars' conceptualization of how reality TV makes the constructed nature of identity plain.

12 For an example of critique of "generational thinking," see Onion 2015.

13 A few writers of the time did acknowledge that Millennials struggled (and continue to struggle) more than their parents did to pay for college tuition, housing, and health insurance (see, e.g., Erickson 2008).

14 Allison Hearn notes that the labor exploitation inherent to reality TV productions impacts bodies differentially: "The twinned processes of labour insecurity and ontological insecurity enacted at the level of politics and in media representations play out most aggressively in the lives and on the bodies of women, the poor, immigrants, migrant workers, the disabled, and gay, lesbian, and transgendered people" (2008, 496–497).

15 Of course, not all Millennials are or were technologically savvy; levels of expertise vary. See Hargittai 2010 for a discussion of this variation.

16 Detailed histories include Banks 1996; Gilbert 2015; Tannenbaum and Marks 2011; various magazine interviews and profiles like Anson's 2000 *Vanity Fair* oral history; and Kaplan 1987, as well as portions of Goodwin 1992 and Schultze et al. 1991.

Chapter 1. "It's Videos, Fool"

1 For more on the transition from network to postnetwork television, see Lotz 2007.

2 As Michael Newman (2010) points out, as early as the 1950s, American newspapers and trade publications began to link up the concepts of youth audiences, television viewing, and attention spans, specifically what kinds of attention spans children had for watching and absorbing TV content.

3 Jackson points out that *American Bandstand* had a lesser-known predecessor, Paul Whiteman's 1949 *TV-Teen Club*, broadcast on WGIL-TV and the new ABC-TV network (1997, ch. 1).

4 In his history of *American Bandstand* in *Rolling Stone* in 2000, Gavin Edwards explains that the show kickstarted the careers of teen idols like Fabian and Frankie Avalon: "Its commercial power was so great rock artists as big as Chuck Berry would stop by to lip-sync their latest singles." A decade later, MTV's *Total Request Live* would premiere, the only other television program to have this much impact on the pop charts.

5 See, for example, Benshoff 2011, Davis and Dickinson 2004, and Ross and Stein 2008 for studies on American teen TV viewership before the 1980s.

6 The writer's guidelines drafted for the *Afterschool Specials* stated that the "prime target audience" for the programming was "the oft-neglected, usually fickle, but extremely important kids eight to fourteen years old" (qtd. in Pike 2011, 136).

7 According to Eric Schaefer (1999), beginning in 1919 and continuing on through the late 1950s, sexual hygiene films were a subset of the exploitation film and the primary visual medium for telling stories about sexual promiscuity and disease carriers. These films made "unacceptable topics" and images, which were normally invisible or covered over within mainstream culture (such as the creation of leper colonies or the banishment of unwed mothers to convents), both visible and central. Audiences went to see these films because they showcased a spectacle of the unknown and the forbidden (1999, 34).

8 Remote controls were just gaining a foothold in the American home in the early 1980s, with the rise of cable programming (Engber 2012).

9 MTV was not the only cable channel airing music videos in the 1980s; it was simply the only channel that aired music videos twenty-four hours per day. Inspired by MTV, NBC launched the long-running *Friday Night Videos* (1983–2002), which allowed viewers to call a 1-900 number and vote for their favorite videos. The Box (originally the Video Jukebox Network) was a music television service launched in 1985 and distributed by satellite and cable providers. As with *Friday Night Videos*, viewers of the Box channel could make requests (Goodwin 1992, 141–142). WTBS, a relatively new superstation, had a music video show called *Night Tracks* (141–142). Both the cable network USA (*Night Flight*) and the subscription channel HBO (*Video Jukebox*) had their

own music-video programming in order to compete with MTV (see Kaplan 1987, 2). Soon after the appearance of these video-based countdown shows, MTV developed its own countdown show, *Dial MTV* (1986–2001) which was ultimately replaced with the iconic *Total Request Live* (TRL), discussed later in this chapter.

10 In September 1981, Bob Pittman, one of MTV's cofounders, told the industry journal *Videography*, "It's ridiculous to think that you have two forms of entertainment—your stereo and your TV—which have nothing to with one another. What we're doing is marrying those two forms so that they work together in unison. . . . MTV is the first attempt to make TV a new form, other than video games and data channels. We're talking about creating a new form using existing technologies" (qtd. in Wicke 1987, 162).

11 Pittman was eventually made CEO of MTV in 1985 and left the channel for other ventures in 1987. Tom Freston took over for Pittman, until he left the channel in 2004 for the media conglomerate Viacom (Anson 2000). Robert M. Bakish has been the CEO of MTV since 2016.

12 As Andrew Goodwin notes, "MTV followed the music industry in defining 'rock' in essentially racist terms, as a form of music that excluded blacks" (1992, 133). Rock music's erasure and whitewashing of the foundational contributions of Black musicians date back to the very beginnings of rock 'n' roll. E. Ann Kaplan argues, in her history of MTV's early years, that "MTV essentially duplicates FM Radio's white rock focus, although FM has perhaps more variety than the cable channel" (1987, 3). For in-depth discussions of the history of rock 'n' roll's exclusion of Black musicians, see DeCurtis 1992, Friedlander 1996, and Szatmary 1987.

13 Pet Benatar recalls, "I got really angry when we shot 'You Better Run.' I kept thinking, *What do they think I am, a runway model? Fuck you!*" (qtd. in Tannenbaum and Marks 2011, 42).

14 Andrew Goodwin adds that the VJs "*anchor* the MTV text, using familiar conventions of the radio DJ and the news presenter" to guide the viewer through the chaotic flow of striking imagery that constituted MTV's first seventeen months on the air (1992, 139).

15 Here I am describing how MTV's first hour was *supposed* to have gone, in terms of segment order, and this is the only version that is currently available online as well as on DVD. However, this debut was reportedly beset with problems. Clips were improperly sequenced, so that Goodman's statement "This is it. Welcome to MTV. Music Television . . ." was aired *last* in the sequence, after all the other VJs introduced themselves. There were also sound problems and brief moments of black screens, when the VJs switched VHS tapes of videos, an inauspicious start. Bob Pittman recalls it this way: "The first hour of MTV was a total, unmitigated disaster. The VJs would announce, 'That was Styx,' right after we'd played REO Speedwagon. . . . Everything that could have gone wrong did go wrong" (qtd. in Tannenbaum and Marks 2011, 43).

16 John Sykes, who produced the first VMAs, remembers, "I really think that award show, along with Michael Jackson's 'Thriller,' were the two events that put MTV on the map" (qtd. in Sanchez 2018).

17 In another interview, Sykes claims, "We saw an opening for a counterculture awards show that would not follow the rules of the traditional ceremonies people were used to seeing. . . . We tried to be the counterculture show because that's what the network was, that's what we were trying to be" (qtd. in Mantzouranis 2020).

18 Jane Hall (1992) writes, "At a time when the broadcast TV networks are battling to hold on to the 40-plus crowd that is the mainstay for their nightly newscasts, MTV is reaching young viewers in 54.5 million U.S. homes with programming that, in its own distinct way, ranges well beyond rock news to cover issues ranging from the environment to warfare, from AIDS to presidential politics."

19 Pittman remembers this period in MTV's history differently: "If anybody at CBS thought that we weren't going to play Michael Jackson, they were out of their minds. Walter claims that he made us play the video. That's such a typical Walter trick, to make himself seem important to his artists" (qtd. in Tannenbaum and Marks 2011, 148–149).

20 Kaplan writes that the success of "Thriller" "convinced record companies of what videos could do and interested several of them in the longer format" (1987, 13).

21 The 1980s films in this cycle include *Wild Style, Breakin', Breakin' 2: Electric Boogaloo, Beat Street, Body Rock, Rappin', Turk 182!, Fast Forward*, and *Krush Groove*.

22 Goodwin argues that MTV's transition to playing more musicians of color was partially facilitated by the success of crossover singles, like Run-DMC's collaboration with Aerosmith on "Walk This Way" and the Fat Boys/Beach Boys cover of "Wipe Out" (1992, 137).

23 Significantly, when MTV shifted from primarily music videos, it lost one of its main venues for Black music and content: *Yo! MTV Raps*.

24 The review-tracking website *Metacritic* rates the first season of *The Real World* as 64/100, based on sixteen critic reviews.

25 Henry Jenkins first deployed the term "participatory culture" to describe this programming, and as a contrast with older notions of media spectatorship: consumers of media content are also producers of media content (2006, 3).

26 See Reuters 2019, Tyko 2019, Whittaker 2019, and Zaveri 2019.

27 This interlinked relationship between celebrity and public discourse precedes reality TV's 2000s-era dominance for several hundred years (see Gamson 1994, 16).

28 For more on the passage from ordinary to celebrity under the frame of reality TV, see Couldry 2008.

29 Nicole Richie is of mixed racial heritage. She was adopted and raised by Lionel Richie and Brenda Harvey-Richie, who are both African American. With

her light skin and straightened blonde hair, Richie's racial identity was purposely ambiguous, unless one was familiar with her backstory.

30 For a detailed analysis of the relationship between MTV reality stars and tabloids in the 2000s, see Meyers 2020.

31 For a useful analysis of the "voice" deployed on MTV's *True Life*, see Ouellette 2015.

32 This subgenre of reality television began with the success of VH1's *The Surreal Life*, which featured numerous B-, C-, and D-list celebrities living in a house together, *Real World*–style. This led to the creation of many other unscripted reality programs starring people who were already famous for something other than starring in a reality TV show.

33 For a detailed history of BET, see Smith-Shomade 2007.

34 These include singing and performing in *American Idol, Rock Star: INXS*, and *Nashville Star*; modeling and acting in *America's Next Top Model, The Starlet*, and *Fight for Fame*; cooking and meal preparation in *Hell's Kitchen* and *Top Chef*; business savvy in *The Apprentice*; clothing design in *Project Runway* and *The Cut*; boxing in *The Contender*; dancing in *Dancing with the Stars* and *So You Think You Can Dance*; and filmmaking in *Project Greenlight*.

35 For example, in April 2020, Tommy Hilfiger's net worth was estimated at $400 million (Celebrity Net Worth 2020).

36 These headlines appeared in, respectively, the *Chicago Sun-Times* (Gilbert 2003), the *New York Times* (Stanley 2003), the *Dallas Morning News* (Mendoza 2003), the *Houston Chronicle* (McFarland 2003), *Newsweek* (Sigesmund and Peyser 2003), and the *Tampa Tribune* (Belcher 2003).

37 A *Daily News of Los Angeles* story profiled the series this way: "another in MTV's fearless sociological studies of the idiotically privileged, following 'The Osbournes' and 'Newlyweds'" (Kronke 2003).

38 In 1996, MTV began to "outsource" its music-video content to other satellite channels like MTV2.

39 The drive toward Instagram-able experiences has even reached the art world, as evidenced by a trend in "made-for-Instagram" exhibits in recent years: the "Rain Room" in London's Barbican Center (2012), "Wonder" at the Smithsonian (2015), and the Museum of Ice Cream in New York City (2017). In "made-for-Instagram" exhibits, patrons can photograph themselves within the installation itself, becoming, momentarily, the "star of the space" (qtd. in Pardes 2017).

40 During our interview, Paula told me, "Even the place where I'm working now, the HR department [will ask], 'Uh, I don't know, weren't you on *The Real World*?' I was just, like, 'Fuck, that was forever ago.'" Beckert interview, June 8, 2018.

Chapter 2. "This Is the True Story . . ."

1 For more on this historic shift, see Holt 2011.

2 The same rationale will be applied to PBS's *An American Family*, discussed later in this chapter, one of the first serialized American reality TV series.

3 When asked if *Candid Camera* was an influence on *The Real World*, Jonathan Murray told me it was not (interview, August 4, 2016). Other quotes from Jonathan Murray in this chapter are from this interview, unless noted otherwise.

4 Allen Funt had the opportunity to use portable audio equipment when serving in World War II, a technology he then brought to *Candid Microphone*, the radio version of the show that would become *Candid Camera* (Kavka 2012, ch. 1).

5 Contemporary practitioners believed TV served to combine "the immediacy of live theatre performance, the space conquering powers of radio, and the visual strategies of the motion picture" (Boddy 1993, 80).

6 The Direct Cinema movement developed in the United States by documentary filmmakers like Richard Leacock and D. A. Pennebaker. This film movement aimed to observe and record an uncontrolled situation by adhering to what these filmmakers called the "philosophy of noninterference" (Sobchack and Sobchack, 1987, 349–353).

7 In an interview with *Cracked* magazine, an anonymous former *Real World* cast member described the "Batphone" that was kept on set: "If you wanted to leave, you had to pick up the Batphone and say 'Hey guys, I wanna go for a run or go downtown and buy some things'" (qtd. in Mannen 2016).

8 Unlike the initial marks profiled in Funt's *Candid Camera* or Milgram's obedience experiments, Bunim-Murray's marks are wholly aware of the experiment in which they are engaging. Kraszewski adds, "Funt's average man in a small crisis did not change the awareness of the unsuspecting person in the skit; it enlightened the audience about an oppressive social structure that permeated spaces of economic equality in the postwar era" (2017, 33).

    The Real World was preceded, one year earlier, by the debut of a Dutch reality series titled *Nummer 28*, which referred to the address of the house where seven strangers lived together for several months. Despite these similarities, Jonathan Murray tells me he had never heard of the series until he read about it in a draft of this chapter. I offer his typed correction here in full:

    > Your footnote is the first time I have heard mention of this series. My belief is that *The Real World* came out of MTV wanting a scripted series about young people starting out their lives in NYC, the inability for us to do a scripted series at a low enough price point, and the work we had already done with the Fox docu-series we developed and shot, "American Families," that was loosely inspired by the PBS series. When we pitched the unscripted *Real World* to MTV, we showed the MTV executive, Lauren Carrao, the pilot for

"American Families," to prove that unscripted television could be as dramatic as scripted television. So, to be clear, I was not aware of "Number 28," when we pitched *The Real World* to MTV. (Murray, personal communication, April 9, 2018)

9   Murray contends that disability is represented by the casting of Jordan Wiseley and Frankie Abernathy. "Jordan, in the Portland season[,] was born with most of his fingers missing on one hand. This disability is discussed by him in the series. Also, Frankie's [San Diego] chronic illness is considered a disability by most people" (Murray, personal communication, April 9, 2018).

10 Beckert interview, June 8, 2018. Other quotes from Paula Beckert in this chapter are from this interview, unless noted otherwise.

11 McGee wrote about her experiences being on *The Real World*, as well as her place in one of the most infamous moments in the franchise's history, in "Slaps, Lies, and Videotape: Irene's True Story of 1998's *The Real World: Seattle*" (2013).

12 When pressed for examples, McGee offered these two hypothetical scenarios: "So, like, if you and I hung up after this interview, and there was somebody eavesdropping on our interview. Then they ask you about the interview and then they say, 'Oh, Irene has different thoughts . . .' and you're, like, 'What thoughts did she have?' and then it gets you paranoid and then we have to live together. Or you and I go out together and pretend everyone wants to be famous, right? So the two of us go to the drugstore together and the cameras follow me around, but not you. Well, what happens to you then? How do *you* feel?" (interview, September 4, 2017). Other quotes from Irene McGee in this chapter are from this interview, unless noted otherwise.

13 Murray, personal communication, April 9, 2018. Murray also told me, "MTV asked that we tell them this before they flew to San Francisco. If they had any concerns, they were advised to speak to their own medical professional before signing on to the series" (personal communication, April 9, 2018).

14 As discussed in the introduction, colorblindness is "a utopian social construct" that "aims to create a model of fairness by which all individuals can be judged fairly and without bias or regard to skin color" (Warner 2015, 8).

15 As of 2020, the preferred term for denoting this identity is "Latinx," which is gender neutral.

16 Thank you to fellow media scholars and *Real World* fans Kristen Warner and Alice Leppert, who helped me think through the moment when this formula shifted.

17 Murray explained, "We discovered that [Ruthie] had a major issue with alcohol. I went back and looked at her application and asked myself, 'How did we miss this?' It said, 'We drink for fun.' But it was my first awareness of binge drinking and how drinking was different on campus in the late '90s than it was when I was in school in the late '70s."

18 The invisible barrier between cast and crew was penetrated immediately, in season 1 of *The Real World*, when Becky Blasband, one of the cast mem-

bers, began to secretly date one of the show's offscreen producers. In season 2, *The Real World: Los Angeles*, the cast members were engaging in some innocent horseplay when things went from "fun" to threatening between David Edwards, an African American comedian, and Tami Akbar, an African American aspiring singer. The scene was intercut with reflective first-person confessionals from Jon Brennan and Beth Stolarczyk, a white production assistant. Both Jon and Beth noted that Tami was displeased with the unveiling of her seminude body on camera. The argument culminated with a house meeting (minus David) wherein the three women, Beth, Tami, and Irene Berrera (a Latinx deputy sheriff), told the other men in the house, Aaron Behle, Dominik Griffin, and Jon (all white men), "We don't feel safe with [David] here. Who knows what he'll do next?" David was asked to leave the series and was then replaced with Glen Naessens, a white musician and devout Christian. This incident, happening early in the series' run, established that some transgressions could lead to expulsion from *The Real World*.

19 Jon Kraszewski notes that *The Real World*'s representations of space also underwent a drastic shift in this season because "the season became a giant ad for [the Palms casino]" (2017, 53).

20 Another change to this series was to include the title and artist of the song playing in the bottom corner of the screen. Kraszewski notes, "With the arrival of YouTube . . . and the normalization of a la carte digital technologies for listening to music," MTV needed a way to sell music to an audience that was no longer watching music videos (2017, 53). In many ways, this shift also prefigures MTV series like *Laguna Beach* and *The Hills*, which sell aspirational lifestyles to youth audiences.

21 See chapter 1 for a discussion of the obsession in the early 2000s with celebrity culture and exhibitionist behavior.

22 *Jersey Shore* also flirted with the possibility of exposing the apparatus in 2012, during season 5. Glimmers of the casts' real-world celebrity, which had previously been quarantined to offscreen space, became visible from time to time. After returning to Seaside Heights, the season 5 cast members returned to their jobs at the Shore Store. Danny, the store manager, displayed underpants for sale emblazoned with *Jersey Shore* catchphrases like "DTF," "Cabs are Here," and "GTL." When the series began back in 2009, the cast were not yet celebrities so their labor at the Shore Store was defined by the usual retail tasks of ringing up customers, stocking shelves, and shirking responsibility. However, by 2012, with their fame solidified, the presence of the *Jersey Shore* cast at the Shore Store *is* their work. While in previous seasons, MTV took great pains to cover up the casts' burgeoning celebrity—keeping paparazzi and fans offscreen—season 5 allowed a few moments of offscreen life to slip onscreen.

Chapter 3. "She's Gonna Always Be Known as . . ."

1 This concept of the girl as ideal consumer is also discussed in Aapola, Gonick, and Harris 2005.

2 Anita Harris's book (2004a) is not specifically about American girlhood, but the conclusions she draws about the relationship between girls, capitalism, consumption, and neoliberalism are a useful frame for reading the way the reality identity cycle represents white girlhood in the 2000s.

3 See Butler and Izadi 2018 or Cogan 2014 for a recap of the full controversy.

4 Jesse Schlotterbeck (2008) usefully summarizes this aesthetic here: "With one camera following the action, reframing must stand in for continuity cuts. Often the trouble of zooming and moving in for close-ups is forgone in favor of humdrum medium or medium-close two-shots. . . . The mobility necessary to capture character interactions belies the presence of a filmmaker in the subjects' midst, moving about to track their actions. . . . [T]hese techniques result in clumsy, imperfectly framed shots, with characters captured from less than ideal angles or distances in terms of narrative purposes and visual appeal."

5 See the introduction to this book for a discussion of the colorblind ideologies at work in MTV texts.

6 See appendix A for a full listing of MTV's identity series and their various spin-offs.

7 Harris notes: "Logically, advertisers can benefit considerably from this new glamour-worker mode of feminine subjectivity, bound up as it is with products, accessories, self-presentation, and lifestyle, all now available to those with increased disposable income (and desired by those without)" (2004a, 19).

8 See McClellan 2008 for a discussion of the ways in which *The Hills* made use of cross-platform marketing.

9 For more on postfeminism, see Negra and Tasker 2007.

10 Kelly Cutrone would go on to star in her own, eight-episode, reality series called *Kell on Earth* for Bravo. The series focused on People's Revolution as well as Cutrone's life as a single, working mother.

11 It is worth noting that Jason Wahler was in the tabloids at this time for legal issues (see Lee 2007).

12 See chapter 1 for a discussion of MTV's *Sorority Life* and the ways in which the white pledges had the "luxury" of representing only themselves (rather than their entire race or ethnic group).

13 See Affuso 2009 for an early analysis of how MTV uses its reality series to sell consumer goods from corporate partners.

14 There are some exceptions to this depiction of Los Angeles. As I have argued elsewhere (2009a), BET's *Baldwin Hills* "effectively straddles the line between projective drama and rhetorical document, offering audiences an opportunity for escape as well as a chance to engage with the challenges and responsibilities faced by Los Angeles teenagers."

15 In the interim between season 2's finale in April of 2007 and the premiere of season 3 in August 2007, tabloids like *Perez Hilton, Us Weekly, The Superficial,* and *Gawker* reported that the show's protagonist and narrator, Lauren Conrad, and her ex-boyfriend, Jason Wahler, had made a sex tape together. Although the story was quickly discredited, rumors spread that it was concocted by Lauren's former roommate (during seasons 1 and 2), Heidi Montag, and her boyfriend, Spencer Pratt. Both women allegedly refused to appear together in publicity photographs promoting the new season and asked that their story lines be filmed separately (Armstrong 2007). For a sampling of the way this scandal was covered in the tabloids, see Agresti 2008, Bartolomeo and Bruce 2008, Grossman 2007, and *OK! Weekly* 2007.

16 To read more about how MTV managed this scandal, see Klein 2009b.

17 See, for example, the *People* cover story "Heidi Montag: Addicted to Plastic Surgery" (Garcia 2010).

18 To read more about how Heidi Montag and Spencer Pratt monetized their *Hills* infamy, see Klein 2009b.

19 Brody Jenner, son of Caitlyn Jenner and stepbrother of most of the cast of *Keeping Up with the Kardashians,* first appeared on reality television in the short-lived series *The Princes of Malibu,* alongside future star of *The Hills* Spencer Pratt. Jenner joined the cast of *The Hills* for its second season, after he began dating Lauren Conrad in 2007.

20 See chapter 2 for a discussion of how *The Real World* turned to self-reflexivity in later seasons.

21 See Ouellette 2014b for more about how teen pregnancy reality series work with advocacy groups.

22 Laurie Ouellette notes that "prosocial television is not a cynical corporate ruse, but a consequence of the wider conflation of the market and society under neoliberalism. MTV operates at the forefront of this transformation" (2018, 154).

23 Here are Sokol Savage's expanded remarks from our interview:

There are . . . a lot of reasons. I can't take responsibility for them, but I can tell you about them. The world of television reflects the world around us, which is, it's kind of racist. So just in the world of TV—in terms of networks . . . there is definitely a perception that Black audiences will watch white stories and white audiences will not watch Black stories. That is something I learned in the last two years, not eight years ago when I started doing this. . . . We pushed very, very hard, even for that first season, to make sure that we had one [woman of color]—and we only had one story. . . . Personally, I think it's a lot like institutional racism. People at the network are all well intentioned, everyone has great ideas, and everyone wants to be inclusive. But when you get down to it, they're making decisions. People tend to not promote . . . people of color. I think that's part of it. We've talked to a lot of groups. We worked closely with the National Campaign to Prevent Unplanned Pregnancy, and I've talked to a lot of groups who do different kinds of social issue work. I talk to a lot of people who worry about race issues, class issues, and they were like, "We don't want more Black women on *16 and Pregnant*." So that's also the flipside. [These groups told me,] "We don't want audiences to think that all the pregnant teenagers are Black."

Sokol Savage interview, October 14, 2016. Other quotes from Dia Sokol Savage in this chapter are from this interview, unless noted otherwise.

24 In chapter 4 I discuss attending one of Maci Bookout's college speaking tours.

25 Faye Woods has compared stereotypes from the UK shows *The Only Way Is Essex* (the Essex Girl, someone who is trashy nouveau riche) and *Made in Chelsea* (the Sloane Girl, a stuck-up rich girl) as a way to demonstrate "the role of excess in the classed femininities and performativity that contribute to these programs' varying displays of nonnaturalism" (2012, 198). MTV offers similar class-based stereotypes of femininity in its programming. See also Tyler and Bennet 2010.

26 As I discuss later in this chapter, *Teen Mom* breaks the fourth wall in season 5, and this moment in which Amber discusses her "fans" on camera is an example.

27 Like the women of *The Hills*, the women who appeared on *16 and Pregnant* and later *Teen Mom* have become celebrities outside of MTV, appearing on the covers of tabloids and at the center of public interest and debate on social media.

28 Sokol Savage interview, October 14, 2016; emphasis mine.

29 See chapter 2 for a discussion of Tony's outburst against MTV's production structures.

30 I am using the term "money shot" as defined by Laura Grindstaff in her study of talk shows, as "joy, sorrow, rage, or remorse expressed in visible, bodily terms" (2002, 19).

31 Farrah also refuses to work in episode 18 when the producers and crew show up to her home. She tells them, "You shouldn't be here today because this production doesn't exist right now." When Farrah refuses to come out and work, that is, to allow the crew to film her life, Larry, an executive producer, becomes irate. The two shout over each other, and Larry yells, "We were here when you were in your cheerleading outfit!"

32 During her time on MTV, Farrah has opened frozen yogurt, furniture, and children's clothing stores, and she has worked as a singer, actress, and author.

Chapter 4. "If You Don't Tan, You're Pale"

1 Sup Dogs's manager, Bret Oliverio, told me that when Pauly D's agent quoted him the booking fee, "I told him we couldn't even afford a fraction of that. I sent his agent a video we made of Doggie Jams 2013, the previous year. It basically showed a bunch of college students having the time of their life. He said he would show it to Pauly D but would be surprised if he agreed to do

the show for less than [the quoted fee]. Pauly D watched the video and loved the college atmosphere and fun nature of the event. He's normally in a Vegas nightclub and Doggie Jams was a totally different type of event. He agreed to do the show to everyone's surprise, for a fraction of his normal fee" (Oliverio, personal communication, December 12, 2018).

2 These eight dimensions are defined as emotional, environmental, financial, intellectual, physical, social, spiritual, and occupational (East Carolina University 2018).

3 See Stephanie Talmadge's (2017) detailed article on sorority uniforms.

4 *Jersey Shore* is produced by 495 Productions, run by SallyAnn Salsano.

5 For a detailed understanding of the concept of subculture, see Hebdige 1979.

6 The Guido subculture in its current form can be traced back to various Italian American street gangs from the 1950s and 1960s, such as the Golden Guineas, Fordham Baldies, Pigtown Boys, Italian Sand Street Angels, and Corona Dukes, among others, who hailed from the Bronx, Queens, and Brooklyn (Tricarico 2007, 49). Many of these gangs were under the tutelage of the local Mafia, who organized youth into crews and put them to work. Much like the 1970s Black, urban youth gangs that sublimated some of the more violent aspects of their subculture into prosocial avenues such as rapping, breakdancing, and graffiti art, over time the violent activities of Italian American youth gangs were translated into stylistic concerns (Tricarico 1991, 48).

7 According to Tricarico, the Guido "neither embraces traditional Italian culture nor repudiates ethnicity in identifying with American culture. Rather it reconciles ethnic Italian ancestry with popular American culture by elaborating a youth style that is an interplay of ethnicity and youth cultural meanings" (1991, 42).

8 See Jon Kraszewski's discussion of how "long-established urban ethnic and racial stereotypes become costumes for reality performances that led to long careers for [people like 'Boston' Rob Mariano and Tiffany 'New York' Pollard] and other reality gamers" (2017, 134).

9 For more on gender performativity, see Butler 2007.

10 One of *Jersey Shore*'s most well-known personalities, Snooki, is not an Italian American by birth. Snooki was born in Santiago, Chile, in 1987. She was adopted at six months old by Italian American parents and raised in New York. Nevertheless, Snooki has embraced the identity-based values and beliefs of her adoptive Italian American parents. Similarly, Jennifer "J Woww" Farley is actually of Irish and Spanish descent.

11 See Isenberg 2016, C. Murray 2012, Putnam 2015, and Vance 2016.

12 In March 2019, the *Associated Press Stylebook* was updated to provide new guidelines for how journalists should use the term "racist" in reporting. One guideline stated, "Do not use racially charged or similar terms as euphemisms for racist or racism when the latter terms are truly applicable" (qtd. in Berendzen 2019).

13. This cycle during the mid-2000s included programs on various cable channels. Representative shows were *Hillbilly Handfishing, Swamp People, Rocket City Rednecks, Redneck Island, My Big Redneck Wedding, Redneck Intervention, Cajun Pawn Stars, River Monsters, Moonshiners, The Legend of Shelby the Swamp Man, Pit Bulls and Parolees, Backyard Oil, Lizard Lick Towing,* and *Here Comes Honey Boo Boo,* among others.

14 See chapter 3 for a discussion of the filming restrictions on *Laguna Beach.*

15 West Virginia's motto is *Montani Semper Liberi,* which translates to "Mountaineers are always free" (Swick 2013), a nod to the state's succession from Virginia in 1862.

16 When this episode cut to a commercial, MTV issued the following statement: "The misuse of guns can lead to damaging consequences. To learn more about this, head to MTV.com."

Chapter 5. "That Moment Is Here"

1 Murray interview, August 4, 2016. Other quotes from Jonathan Murray in this chapter are from this interview, unless noted otherwise.

2 Responding to complaints that *Washington Heights* was not "Dominican enough," J.P. told a reporter, "It's a story about *us*. It's not called Dominican Heights" (qtd. in Llenas 2013; emphasis mine).

3 One exception among Goin's interviewees was Leta, an eighteen-year-old Dominican American who enjoyed the show because it "resonate[d] with her on both generational and cultural levels" (2015, 167). That is, Goin suspects Leta enjoyed the series more due to a generational affiliation; she is roughly the same age as the series' cast members and can readily identify with their speech patterns, leisure activities, and attitudes.

Conclusion

1 Joseph interview, 2015. Other quotes from Max Joseph in this chapter are from this interview, unless noted otherwise.

2 Information about mass shootings is found in R. Arthur 2017.

3 For more on the complicated relationship between Millennials and the internet, see Bolton et al. 2013, Geraci and Nagy 2004, Nielsen 2014, Selwyn 2009, and Vaidhyanathan 2008.

4 Joseph told me, "Yes, a lot of the time I'm like, 'Goddamn it, why didn't you do more research?' and we do chastise those people. Most of the time it's pretty hypocritical because if they did do it, they wouldn't end up on the show. We wouldn't have a show!"

5 For more discussion of the construction of identities online, see Davis and Jurgenson 2011.

6 Joseph told me, "When you get these two people in a room, finally, and let's

say they are who they say they are, it almost never works out! In real life it can more than it does on the show. But on the show [it doesn't]."

7 See chapter 2 for an in-depth analysis of Cory's whiteness epiphany.

8 See chapter 1 for a discussion of *Yo! MTV Raps*.

9 See Higgins 2016; Khazan 2013; Lister, Sciutto, and Ilylushina 2017; and MacKinnon 2019.

REFERENCES

Aapola, Sinikka, Marnina Gonick, and Anita Harris. 2005. *Young Femininity: Girlhood, Power, and Social Change.* New York: Palgrave Macmillan.

Adams, Erik, Noel Murray, Donna Bowman, Emily Todd VanDerWerff, Phil Dyess-Nugent, Ryan McGee, and Meredith Blake. 2012. "A New Form of Reality TV Emerges from the Sands of Laguna Beach." *AV Club.* August 16. https://tv.avclub.com/a-new-form-of-reality-tv-emerges-from-the-sands-of-lagu-1798232888.

Affuso, Elizabeth. 2009. "'Don't Just Watch It, Live It': Technology, Corporate Partnerships and *The Hills.*" *Jump Cut*, no. 51. https://www.ejumpcut.org /archive/jc51.2009/Hills-Affuso/text.html.

Agresti, Amy. 2008. "The Feud Gets Worse." *Us Weekly*, May 19, 58–63.

Akosua. 2013. "Washington Heights: A Show Abandoned." *Mandawhite*, March 7. https://mandawhite.wordpress.com/2013/03/07/washington-heights-a-show -abandoned/.

Allen, Renqiua. 2019. "The Missing Black Millennial." *New Republic*, February 20. https://newrepublic.com/article/153122/missing-black-millennial.

Alzayat, Dima. 2011. "On Location: MTV's 'Buck Wild' Denied West Virginia Tax Credit." *Los Angeles Times*, December 7. http://articles.latimes.com/2011 /dec/07/business/la-fi-ct-mtv-tax-credits-20111207.

Anderson, Monica, and Jingjing Jiang. 2018. "Teens, Social Media & Technology 2018." *Pew Research Center*, May 31. https://www.pewinternet.org/2018 /05/31/teens-social-media-technology-2018/.

Andrejevic, Mark. 2004. *Reality TV: The Work of Being Watched.* Lanham, MD: Rowman and Littlefield.

Andrejevic, Mark. 2014. "When Everyone Has Their Own Reality Show." In *Companion to Reality Television*, edited by Laurie Ouellette, 40–56. Hoboken, NJ: Wiley Blackwell.

Angelo, Megan. 2014. "Secrets of *The Real World*: How It Actually Casts People, Shoots Hookups, and Decorates Those Crazy Houses." *Glamour*, December 9. https://www.glamour.com/story/real-world-behind-the-scenes.

Anson, Robert Sam. 2000. "Birth of an MTV Nation." *Vanity Fair*, November. https://www.vanityfair.com/news/2000/11/mtv200011.

Apollon, Dom. 2011. "Don't Call Them 'Post-Racial.' Millennials Say Race Matters to Them." *Colorlines*, June 7. https://www.colorlines.com/articles /dont-call-them-post-racial-millennials-say-race-matters-them.

Arango, Tim. 2009. "Make Room, Cynics; MTV Wants to Do Some Good." April 18. https://www.nytimes.com/2009/04/19/business/media/19mtv.html.

Armstrong, Jennifer. 2007. "'The Hills' Are Alive." *Entertainment Weekly*, August 9.

Arthur, Kate. 2008. "The Speidi Chronicles." *Los Angeles Times*, May 11. http:// articles.latimes.com/2008/may/11/entertainment/ca-hills11.

Arthur, Kate. 2014. "Looking Back at 'The Real World: San Francisco,' the Show That Changed the World." *Buzzfeed*, January 4. https://www.buzzfeed.com /kateaurthur/real-world-san-francisco-pedro-zamora-rachel-campos# .ab3mxYE1M.

Arthur, Rob. 2017. "No Matter How You Measure Them, Mass Shooting Deaths Are Up." *FiveThirtyEight*, November 7. https://fivethirtyeight.com/features /no-matter-how-you-measure-them-mass-shooting-deaths-are-up/.

Balderrama, Anthony. 2007. "Generation Y: Too Demanding at Work?" CNN, December 26. http://www.cnn.com/2007/LIVING/worklife/12/26/ cb .generation/ index.html.

Banet-Weiser, Sarah. 2012. *Authentic: The Politics of Ambivalence in a Brand Culture*. New York: New York University Press.

Banet-Weiser, Sarah. 2015. "'Confidence You Can Carry!': Girls in Crisis and the Market for Girls Empowerment Organizations," *Continuum* 29 (2): 182–193.

Banks, Jack. 1996. *Monopoly Television: MTV's Quest to Control the Music*. Boulder, CO: Westview.

Barshad, Amos. 2011. "A Conversation with Famously Reclusive *Tree of Life* Director Terrence Malick." *Vulture*, May 27. https://www.vulture.com/2011 /05/a_fake_interview_with_the_famo.html.

Barshad, Amos. 2013. "Why the Hell Did MTV Make a Show about Washington Heights?" *Grantland*, January 16. http://grantland.com/hollywood -prospectus/why-the-hell-did-mtv-make-a-show-about-washington-heights/.

Bartolomeo, Joey, and Leslie Bruce. 2008. "How I Was Stabbed in the Back." *Us Weekly*, March 31, 42–47.

Bauder, David. 1999. "Teen Music Fans' Energy at the Heart of 'TRL.'" *Columbian*, October 17.

Belcher, Walt. 2003. "Specials on HBO and MTV May Be a Little Too Rich for Some Viewers." *Tampa Tribune*, October 27.

Bennett, Jessica. 2015. "When Your Punctuation Says It All (!)."*New York Times*, February 27.

Benshoff, Harry. 2011. *Dark Shadows*. Detroit, MI: Wayne State University Press.

Berendzen, Gerri. 2019. "AP Stylebook Adds New Umbrella Entry for Race-Related Coverage." *ACES: The Society for Editing*. March 29. https://aceseditors.org/news/2019/ap-stylebook-adds-new-umbrella-entry-for-race-related-coverage-issues-new-hyphen-guidance-and-other-changes.

Blake, Meredith. 2011. "The Real World: 'This Is the True Story . . .'" *AV Club*, June 6. https://tv.avclub.com/the-real-world-this-is-the-true-story-1798169103.

Boddy, William. 1993. *Fifties Television: The Industry and Its Critics*. Urbana: University of Illinois Press.

Bodroghkozy, Aniko. 2001. *Groove Tube: Sixties Television and Youth Rebellion*. Durham, NC: Duke University Press.

Bolton, Ruth, A. Parasuraman, Ankie Hoefnagels, Nanne Migchels, Sertan Kabadayi, Thorsten Gruber, Yuliya Komarova Loureiro, and David Solnet. 2013. "Understanding Generation Y and Their Use of Social Media: A Review and Research Agenda." *Journal of Service Management* 24 (3): 245–267. https://doi.org/10.1108/09564231311326987.

Bookout, Maci. 2015. *Bulletproof*. New York: Post Hill.

Boston Herald. 2003. "HOTLINE: MTV's So-Called 'Reality' Fills Fall Season." September 3.

boyd, danah. 2014. *It's Complicated: The Social Lives of Networked Teens*. New Haven, CT: Yale University Press.

Boyer, Peter J. 1988. "MTV Changes Image: But Game Shows?" *Chicago Tribune*, May 19. https://www.chicagotribune.com/news/ct-xpm-1988-05-19-8803180303-story.html.

Brooks, Caryn. 2009. "Italian Americans and the G Word: Embrace or Reject?" *Time*, December 12. http://www.time.com/time/nation/article/0,8599,1947338,00.html.

Brumberg, Joan Jacobs. 1997. *The Body Project: An Intimate History of American Girls*. New York: Random House.

Burton, Nylah. 2019. "The Young Activists of Color Who Are Leading the Charge against Climate Disaster." *Vox*, October 11. https://www.vox.com/identities/2019/10/11/20904791/young-climate-activists-of-color.

Butler, Bethonie, and Elahe Izadi. 2018. "Everything You Forgot about Janet Jackson and Justin Timberlake's 2004 Super Bowl Controversy." *Washington Post*, February 1. https://www.washingtonpost.com/news/arts-and-entertainment/wp/2017/10/23/everything-you-forgot-about-janet-jackson-and-justin-timberlakes-2004-super-bowl-controversy/?utm_term=.f2606ecefe85.

Butler, Judith. 2007. *Gender Trouble: Feminism and the Subversion of Identity*. New York: Routledge.

Cantor, Brian. 2013. "MTV's 'Washington Heights' Premiere Flops in the Ratings." *Headline Planet*, January 10. https://headlineplanet.com/home/2013/01/10/mtvs-washington-heights-premiere-flops-in-the-ratings/.

Cappelli, Ottorino. 2011. "The Name of the Guido: An Exercise in Italian/American Identity Politics." In *Guido: Italian/American Youth and Identity Politics*, edited by Letizia Airos and Ottorino Cappelli, 10–13. New York: Bordighera.

CCTA. 2020. "History of Cable." California Cable and Telecommunications Association. Accessed June 12. calcable.org/learn/history-of-cable/.

Celebrity Net Worth. 2020. "Tommy Hilfiger Net Worth." Accessed May 1. https://www.celebritynetworth.com/richest-businessmen/richest-designers/tommy-hilfiger-net-worth/.

Change.org. 2012. "Bring Back 'Washington Heights' for Another Season!" https://www.change.org/p/mtv-bring-back-washington-heights-for-another-season.

Chen, Adrien. 2013. "Don't Be a Stranger." *New Inquiry*, February 13. https://thenewinquiry.com/dont-be-a-stranger/.

Ciampaglia, Dante A. 2018. "What Is a Millennial? Birthyear Guidelines Set for How to Define Generations." *Newsweek*, March 1.

Clement, Scott. 2015. "Millennials Are Just about as Racist as Their Parents." *Washington Post*, April 7. https://www.washingtonpost.com/news/wonk/wp/2015/04/07/white-millennials-are-just-about-as-racist-as-their-parents/?utm_term=.78a5cd2aafo1.

Cogan, Marin. 2014. "In the Beginning, There Was a Nipple." ESPN, January 28. http://www.espn.com/espn/feature/story?id=10333439&_slug_=wardrobe-malfunction-beginning-there-was-nipple.

Cohn, Nik. 1976. "Tribal Rights of the New Saturday Night." *New York Magazine*, June 17. http://nymag.com/nightlife/features/45933/.

Conlin, Michelle. 2008. "Youth Quake; They're Called Millennials—and They're Fed Up." *Business Week*, January 21.

Copeland, Libby. 2003. "Strutting Season: At the Jersey Shore, Guidos Are Pumped for the Prime of Their Lives." *Washington Post*, July 6.

Corner, John. 2002. "Performing the Real: Documentary Diversions." *Television and New Media* 3 (3): 255–270.

Corsani, Antonella. 2007. "Beyond the Myth of Woman: The Becoming-Transfeminist of (Post-Marxism)." *SubStance* 36 (1): 107–138.

Coscarelli, Joe. 2011. "Bridge and Tunnel Traps Now Competing with Hipster Traps on NYC Sidewalks." *Village Voice*, March 18. https://www.villagevoice.com/2011/03/18/bridge-and-tunnel-traps-now-competing-with-hipster-traps-on-nyc-sidewalks/.

Couldry, Nick. 2008. "Reality TV, or the Secret Theater of Neoliberalism." *Review of Education, Pedagogy, and Cultural Studies* 30 (3): 3–13.

Coupland, Douglas. 1991. *Generation X: Tales for an Accelerated Culture*. New York: St. Martin's.

Davis, Glyn, and Kay Dickinson. 2004. *Teen TV: Genre, Consumption, and Identity*. London: Bloomsbury.

Davis, Jenny, and Nathan Jurgenson. 2011. "Prosuming Identity Online." *Society*

Pages, September 12. https://thesocietypages.org/cyborgology/2011/09/12
/prosuming-identity-online/.

DeCurtis, Anthony, ed. 1992. *Present Tense: Rock and Roll Culture*. Durham, NC:
Duke University Press.

Dickstein, Martin. 1975. "New York Is a Nice Place to Visit." *Db: The Sound Engineering Magazine* 9 (7): 12–19.

Dimock, Michael. 2019. "Defining Generations: Where Millennials End and
Generation Z Begins." Pew Research Center. January 17. https://www
.pewresearch.org/fact-tank/2019/01/17/where-millennials-end-and
-generation-z-begins/.

Dodero, Camille. 2011. "Meet the Original JWoww and Snooki, Would-Be Stars
of *Bridge & Tunnel*." *Village Voice*, August 5. https://longform.org/posts
/meet-the-original-jwoww-and-snooki-would-be-stars-of-bridge-tunnel.

Doonan, Simon. 2010. "How Snooki Got Her Gucci: The Dirt on Purses."
Observer, August 17. https://observer.com/2010/08/how-snooki-got-her
-gucci-the-dirt-on-purses/.

Dovey, Jon. 2000. *Freakshow: First Person Media and Factual Television*. London: Pluto.

Dreher, Rod. 2016. "Trump: Tribune of Poor White People." *American Conservative*, July 22. https://www.theamericanconservative.com/dreher
/trump-us-politics-poor-whites/.

Dyer, Richard. 1986. *Heavenly Bodies*. New York: St. Martin's.

Dyer, Richard. 1997. *White*. London: Routledge.

East Carolina University. 2018. "Wellness Passport & Recreational Programs."
Accessed July 1. https://crw.ecu.edu/wellness-fitness/wellness-passport
-educational-programs/#attending.

Edwards, Gavin. 2000. "The New American Bandstand." *Rolling Stone*, February 17, 13, 16.

El Nasser, Haya. 2014. "US Birthrate Continues to Slow Because of Recession."
Al Jazeera America, December 10. http://america.aljazeera.com/articles
/2014/12/10/census-populationdiversity.html.

Engber, Daniel. 2012. "Ugly Buttons: How Did the Remote Control Get So Awful
and Confusing?" *Slate*, June 27. https://slate.com/human-interest/2012/06
/the-history-of-the-remote-control-why-are-they-so-awful.html.

Erickson, Tammy. 2008. "Gen Y: Really All That Narcissistic?" *Business Week
Online*, March 3. http://www.businessweek.com/managing/content
/feb2008/ ca20080228_450510.htm.

Foucault, Michel. 1969. *L'archéologie du savoir* [The archeology of knowledge].
Paris: Editions Gallimard.

Fox, Margalit. 2015. "Paul Almond, Who Directed First 'Seven Up!,' Dies at 83."
New York Times, April 14.

Franklin, Nancy. 2008. "Frenemy Territory: The Hills Are Alive with the Sound
of Girl Talk." *New Yorker*, April 12. https://www.newyorker.com/magazine
/2008/04/21/frenemy-territory.

Fretts, Bruce. 1995. "The 'Real World' Returns for Fourth Season." *Entertainment Weekly*, July 21. http://ew.com/article/1995/07/21/real-world-returns-fourth -season/.

Friedlander, Paul. 1996. *Rock and Roll: A Social History*. Boulder, CO: Westview.

Frontline. 2001. "The Merchants of Cool: A Report on the Creators & Marketers of Popular Culture for Teenagers." February 27. https://www.pbs.org/wgbh /frontline/film/showscool/.

Fry, Richard, and Kim Parker. 2018. "Early Benchmarks Show 'Post-Millennials' on Track to Be Most Diverse, Best-Educated Generation Yet." Pew Research Center, November 15. https://www.pewsocialtrends.org/2018/11/15/early -benchmarks-show-post-millennials-on-track-to-be-most-diverse-best -educated-generation-yet/.

Gamson, Joshua. 1994. *Claims to Fame: Celebrity in Contemporary America*. Berkeley: University of California Press.

Gans, Herbert. 1979. "Symbolic Ethnicity: The Future of Ethnic Groups and Cultures in America." *Ethnic and Racial Studies* 2 (1): 1–20.

Garber-Paul, Elisabeth. 2009. "MTV: Teen Pregnancy Meets Reality Television." *Rewire.News*, May 20.

Garcia, Jennifer. 2010. "Heidi Montag: Addicted to Plastic Surgery." *People*, January 13. https://people.com/bodies/heidi-montag-addicted-to-plastic -surgery/.

Gay, Jason. 2008. "The Stars of 'The Hills': Are They for Real?! Why MTV's 'Laguna Beach' Spin-Off Is the Show You Love to Hate—or Hate to Love." *Rolling Stone*, May 15. https://www.rollingstone.com/tv/tv-news/the-stars -of-the-hills-are-they-for-real-100782/.

Geraci, John C., and Judit Nagy. 2004. "Millennials—the New Media Generation." *Young Consumers* 5 (2): 17–24.

Gessen, Masha. 2018. "The Fifteen-Year-Old Climate Activist Who Is Demanding a New Kind of Politics." *New Yorker*, October 2.

Gilbert, Matthew. 2003. "Clueless Rich Girls Take Primetime by Storm." *Chicago Sun-Times*, December.

Gilbert, Sara. 2015. *Built for Success: The Story of MTV*. Mankato: Creative Paperbacks.

Gill, Rosalind. 2007. "Postfeminist Media Culture: Elements of a Sensibility." *European Journal of Cultural Studies* 10 (2): 147–166.

Gillan, Jennifer. 2015. *Television Brandcasting: The Return of the Content-Promotion Hybrid*. New York: Routledge.

Goin, Keara. 2015. "Dominican Identity in Flux: Media Consumption, Negotiation, and Afro-Caribbean Subjectivity in the U.S." PhD dissertation, University of Texas at Austin.

Goodwin, Andrew. 1992. *Dancing in the Distraction Factory: Music Television and Popular Culture*. Minneapolis: University of Minnesota Press.

Gorman, Bill. 2008. "The Hills Tops Cable TV Time-Shifting with 35.5%

Increase." *TV by the Numbers*, May 28. http://tvbythenumbers.com
/2008/05/28/ the-hills-tops-cable-tv-time-shifting-with-355-increase/3926.

Grindstaff, Laura. 2002. *The Money Shot: Trash, Class, and the Making of TV Talk Shows*. Chicago: University of Chicago Press.

Grindstaff, Laura. 2011a. "From *Jerry Springer* to *Jersey Shore*: The Cultural Politics of Class in/on US Reality Programming." In *Reality Television and Class*, edited by Helen Wood and Beverley Skeggs, 197–209. London: Palgrave Macmillan.

Grindstaff, Laura. 2011b. "Just Be Yourself—Only More So: Ordinary Celebrity in the Era of Self-Service Television." In *The Politics of Reality Television: Global Perspectives*, edited by Marwan Kraidy and Katherine Sender, 44–58. New York: Routledge.

Grindstaff, Laura. 2014. "DI(t)Y Reality-Style: The Cultural Work of Ordinary Celebrity." In *Companion to Reality Television*, edited by Laurie Ouellette, 324–344. Hoboken, NJ: Wiley Blackwell.

Grindstaff, Laura, and Susan Murray. 2015. "Reality Celebrity: Branded Affect and the Emotion Economy." *Public Culture* 27 (1): 109–135.

Grossman, Peter. 2007. "Why I Called Off My Wedding." *Us Weekly*, December 31, 54–59.

Halbfinger, David M. 1998. "In Washington Heights, Drug War Survivors Reclaim Their Stoops." *New York Times*, May 18. http://academics.wellesley
.edu/Chemistry/Chem102/war/html%20pages/ny-heights-crime.html.

Hall, Jane. 1992. "Like, Here's the News." *Los Angeles Times*, February 16.

Hall, Stuart. 1996. "Who Needs 'Identity'?" In *Questions of Cultural Identity*, edited by Stuart Hall and Paul du Gay, 1–17. London: Sage.

Hargittai, Eszter. 2010. "Digital Na(t)ives? Variation in Internet Skills and Uses among Members of the 'Net Generation.'" *Sociological Inquiry* 80 (1): 92–113.

Hargraves, Hunter. 2014. "Tan TV: Reality Television's Postracial Delusion." In *Companion to Reality Television*, edited by Laurie Ouellette, 283–306. Hoboken, NJ: Wiley Blackwell.

Harris, Anita. 2004a. *Future Girl: Young Women in the Twenty-First Century*. New York: Routledge.

Harris, Anita. 2004b. "Jamming Girl Culture: Young Women and Consumer Citizenship." In *All about the Girl: Culture, Power, and Identity*, edited by Anita Harris, 163–172. New York: Routledge.

Harris, Neil. 1981. *Humbug: The Art of P. T. Barnum*. Chicago: University of Chicago Press.

Hatch, Kristen. 2013. "*Here Comes Honey Boo Boo* and the Spectacle of the Ungovernable Child." *Flow: A Critical Forum on Television and Media Culture*, May 6. https://www.flowjournal.org/2013/05/here-comes-honey
-boo-boo/.

Hay, Carla. 2001. "Proper Role of Music TV Debated in U.S." *Billboard*, February 17.

Hearn, Allison. 2008. "Insecure: Narratives and Economies of the Branded Self in Transformation Television." *Continuum: Journal of Media & Cultural Studies* 22 (4): 495–504.

Hearn, Allison. 2010. "Reality Television, *The Hills*, and the Limits of the Immaterial Labour Thesis." *Triple C* 8 (1): 60–76.

Hearn, Allison. 2014. "Producing 'Reality': Branded Content, Branded Selves, Precarious Futures." In *Companion to Reality Television*, edited by Laurie Ouellette, 437–456. Hoboken, NJ: Wiley Blackwell.

Hebdige, Dick. 1979. *Subculture: The Meaning of Style*. London: Methuen.

Heffernan, Virginia. 2004. "Surfing on a Wave of Adolescent Angst." *New York Times*, September 28. https://www.nytimes.com/2004/09/28/arts/television/surfing-on-a-wave-of-adolescent-angst.html.

Higgins, Andrew. 2016. "Effort to Expose Russia's 'Troll Army' Draws Vicious Retaliation." *New York Times*, May 30.

Hill, Annette. 2005. *Reality TV: Audience and Popular Factual Television*. London: Routledge.

Hirschorn, Michael. 2007. "The Case for Reality TV." *Atlantic*, May 2007. https://www.theatlantic.com/magazine/archive/2007/05/the-case-for-reality-tv/305791/.

"HIV and AIDS—United States, 1981–2000." 2001. *Journal of the American Medical Association* 285 (24): 3083–3084. https://jamanetwork.com/journals/jama/fullarticle/1844004.

Hochman, Steve. 1999. "MTV Aims to Keep It Totally Honest on 'Total Request Live.'" *Los Angeles Times*, December 5.

Holmes, Elizabeth. 2011. "Abercrombie and Fitch Offers to Pay 'The Situation' to Stop Wearing Its Clothes." *Wall Street Journal*, August 16. https://blogs.wsj.com/speakeasy/2011/08/16/abercrombie-and-fitch-offer-to-pay-the-situation-to-stop-wearing-their-clothes/.

Holt, Jennifer. 2011. *Empires of Entertainment: Media Industries and the Politics of Deregulation, 1980–1996*. New Brunswick, NJ: Rutgers University Press.

Hoover, Maddie, Hannah Teklits, and Ethan Eshbach. 2019. "*Catfish*: The Untold Story of Facebook." *Cinemablography*, January 7. http://www.cinemablography.org/catfish.html.

Horning, Rob. 2012a. "Facebook and Living Labor." *New Inquiry*, May 17. https://thenewinquiry.com/blog/facebook-and-living-labor/.

Horning, Rob. 2012b. "Hi Haters!" *New Inquiry*, November 27. https://thenewinquiry.com/hi-haters/.

Howe, Neil, and William Strauss. 2000. *Millennials Rising: The Next Great Generation*. New York: Random House.

Huber, Patrick. 1995. "A Short History of Redneck: The Fashioning of a Southern White Masculine Identity." *Southern Cultures* 1 (2): 145–166.

Hyman, Vicki. 2009a. "'Jersey Shore' Cast Members Say Guido Is a Lifestyle, Not a Slur." *Star-Ledger*, December 2. http://www.nj.com/entertainment/celebrities/index.ssf/2009/12/jersey_shore_cast_members_say.html.

Hyman, Vicki. 2009b. "'Jersey Shore' Offends Italian-American Group; President Protests Use of 'Guido.'" *Star-Ledger*, November 24. http://www.nj.com/entertainment/celebrities/index.ssf/2009/11/jersey_shore_offends_italian-a.html.

Imre, Aniko, and Annabel Tremlett. 2011. "Reality TV without Class: The Post-Socialist Anti-Celebrity Docusoap." In *Reality Television and Class*, edited by Helen Wood and Beverley Skeggs, 88–103. London: British Film Institute.

Isenberg, Nancy. 2016. *White Trash: The 400-Year Untold History of Class in America*. New York: Penguin Books.

Israel, Betsy. 1994. "HIV, and Positive, Pedro Zamora of MTV's *Real World* Lived His Too-Brief Life to Its Limit." *People*, November 28. https://people.com/archive/hiv-and-positive-vol-42-no-22/.

Jackson, John. 1997. *American Bandstand: Dick Clark and the Making of a Rock 'n' Roll Empire*. Oxford: Oxford University Press.

Jargon, Julie. 2014. "McDonald's Faces 'Millennial' Challenge." *Wall Street Journal*, August 24.

Jayson, Sharon. 2007. "Gen Y's Goal? Wealth and Fame." *USA Today*, January 10. http://www.usatoday.com/news/nation/2007-01-09-gen-y-cover_x.htm.

Jenkins, Henry. 2006. *Convergence Culture: Where Old and New Media Collide*. New York: New York University Press.

Jones, Steve. 2005. "MTV: The Medium Was the Message." *Critical Studies in Media Communication* 22 (1): 83–88.

Jost, François. 2011. "When Reality TV Is a Job." In *The Politics of Reality Television: Global Perspectives*, edited by Marwan Kraidy and Katherine Sender, 31–43. New York: Routledge.

Jurgenson, Nathan. 2012. "The Facebook Eye." *Atlantic*, January 13. https://www.theatlantic.com/technology/archive/2012/01/the-facebook-eye/251377/.

Kaiser Family Foundation. 2010. "Generation M2: Media in the Lives of 8- to 18-Year-Olds." January 20. https://www.kff.org/other/event/generation-m2-media-in-the-lives-of/.

Kaplan, E. Ann. 1987. *Rocking around the Clock: Music Television, Postmodernism, and Consumer Culture*. New York: Routledge.

Kaufman, Debra. 2008. "Heading for *The Hills*." *Studio Daily*, August 2. https://www.studiodaily.com/2006/08/heading-for-the-hills/.

Kavka, Misha. 2012. *Reality TV*. Edinburgh: Edinburgh University Press. Ebook.

Kavka, Misha. 2014. "A Matter of Feeling: Mediated Affect in Reality Television." In *Companion to Reality Television*, edited by Laurie Ouellette, 459–477. Hoboken, NJ: Wiley Blackwell.

Keeler, Amanda Renee. 2016. "Premature Adulthood: Alcoholic Moms and Teenage Adults in the ABC *Afterschool Specials*." *Quarterly Review of Film and Video* 33 (6): 483–500.

Khazan, Olga. 2013. "Russia's Online-Comment Propaganda Army." *Atlantic*, October 9. https://www.theatlantic.com/international/archive/2013/10/russias-online-comment-propaganda-army/280432/.

Klein, Amanda Ann. 2009a. "ʙᴇᴛ's *Baldwin Hills*: Injecting Race and Class into the Projective Drama." *Flow: A Critical Forum on Television and Media Culture*, November 12. https://www.flowjournal.org/2009/11/bet %E2%80%99s-baldwin-hills-injecting-race-and-class-into-the-projective -drama-amanda-klein-east-carolina-university/.

Klein, Amanda Ann. 2009b. "Postmodern Marketing, Generation Y and the Multi-Platform Viewing Experience of ᴍᴛᴠ's *The Hills*." *Jump Cut*, no. 51. https://www.ejumpcut.org/archive/jc51.2009/HillsKlein/.

Klein, Amanda Ann. 2010. "Window Dressing: Spectacular Costuming in ᴍᴛᴠ's *The Hills*." *Flow: A Critical Forum on Television and Media Culture*, January 22. https://www.flowjournal.org/2010/01/window-dressing-spectacular -costuming-in-mtvs-the-city-amanda-ann-klein-east-carolina-university/.

Klein, Amanda Ann. 2011a. *American Film Cycles: Reframing Genres, Screening Social Problems, and Defining Subcultures*. Austin: University of Texas Press.

Klein, Amanda Ann. 2014. "Abject Femininity and Compulsory Masculinity on the *Jersey Shore*." In *Reality Gendervision: Decoding Sexuality and Gender on Transatlantic Reality ᴛᴠ*, edited by Brenda Weber, 149–169. Durham, NC: Duke University Press.

Klein, Amanda Ann. 2018. "Genre." In *The Craft of Criticism: Critical Media Studies in Practice*, edited by Mary Celeste Kearney and Michael Kackman, 195–206. New York: Routledge.

Klein, Amanda Ann, and R. Barton Palmer, eds. 2016. *Cycles, Sequels, Spin-Offs, Remakes, and Reboots: Multiplicities in Film and Television*. Austin: University of Texas Press.

Kleinhans, Chuck. 2008. "Webisodic Mock Vlogs: HoShows as Commercial Entertainment New Media." *Jump Cut*, no. 50. https://www.ejumpcut.org /archive/jc50.2008/WeHoGirls/index.html.

Kraidy, Marwan, and Katherine Sender, eds. 2011. *The Politics of Reality Television: Global Perspectives*. New York: Routledge.

Kraszewski, Jon. 2009. "Country Hicks and Urban Cliques: Mediating Race, Reality, and Liberalism on ᴍᴛᴠ's *The Real World*." In *Reality ᴛᴠ: Remaking Television Culture*, edited by Susan Murray and Laurie Ouellette, 179–196. New York: New York University Press.

Kraszewski, Jon. 2010. "Multiracialism on *The Real World* and the Reconfiguration of Politics in ᴍᴛᴠ's Brand during the 2000s." *Popular Communication* 8 (2): 132–146.

Kraszewski, Jon. 2017. *Reality ᴛᴠ*. New York: Routledge.

Kristeva, Julia. 1982. *Powers of Horror: An Essay on Abjection*. Translated by Leon S. Roudiez. New York: Columbia University Press.

Kronke, David. 2003. "Lifestyles of the Rich and Extremely Obnoxious." *Daily News of Los Angeles*, October 27.

Lee, Esther. 2014. "Farrah Abraham's Teen Mom Costars Amber Portwood and Catelynn Lowell Want Her Fired." *Us Weekly*, March 19. https://www.us

magazine.com/entertainment/news/farrah-abrahams-teen-mom-costars
-amber-portwood-and-catelynn-lowell-want-her-fired-2014193/.

Lee, Ken. 2007. "Jail Time for Jason Wahler of *The Hills*." *People*, March 6. http://
www.people.com/people/article/0,,20014216,00.html.

Leung, Louis. 2003. "Impacts of Net-Generation Attributes, Seductive Properties
of the Internet, and Gratifications-Obtained on Internet Use." *Telematics
and Informatics* 20 (2): 107–129.

Levine, Ed. 1983. "TV Rocks with Music." *New York Times*, May 8. https://www
.nytimes.com/1983/05/08/magazine/tv-rocks-with-music.html.

Levine, Elana. 2006. "The New Soaps? *Laguna Beach, The Hills*, and the Gendered Politics of Reality 'Drama.'" *Flow: A Critical Forum on Television
and Media Culture*, August 18, 2006. https://www.flowjournal.org/2006/08
/the-new-soaps-laguna-beach-the-hills-and-the-gendered-politics-of
-reality-drama/.

Levine, Elana. 2007. *Wallowing in Sex: The New Sexual Culture of 1970s American Television*. Durham, NC: Duke University Press.

Lister, Tim, Jim Sciutto, and Mary Ilyushina. 2017. "Exclusive: Putin's 'Chef,' the
Man behind the Troll Factory." *CNN*, October 18.

Llenas, Bryan. 2013. "MTV's 'Washington Heights' Stars Say Show Isn't about
Being Dominican." *Fox News*, January 20. https://www.foxnews.com
/entertainment/mtvs-washington-heights-stars-say-show-isnt-about-being
-dominican.

Lotz, Amanda. 2007. *The Television Will Be Revolutionized*. New York: New
York University Press.

Lukow, George. 1991. "The Antecedents of MTV: Soundies, Scopitones and Snad-
ers, and the History of an Ahistorical Form." In *Art of Music Video: 10
Years Later*, edited by Michael Nash, 6–9. Long Beach, CA: Long Beach
Museum of Art.

Lynne, Amanda. 2016. "'Teen Mom 4' Coming: MTV Casting New Show."
Inquisitr, January 4. https://www.inquisitr.com/2680604/teen-mom-4
-coming-mtv-casting-new-show/.

MacKinnon, Amy. 2019. "The Evolution of a Russian Troll." *Foreign Policy*, July
10.

Mannen, Amanda. 2016. "I Was on MTV's *The Real World*: It Was Not Like You
Think." *Cracked*, July 13. http://www.cracked.com/personal-experiences
-2036-inside-manufactured-life-real-world-cast-member.html.

Mannheim, Karl. 1972. "The Problem of Generations." In *Karl Mannheim: Essays*, edited by Paul Kecskemeti, 276–322. New York: Routledge. First published 1952.

Mantzouranis, Tom. 2020. "The Inside Story of How the First MTV VMAS
Created a Tradition of Making Censors Sweat." *Uproxx*. Accessed April 27.
https://uproxx.com/music/mtv-vmas-1984-madonna-like-a-virgin-michael
-jackson-thriller/.

Marks, Craig. 2017. "Classic Power Squad: MTV Founders Reunite, Reflect on

'Life Changing' Channel." *Billboard*, February 9. https://www.billboard
.com/articles/business/7685112/mtv-founders-reunite-channel.

Marwick, Alice. 2013. *Status Update: Celebrity, Publicity, and Branding in the So-cial Media Age*. New Haven, CT: Yale University Press.

McCarthy, Anna. 2004. "Laguna Beach." *Flow: A Critical Forum on Television and Media Culture*, December 3. https://www.flowjournal.org/2004/12 /laguna-beach/.

McCarthy, Anna. 2009. "Stanley Milgram, Allen Funt, and Me." In *Reality TV: Remaking Television Culture*, edited by Susan Murray and Laurie Ouellette, 19–39. New York: New York University Press.

McClellan, Steve. 2008. "'The Hills' Is Alive: MTV Research Links Cross-Platform Marketing to Brand Affinity among Web Users." *AdWeek*, May 5. https://www.adweek.com/tv-video/hills-alive-95687/2/.

McFarland, Melanie. 2003. "Poor Little Rich Kids: Wealthy Offspring Flaunt Riches with Little Sympathy." *Houston Chronicle*, October 27.

McGee, Irene. 2013. "Slaps, Lies, and Videotape: Irene's True Story of 1998's *The Real World: Seattle*." *Vulture*, November 22. https://www.vulture.com/2013 /11/real-world-seattle-irene-slap-her-story.html.

Mendoza, Manuel. 2003. "Puttin' on the Rich: The New Trend in Following the Money Is with a TV Camera." *Dallas Morning News*, October 27.

Meyers, Erin. 2013. "The 'Reality' of Contemporary Stardom." *Flow: A Critical Forum on Television and Media Culture*, November. http://flowtv.org/2013 /11/the-reality-of-contemporary-stardom/.

Meyers, Erin. 2014. "Tabloids, Reality Television, and the 'Ordinary' Celebrity." *Flow: A Critical Forum on Television and Media Culture*, February 11. https://www.flowjournal.org/2014/02/tabloids-reality-television-and-the -ordinary-celebrity/.

Meyers, Erin. 2020. *Extraordinarily Ordinary: Us Weekly and the Rise of Reality Television Celebrity*. New Brunswick, NJ: Rutgers University Press.

Miller, Lisa. 2018. "Teens Already Know How to Overthrow the Government." *The Cut*, March 16. https://www.thecut.com/2018/03/parkland-students-emma-gonzalez-david-hogg.html.

Mittell, Jason. 2015. *Complex TV: The Poetics of Contemporary Storytelling*. New York: New York University Press.

Mole, Tom. 2004. "Hypertrophic Celebrity." *M/C Journal* 7 (5). http://journal .media-culture.org.au/0411/08-mole.php.

Muñoz, José Esteban. 1998. "Pedro Zamora's *Real World* of Counterpublicity: Performing an Ethics of the Self." In *Living Color: Race and Television in the United States*, edited by Sasha Torres, 195–218. Durham, NC: Duke University Press.

MTV. 2020. "MTV Casting Calls." Accessed June 12. http://www.mtv.com/mtv -casting-calls.

Murray, Charles. 2012. *Coming Apart: The State of White America, 1960–2010*. New York: Crown Forum.

Murray, Susan. 2009. "I Think We Need a New Name for It." In *Reality TV: Re-making Television Culture*, edited by Susan Murray and Laurie Ouellette, 40–56. New York: New York University Press.

Nakamura, Reid. 2018. "Nev Schulman Tells Us How the Hell This 'Catfish' Thing Is Still Happening in 2018." *The Wrap*, July 11. https://www.thewrap.com/nev-schulman-tells-us-how-this-catfish-thing-keeps-happening-in-2018/.

National Italian American Foundation. 2013. "National Italian American Foundation Official Statement: MTV's 'Jersey Shore.'" Accessed August 1. http://www.niaf.org/news/index.asp?id=699.

Negra, Diane, and Yvonne Tasker, eds. 2007. *Interrogating Postfeminism: Gender and the Politics of Popular Culture*. Durham, NC: Duke University Press.

Neuborne, Ellen, and Kathleen Kerwin. 1999. "Generation Y." *Business Week Online*, February 15. http://www.businessweek.com/1999/99_07/b3616001.htm.

Newman, Michael. 2010. "New Media, Young Audiences and Discourses of Attention: From *Sesame Street* to 'Snack Culture.'" *Media, Culture & Society* 32 (4): 581–596.

Ng, E. S., L. Schweitzer, and S. T. Lyons. 2010. "New Generation, Great Expectations: A Field Study of the Millennial Generation." *Journal of Business and Psychology* 25 (2): 281–292.

Nichols, Bill. 2001. *Introduction to Documentary*. Bloomington: Indiana University Press.

Nielsen. 2013. "Tops of 2013." December 17. https://www.nielsen.com/us/en/insights/news/2013/tops-of-2013-tv-and-social-media.html.

Nielsen. 2014. "Millennials: Technology = Social Connection." February 26. https://www.nielsen.com/us/en/insights/article/2014/millennials-technology-social-connection/.

Nielsen. 2016. "Young, Connected and Black." October 17. https://www.nielsen.com/us/en/insights/reports/2016/young-connected-and-black.html.

NPR. 2008. "The Fall of 'TRL' and the Rise of Internet Video." November 12. http://www.npr.org/templates/story/story.php?storyId=96869060.

Oake, Jonathon I. 2004. "*Reality Bites* and Generation X as Spectator." *Velvet Light Trap*, no. 53, 83–97.

O'Connor, John. 1992. "'The Real World,' According to MTV." *New York Times*, July 9. https://www.nytimes.com/1992/07/09/arts/review-television-the-real-world-according-to-mtv.html.

OK! Weekly. 2007. "Has L.C. Gone XXX?" April 23, 31.

Onion, Rebecca. 2015. "Against Generations." *Aeon*, May 19. https://aeon.co/essays/generational-labels-are-lazy-useless-and-just-plain-wrong.

Ouellette, Laurie. 2006. "Do Good TV?" *Flow: A Critical Forum on Television and Media Culture*, February 24. https://www.flowjournal.org/2006/02/do-good-tv/.

Ouellette, Laurie. 2014a. "Introduction." In *Companion to Reality Television*, edited by Laurie Ouellette, 1–8. Hoboken, NJ: Wiley Blackwell.

Ouellette, Laurie. 2014b. "It's Not TV, It's Birth Control: Reality TV and the 'Problem' of Teenage Pregnancy." In *Reality Gendervision: Decoding Sexuality and Gender on Transatlantic Reality TV*, edited by Brenda Weber, 236–258. Durham, NC: Duke University Press.

Ouellette, Laurie. 2015. "True Life: The Voice of Television Documentary." In *Contemporary Documentary*, edited by Daniel Marcus and Selmin Kara, 107–123. New York: Routledge.

Ouellette, Laurie. 2018. "#Prosocial Television." In *Networks to Netflix: A Guide to Changing Channels*, edited by Derek Johnson, 147–156. New York: Routledge.

Ouellette, Laurie, and James Hay. 2008. *Better Living through Reality TV: Television and Post-Welfare Citizenship*. Malden, MA: Blackwell.

Palmer, Gareth. 2011. "Organic Branding: The Self, Advertising and Life-Experience Formats." In *Reality Television and Class*, edited by Helen Wood and Beverley Skeggs, 132–143. London: Palgrave Macmillan.

Pardes, Arielle. 2017. "Selfie Factories: The Rise of the Made-for-Instagram Museum." *Wired*, September 27. https://www.wired.com/story/selfie -factories-instagram-museum/.

Pickens, Therí A. 2015. "Shoving Aside the Politics of Respectability: Black Women, Reality TV, and the Ratchet Performance." *Women and Performance: A Journal of Feminist Theory* 25 (1): 41–58.

Pike, Kristen. 2011. "Lessons in Liberation: Schooling Girls in Feminism and Femininity in 1970s ABC Afterschool Specials." *Girlhood Studies: An Interdisciplinary Journal* 4 (1): 95–113.

Pittman, Robert W. 1990. "How 'TV Babies' Learn." *New York Times*, January 24.

Poniewozik, James. 2008. "Don't Hate It Because It's Beautiful." *Time*, August 7. http://content.time.com/time/magazine/article/0,9171,1830407,00.html.

Putnam, Robert D. 2015. *Our Kids: The American Dream in Crisis*. New York: Simon and Schuster.

Radar Online. 2013. "Teen Mom Farrah Abraham Pockets $1.5M for XXX Sex Tape." April 30. https://radaronline.com/exclusives/2013/04/farrah -abraham-1-5-million-dollars-sex-tape-teen-mom/.

Reichelt, Lisa. 2007. "Ambient Intimacy." *Disambiguity*, March 1. http://www .disambiguity.com/ambient-intimacy/.

Reuters. 2019. "Colombia Orders Uber to Improve Data Security after 2016 Breach." July 23. https://www.reuters.com/article/us-uber-colombia /colombia-orders-uber-to-improve-data-security-after-2016-breach -idUSKCN1UI2E2.

Rich, Robert. 2013. "The Great Recession (December 2007–June 2009)." *Federal Reserve History*, November 22. https://www.federalreservehistory.org /essays/great_recession_of_200709.

Rikleen, Lauren Stiller. 2008. "How the 'Millennial' Generation Works." *Young Lawyer* 1–2, July 14. http://www.proquest.com.jproxy.lib.ecu.edu/.

Rochlin, Margy. 2005. "An MTV Coming of Age That Went Far on Charm." *New*

York Times, August 30. http://www.nytimes.com/2005/08/30/arts
/television/30lagu.html.

Ross, Sharon Marie, and Louisa Ellen Stein. 2008. *Teen TV: Essays on Programming and Fandom.* Jefferson, NC: MacFarland.

Ruoff, Jeffrey. 2002. *An American Family: A Televised Life.* Minneapolis: University of Minnesota Press.

Ryan, Maureen. 2004. "Visit 'Laguna Beach' for a Truly Boring Day." *Chicago Tribune*, September 28. http://www.chicagotribune.com/news/ct-xpm
-2004-09-28-0409280042-story.html.

Samuels, David. 2004. "The Rap on Rap: The 'Black Music' That Isn't Either." In *That's the Joint! The Hip-Hop Studies Reader*, edited by Murray Forman and Mark Anthony Neal, 147–153. New York: Routledge.

Sanchez, Omar. 2018. "Hollywood Flashback: Madonna Rolled around Onstage, the Cars Topped Michael Jackson at First VMAs." *Hollywood Reporter*, August 15. https://www.hollywoodreporter.com/news/vmas-flashback
-madonna-rolled-around-onstage-1984-like-a-virgin-1134889.

Scahill, Andrew. 2012. "Pigmalion: Animality and Failure in *Here Comes Honey Boo Boo*." *Flow: A Critical Forum on Television and Media Culture*, September 10. https://www.flowjournal.org/2012/09/pigmalion-animality/.

Schaefer, Eric. 1999. *"Bold! Daring! Shocking! True!": A History of Exploitation Films, 1919–1959.* Durham, NC: Duke University Press.

Scheff, Sue. 2017. *Shame Nation: The Global Epidemic of Online Hate.* Naperville, IL: Sourcebooks.

Schillaci, Sophie. 2012. "West Virginia Senator 'Repulsed' by MTV's 'Jersey Shore' Replacement 'Buckwild.'" *Hollywood Reporter*, December 7. https://www
.hollywoodreporter.com/news/buckwild-sen-joe-manchin-repulsed-399296.

Schlotterbeck, Jesse. 2008. "What Happens When Real People Start Getting Cinematic: Laguna Beach and Contemporary t.v. Aesthetics." *Scope: An Online Journal of Film*, no. 12. https://www.nottingham.ac.uk/scope
/documents/2008/october-2008/schlotterbeck.pdf.

Schonfeld, Zach. 2018. "The Oldest Millennials Were Born in 1981. Are They Even Really Millennials?" *Newsweek*, March 20. https://www.newsweek
.com/2018/03/30/what-millennial-born-1981-generation-x-pew-853416.html.

Schnurr, Samantha. 2018. "Jersey Shore Stars' Plastic Surgery Transformations." *E! Online*, April 12. https://www.eonline.com/news/927046/jersey-shore
-stars-plastic-surgery-transformations.

Schultze, Quentin James, Roy M. Anker, Quentin Schultze, James D. Bratt, Lambert Zuidervaart, John Worst, and William Romanowski. 1991. *Dancing in the Dark: Youth, Popular Culture, and the Electronic Media.* Grand Rapids, MI: William B. Eerdmans.

Schuyler Center for Analysis and Advocacy. 2008. "Teenage Births: Outcomes for Young Parents and Their Children." December. http://www.scaany.org
/documents/teen_pregnancy_dec08.pdf.

Seidman, Robert. 2010. "Ratings Juggernaut 'Jersey Shore' Helps MTV to Best

Summer Ratings in Three Years." *TV by the Numbers*, September 1. https://
tvbythenumbers.zap2it.com/network-press-releases/ratings-juggernaut
-jersey-shore-helps-mtv-to-best-summer-ratings-in-three-years/.

Selwyn, Neil. 2009. "The Digital Native—Myth and Reality." *Aslib Proceedings:
New Information Perspectives* 61 (4): 364–379.

Serpe, Gina. 2012. "*Teen Mom*'s Farrah Abraham Shows Off Brand-New Face
after Plastic Surgery." *E! Online*, October 4. https://www.eonline.com/de
/news/356837/teen-mom-s-farrah-abraham-shows-off-brand-new-face
-after-plastic-surgery.

Shales, Tom. 1992. "'Real World': MTV's Ego Trap." *Washington Post*, May 28.
https://www.washingtonpost.com/archive/lifestyle/1992/05/28/real-world
-mtvs-ego-trap/1f3b2597-c056-42e7-8f33-88760059b03d/?noredirect=on
&utm_term=.bed4cd79f134.

Sharpe, Jennifer. 2006. "Rise and Fall of the Scopitone Jukebox." *NPR*, August 9.
https://www.npr.org/templates/story/story.php?storyId=5630027.

Sigesmund, B. J., and Marc Peyser. 2003. "Heir Heads—Reality TV Is Obsessed
with People Trying to Get Rich." *Newsweek*, October 20.

Skeggs, Beverley. 1997. *Formations of Class and Gender: Becoming Respectable*.
London: Sage.

Smith, Lynn. 2005. "There's Laguna, and Then There's MTV's 'Laguna.'" *Los
Angeles Times*, November 5. http://articles.latimes.com/2005/nov/05
/entertainment/et-laguna5.

Smith-Shomade, Beretta E. 2007. *Pimpin' Ain't Easy: Selling Black Entertainment
Television*. New York: Routledge.

Sobchack, Thomas, and Vivian C. Sobchack. 1987. *An Introduction to Film*. 2nd
ed. Glenview: Scott, Foresman, and Company.

Squires, Catherine R. 2014. "The Conundrum of Race and Reality Television."
In *Companion to Reality Television*, edited by Laurie Ouellette, 264–282.
Hoboken, NJ: Wiley Blackwell.

Stack, Tim. "They Shoot. She Scores." *Entertainment Weekly*, August 8, 26–31.

Stanley, Alessandra. 2003. "With a Rich Girl Here and a Rich Girl There." *New
York Times*, December 2. https://www.nytimes.com/2003/12/02/arts
/television-review-with-a-rich-girl-here-and-a-rich-girl-there.html.

Stein, Joel. 2013. "Millennials: The Me, Me, Me Generation: Millennials Are
Lazy, Entitled Narcissists Who Still Live with Their Parents. Why They'll
Save Us All." *Time*, May 20.

Story, Louise. 2005. "Forget about Milk and Bread. Give Me Gossip!" *New York
Times*, June 13. https://www.nytimes.com/2005/06/13/business/media
/forget-about-milk-and-bread-give-me-gossip.html.

Susman, Gary. 2004. "MTV Plans 'O.C.'-ish 'Reality Drama.'" *Entertainment
Weekly*, June 26. https://ew.com/article/2004/06/26/mtv-plans-oc-ish
-reality-drama/.

Swick, Gerald D. 2013. "Virginia's Great Divorce." *History Net*, March 5. https://
www.historynet.com/virginias-great-divorce.htm.

Szatmary, David P. 1987. *Rockin' in Time: A Social History of Rock-and-Roll.* 3rd ed. Upper Saddle River, NJ: Prentice Hall.

Talmadge, Stephanie. 2017. "The Sisterhood of the Exact Same Pants." *Racked*, August 30. https://www.racked.com/2017/8/30/16218066/sorority-dress -code-rush-t-shirts.

Tan, Cheryl Lu-Lien. 1999. "The Cult of Noncelebrity Takes MTV beyond Its Music." *Los Angeles Times*, November 23. http://articles.latimes.com/1999 /nov/23/entertainment/ca-36619.

Tannenbaum, Rob. 2014. "The Real Story behind Madonna's Iconic 'Like a Virgin' Performance at the 1984 VMAs." *Billboard*, October 28. https:// www.billboard.com/articles/news/6296887/madonna-1984-mtv-vmas -performance.

Tannenbaum, Rob, and Craig Marks. 2011. *I Want My MTV: The Uncensored Story of the Music Video Revolution.* New York: Penguin.

Taylor, Lisa. 2011. "'I'm a Girl, I Should be a Princess': Gender, Class Entitlement and Denial in *The Hills*." In *Reality Television and Class*, edited by Helen Wood and Beverley Skeggs, 119–131. London: Palgrave Macmillan.

Thornton, Sarah. 1997. "The Social Logic of Subcultural Capital." In *The Subcultures Reader*, edited by Ken Gelder and Sarah Thornton, 200–209. London: Routledge.

Tolson, Andrew. 2011. "'I'm Common and My Talking Is Quite Abrupt' (Jade Goody): Language and Class in *Celebrity Big Brother*." In *Reality Television and Class*, edited by Helen Wood and Beverley Skeggs, 45–59. London: Palgrave Macmillan.

Tricarico, Donald. 1991. "Guido: Fashioning an Italian-American Youth Style." *Journal of Ethnic Studies* 19 (1): 41–66.

Tricarico, Donald. 2007. "Youth Culture, Ethnic Choice, and the Identity Politics of Guido." *Voices in Italian Americana* 18 (1): 34–86.

Tucker, Ken. 1992. "The Real World." *Entertainment Weekly*, May 22. http:// ew.com/article/1992/05/22/real-world-5/.

Turner, Graeme. 2014. *Understanding Celebrity.* 2nd ed. Los Angeles: Sage.

Twenge, Jean. 2006. *Generation Me: Why Today's Young Americans Are More Confident, Assertive, Entitled—and More Miserable Than Ever Before.* New York: Simon and Schuster.

Tyko, Kelly. 2019. "Consumers Must Deal with More Red Tape to Get Cash from Equifax Settlement." *USA Today*, September 10.

Tyler, Imogen, and Bruce Bennett. 2010. "'Celebrity Chav': Fame, Femininity and Social Class." *European Journal of Cultural Studies* 13 (3): 375–393.

Us Weekly. 2018. "Farrah Abraham through the Years." November 6. https:// www.usmagazine.com/celebrity-news/pictures/farrah-abraham -through-the-years/.

Vaidhyanathan, Siva. 2008. "Generational Myth: Not All Young People Are Tech-Savvy." *Chronicle Review* 55 (4): B7.

Vaillancourt, Daniel. 1994. "Pedro Zamora Tells All." *The Peak*, July 11. https://

web.archive.org/web/20110514145901/http:/www.peak.sfu.ca/gopher/94-2
/issue11/zamora.ans.

Vance, J. D. 2016. *Hillbilly Elegy: A Memoir of a Family and Culture in Crisis.*
New York: HarperCollins.

Varallo, Sharon. 2008. "Motherwork in Academe: Intensive Caring for the Millennial Student." *Women's Studies in Communication* 31 (2): 151–157.

Verevis, Constantine. 2016. "The Cinematic Return." *Film Criticism* 40 (1). http://
dx.doi.org/10.3998/fc.13761232.0040.134.

Viacom. 2009. "MTV Chronicles the Challenges of Teen Pregnancy in '16 &
Pregnant' Premiering on Thursday, June 11th at 10pm ET/PT." May 18.
https://ir.viacom.com/news-releases/news-release-details/mtv-chronicles
-challenges-teen-pregnancy-16-pregnant-premiering.

Vice News. 2017. "Charlottesville: Race and Terror." August 21. https://news
.vice.com/en_us/article/qvzn8p/vice-news-tonight-full-episode
-charlottesville-race-and-terror.

Wallace, Benjamin. 2013. "Diamond in the Mud: The Death of *Buckwild* Star
Shain Gandee and the Search for Authenticity in Reality TV." *Vulture*, September 15. https://www.vulture.com/2013/09/mtv-buckwild-shain-gandee
.html.

Wang, Grace. 2010. "A Shot at Half-Exposure: Asian Americans in Reality TV
Shows." *Television and New Media* 11 (5): 404–427.

Warner, Kristen J. 2013. "They Gon' Think You Loud Regardless: Ratchetness, Reality Television, and Black Womanhood." *Camera Obscura* 30 (1): 129–153.

Warner, Kristen J. 2015.*The Cultural Politics of Colorblind Casting.* New York:
Routledge.

Warner, Kristen J. 2017. "In the Time of Plastic Representation." *Film Quarterly*
71 (2). https://filmquarterly.org/2017/12/04/in-the-time-of-plastic
-representation/.

Waters, Mary C. 1996. "Optional Ethnicities: For Whites Only?" In *Origins and
Destinies: Immigration, Race, and Ethnicity in America*, edited by Silvia Pe-
draza and Rubén G. Rumbaut, 444–454. Belmont, MA: Wadsworth.

Weber, Brenda. 2009. *Makeover TV: Selfhood, Citizenship, and Celebrity.* Durham, NC: Duke University Press.

Weprin, Alex. 2009. "Can MTV Get Its Groove Back?" *Broadcasting and Cable*,
February 23. http://www.broadcastingcable.com/article/174551-Cover
_Story_Can_MTV_Get_Its_Groove_Back_.php?.

Whittaker, Zack. 2019. "A Huge Database of Facebook Users' Phone Numbers
Found Online." *Tech Crunch*, September 4. https://techcrunch.com/2019
/09/04/facebook-phone-numbers-exposed/.

Wicke, Peter. 1987. *Rock Music: Culture, Aesthetics and Sociology.* Translated by
Rachel Fogg. Cambridge: Cambridge University Press.

Williams, Linda. 1998. "Melodrama Revised." In *Refiguring American Film
Genres: Theory and History*, edited by Nick Browne, 42–88. Berkeley: University of California Press.

Wilson, Julie. 2014. "Reality Television Celebrity: Star Consumption and Self-Promotion in Media Culture." In *Companion to Reality Television*, edited by Laurie Ouellette, 421–436. Hoboken, NJ: Wiley Blackwell.

Wood, Helen, and Beverley Skeggs, eds. 2011b. *Reality Television and Class.* London: Palgrave Macmillan.

Woods, Faye. 2012. "Classed Femininity, Performativity, and Camp in British Structured Reality Programming." *Television and New Media* 15 (3): 197–214.

Wu, Tim. 2016. *The Attention Merchants: The Epic Scramble to Get Inside Our Heads.* New York: Vintage Books.

Yabroff, Jennie. 2008. "Here's Looking at You, Kids." *Newsweek*, March 24. http://www.newsweek.com/id/123484.

Yeaton, Kathryn. 2008. "Recruiting and Managing the 'Why?' Generation: Generation Y." *CPA Journal* 78 (4): 69.

Zara, Christopher. 2015. "MTV Ratings Decline Raises Relevance Questions as Young People Cut Cable Cord for Devices." *International Business Times*, April 14. https://www.ibtimes.com/mtv-ratings-decline-raises-relevance-questions-young-people-cut-cable-cord-devices-1881468.

Zaveri, Mihir. 2019. "Russian Man Pleads Guilty in 'Massive' Hacking Scheme." *New York Times*, September 23. https://www.nytimes.com/2019/09/23/business/russian-hacking-jpmorgan.html.

INDEX

Bosworth, Lo (cast member, *Laguna Beach*), 95, 104
Boulet, Tyler (cast member, *Buckwild*), 142, 145, 147
boundaries between public and private, 63–64
Bow Wow (rapper), 181
Box, The (Video Jukebox Network), 199n9
boy bands, 46
boyd, dana, 177
Bradley, Shae (cast member, *Buckwild*), 144, 145
branding, 2; MTV overhauls, 37; "preemptive product placement/unbranding," 131–132. *See also* self-branding
"Brass in Pocket" (Pretenders), 35
Brennan, Jon (cast member, *The Real World*), 71–72
Bridge and Tunnel (MTV reality show), 128–129, 138–139
"bridge and tunnel" (B&T) crowd, 130
Brown, Julie, 38
Buckwild (MTV reality show), 6, 7, 8, 22, 123, 127, 139–149, 151, 198n9; dangerous behaviors in, 142, 144, 146, 148; freedom, theme of, 142, 146, 210n15; marginalization of nonwhite cast member, 144–145; muddin', 142, 148; nondiegetic music in, 142–143; promotion of, 162; ridicule of Redneck identity, 22, 141, 154, 158, 185; same-sex bonding in, 144
Buggles, 1, 2, 33, 40, 197n1
Bunim, Mary-Ellis, 42, 58, 60, 68, 71, 74–76, 132
Buzzfeed personality tests, 15–16

Cable Communications Policy Act, 37
cable television, 31, 32, 37, 199n8, 199–200n9
camcorder era (1989–1999), 18, 42, 67, 89
Campos, Rachel (Campos-Duffy) (cast member, *The Real World*), 75, 78, 87
Candid Camera (television show), 20, 60–63, 62, 69, 72

Can-Do Girl identity, 19, 21, 89–123, 171, 184; economy of identity and, 122; of *The Hills*, 97–102; inability to live up to, 104–105; of *Laguna Beach*, 91–102. *See also* aspirational identity and stories; *City, The* (MTV reality show); *Hills, The* (MTV reality show); *Laguna Beach: The Real Orange County* (MTV reality show)
Cannatella, Trishelle (cast member, *The Real World*), 81, 82
Cantwell, Christopher, 150
Carceres, Jimmy (cast member, *Washington Heights*), 157–158, 161
"career women," 99
Cars, 36
casting, 6, 9–10, 70–77; "colorblind," 17, 162; "diversity" as concept in, 9, 58, 70–73, 81, 90, 153, 184–186, 204n9; female-centered, 90; of homogenous groups, 153–154; racial bias in, 107, 207–208n23; "seven strangers" model, 42, 57, 69–70, 74, 80, 82, 90, 153, 203–204n8
cast members, 19; betterment as goal of, 20–21, 50–52, 110–112; feedback given to, 69; increased self-consciousness and performativity of, 84; Latinx, 43, 55, 74–79, 77; as progeny of reality shows, 6; of *Real World*, 21; self-selecting, 176–177; self-surveillance, 16, 42–43, 112, 122–123. *See also* nonwhite cast members
Catfish (film documentary), 175–176
Catfish (MTV reality show), 4, 6, 19, 22–23, 127, 172, 173–183, 182, 185; aesthetics of, 182–183; ratings, 183; research on identities of Catfish, 178–179; self-selecting cast members, 176–177
Catfish identity (*Catfish*), 23, 173, 175–183
cautionary identity, 107–108, 127, 136–137, 184–185. *See also* At-Risk Girl identity
Cavallari, Kristin (cast member, *Laguna Beach*), 95, 96, 105
"celebreality" programming, 50, 53

celebrity, 89; democratization of, 46; "famous for being famous," 48, 83; "ordinary," 9, 47–50, 92, 208n27; "private side discourses," 48; tabloid, 47–49, 103–104, 207n15

Celebrity Big Brother (reality show), 85

Challenge, The (MTV show), 59

Charlottesville, Virginia, "Unite the Right" rally, 150–151

Chen, Adrien, 177

choice, 2, 44–45, 98–102, 106–108; class-based rhetoric of, 100–101, 110, 146, 149; fetishization of, 98–99; "good" vs. "bad," 21–22, 106, 110–111; sense of freedom of, 102; white ethnic, 131

Christie, Chris, 141

citizenship, 15, 61, 90, 142

City, The (MTV reality show), 6, 8, 21, 88, 101–102

Clark, Dick, 26, *26*

closed-circuit television (CCTV), 42, 67

Club MTV program, 38

Colletti, Stephen (cast member, *Laguna Beach*), 93, 95, 96

colorblind ideology, 9, 17, 149, 162, 183, 204n14

Columbia (space shuttle), 32

"Come Clean" (Duff), 95–96

"coming clean," 96, 117–118

communication gap, 29

competition format, 51

confession, 84–86, 118, 165, 167–169; as compulsion, 66; cultures of, 18–19, 59; first-person aesthetic, 168, 205n18; identity confession, 8–9, 51, 71–72, 85, 88, 129, 133, 144, 146, 163; as marker of authenticity, 59; as performance of self, 72; in *Real World*, 76; "talking head" style, 137

Conrad, Lauren (aka LC) (cast member, *Laguna Beach/The Hills*), 21, 90, 93–101, 103–104, 123, 132, 146, 153, 207n15

consumption, 56, 90–91; prioritization of in *The City*, 101–102; rationalization of, 84; white girls as consumer citizens, 90, 206n7

co-optation, spectacle of, 52

Cops (television show), 42, 67

Corner, John, 84

Corsani, Antonella, 147

countdown-based programming, 199–200n9; *Total Request Live*, 3–4, 43–47

Coupland, Douglas, 197n2

Couples' Therapy (VH1 series), 117, 122

courtroom drama, 59

Crawford, Cindy, 41

crime and law enforcement series, 42, 67

cultural capital, 23, 130, 132, 137, 152, 159–160

Culture Club, 35

culture of praise, 13–14

Cunningham, Todd, 13, 43–44, 46

Current Affair, A (television show), 42, 67

Curry, Ian, 179

Cutrone, Kelly (cast member, *The Hills*), 99, 101, 206n10

Daily Stormer, 150, 151

Daly, Carson, 3–4, 43, 44, 45, 46

Daniels, Susanne, 148

Dark Shadows (soap opera), 27

data breach scandals, 45–46

David (cast member, *Virgin Territory*), 168–169

Dawn: Portrait of a Teenage Runaway (made-for-TV movie), 28

"dayparting" format, 38, 41

Dee (cast member, *Catfish*), 181–182

Deen, James (adult film star), 112

defense, poetics of, 76

DelVecchio, Paul (DJ Pauly D, cast member, *Jersey Shore*), 124–126, *126*, 134, 138, 208–209n1

Dial MTV, 200n9

digital music platforms, 4, 20, 47, 56

DiMino, Andre, 129

Direct Cinema, 66, 87

DiSanto, Tony, 103, 104, 106, 128

DiVello, Adam, 94, 105

"diversity," 17, 56, 87–88, 132, 149; casting for, 9, 58, 70–73, 81, 90, 153,

Lowell, Catelynn (cast member, *Teen Mom*), 109, *110*, 114, 115, 117
Lowenthal, Barry, 172
Lukow, George, 30
Lyon, Jay (cast member, *The City*), 102

Maas, James, 61
Made (MTV reality show), 20, 50–52, 90
Madonna, 36–37
makeover television, 50–52
Malick, Terence, 180
Mallory, Davis (cast member, *The Real World*), 58
Maloof, George, 82
Manchin, Joe, III, 141
Mann, Michael, 103
Mannheim, Karl, 11
marginalized communities/youth, 8–9, 17, 74–76, 145, 158
Marjorie (cast member, *Virgin Territory*), 171
Marks, Craig, 29, 41
Marwick, Alice, 4, 15, 98
Mary Tyler Moore Show, The (television show), 99
McCarthy, Anna, 18, 61, 95
"McDonald's Faces 'Millennial' Challenge" (*Wall Street Journal*), 2
McGee, Irene (cast member, *The Real World*), 21, 56, 59, 68, 70–73, 83, 204nn11–12; on alcohol use in reality TV, 80–81
McGroarty, Bob, 31
Mead, Margaret, 64
Media Kitchen, 172
media scholarship, 5–6, 12–14, 18, 60
melodrama, 59, 94–95, 105, 117
"Me Me Me Generation, The" (*Time*), 2–3
men's rights activists, 151
Merchants of Cool (*Frontline*), 13
Meyers, Erin, 48, 50
Michael (cast member, *Catfish*), 181
Midler, Bette, 36
Milgram, Stanley, 20, 61, 63
Millennials (born 1981–1996), 2, 197n3; African American, 17; defining, 11–17;

diversity of, 4, 16–17; employment chances, 14, 114–116, 146–147, 159, 198n13; as homogeneous, 3, 11; identity as concern of, 23, 46–47, 55, 171–172; industry-destroying stereotype of, 2–3; parenting of, 13–14; participation in media, preference for, 15–16, 44–45, 56, 201n25; Pew Research Center definition, 12–13. *See also* social media
Millennials Rising: The Next Great Generation (Howe and Strauss), 12
Miranda, Lin-Manuel, 155
Montag, Heidi (cast member, *The Hills*), 104–105, 128, 136, 139, 207n15
Moore, Mary Tyler, 99
Moore, Nia (cast member, *The Real World*), 58
Mortensen, Colin (cast member, *The Real World*), 81
MTV: aging of youth audience, 37, 41; Armstrong commercial, *21*, 24, 32–33; audience appeal choices, 176; audience research, 3, 13, 20, 31–32, 43–44, 47, 50, 56; beginning of, 29–37, 200n15; Black artists blocked by, 38–39; brand overhauls, 37; celebrity-centered series, 89; "dayparting" format, 38, 41; executives, 13, 200nn10–11; failed series, 153–172; focus groups, 13, 20; "Golden Age" (1981–1992), 29, 41–42; history of, 1981–2003, 18, 24–56; identity on, defined, 6–11; industrial context for, 19; influence on taste, 35–36; launch of, 1–2, 19; "Music Television" dropped from logo, 55; product as MTV itself, 24; programming shifts, 18, 38, 186–187; as public corporation, 36; ratings, 1980s, 37; ratings, 2010, 138; ratings, 2012, 172; ratings, *Catfish*, 183; ratings, *The Hills*, 101; ratings, *Jersey Shore* and *Buckwild*, 154; ratings, *Laguna Beach*, 93; ratings, *The Real World*, 43, 74, 84, 93; ratings, TRL, 44; ratings, *Washington Heights*, 162, 185; ratings drop in 1990s, 2–3;

public discourses, 6, 11, 13, 18–19, 28, 43, 53, 185, 201n27; about *Laguna Beach*, 92–93

"pull" vs. "push," 8, 131

Quinn, Martha, 29–30, 35

race, 7, 16–17; conflict and, 58–59, 77–78; representatives of, 54–55, 139, 206n12; as self-management project, 132

racism, 59, 207–208n23; euphemisms for, 140, 209n12

radio, 2, 25, 29–30, 37, 200n12

Rainey, David "Puck" (cast member, *The Real World*), 76, 78, 87

Rakim, 40

rap music, 33, 39

Rasuk, Fred (cast member, *Washington Heights*), 161

Rasuk, Rico (cast member, *Washington Heights*), 161

ratchet imaginary, 11, 198n11

Ray, Robert, 151

Raymond, Alan, 63

Raymond, Susan, 63, 65

real-estate "bubble" of the early 2000s, 91

realism, 61–62

"realist" aesthetic, 84, 94–95, 137–138

reality identity cycle (2004–2018), 15, 18, 23, 43, 46–47, 80; audience participation in process, 84; direct precursors to, 49–55; extradiegetic narrative in, 104–105; functions of subjects, 127; *Laguna Beach* as first series in, 90; pedagogical roles, 127. *See also* production cycles

reality television: camcorder era (1989–1999), 18, 42; celebrity status and, 47–49; colorblind programming, 17, 79, 97, 162; as cost-cutting measure, 3, 20, 41–43, 58, 60, 92; economies of celebrity (2002–), 18; hopefuls, self-branding of, 7–8, 10; labor exploitation in, 15, 198n14; as mediated space, 58; "more real," 128; on MTV, 49–55; public performance of private, 10;

scripted, 2–3, 42–43, 52, 67–70, 86, 91–94, 99, 117–118, 177, 203–204n8; second-generation (1999–2005), 18, 51; self-reflexivity of, 84–87, 105; "self-serve," 4, 9; shopping environments in, 101–102; sleight of hand revealed, 105; surveillance and competition formats (1999–2005), 18; third generation of, 89–90. *See also* casting; cast members; nonfiction programming; television; *individual programs*

Reality TV (Kavka), 18, 42

"real life," 48, 62; commodification of, 140–141; fourth wall and, 68

Real World, The (MTV reality show), 4, 8–9, 42–43, 56, 57–88, 183–184; addiction and mental health concerns in, 80–83; *An American Family* as precursor to, 63–66, 65; attention economy, competition within, 69; audience research, 56; *Candid Camera* as precursor to, 60–63, 62; confession and visible suffering emphasized, 59; "diversity" of identities in, 9, 58, 69–73, 87–88, 153; first season, 74–80, 75; "fly on the wall" observational mode, 66, 87; historical context, 57; montage of living space, 82; neutrality dispensed with, 84–85; no contact between cast and crew, 68–69; opening statement, 57; partying required of cast members, 83; "Planes, Trains and Paddywagons" episode, 75; in postdocumentary context, 83–87; precedents for, 60–66; producing, 67–69; production process made visible, 84; ratings, 43, 74, 84, 93; *Real World: Ex-plosion*, 85; *Real World: Hawaii*, 80–81; *Real World: Key West*, 19, 21, 59; *Real World: Las Vegas*, 81–83; *Real World: San Francisco*, 43, 74; *Real World: Seattle*, 21, 59; *Real World: Skeletons*, 85–86, 116; reviews of, 43, 74; sex in, 82–83; shift in formula, 80–83; success of, 20–21; surveillance technologies in, 68; "White Like Me" episode, 77–78, 149, 183–184

Rebel without a Cause (movie), 28
reboots, 175, 185–186
record industry, 30–31, 35, 44–45
Redneck identity, 6, 7, 8, 91, 139–149,
198n9; as badge of honor, 127; recla-
mation of, 141–142, 151; ridicule of,
22, 123, 141, 154, 185. See also *Buckwild*
(MTV reality show)
Reese, Frankie (cast member, *Washington Heights*), 160, 161
Reeve, Elle, 150–151
regional and ethnic others, 22, 124–152
Reichelt, Leisa, 179
remote controls, 29, 199n8
representation, 7–8; "plastic," 162–163
reunion shows, 117, 122, 136
Richard, Cliff, 35
Rich Girls (MTV reality show), 20, 52–53
Richie, Nicole, 48, 201–202n29
ridicule, 123, 159; of Guido identity,
132–133, 138, 154, 185; of Redneck iden-
tity, 22, 141, 154, 158, 185
Rikleen, Lauren Stiller, 13
Robinson, James, III, 31, 41
rock music, 25–27, 31–40, 46; as some-
thing to fight for, 46–47; whitewashed
approach to, 26–27, 220n12
"rock promos," 31
"Rock Your Body" (Timberlake), 92
Rogoff, Patti, 32
Roman, Paul, 94
Ross, Sharon, 27
Ross, Steve, 31
Run-DMC, 40, 201n22
Ruoff, Jeffrey, 66
Ryan, Maureen, 93

Saldana, Reyna (cast member, *Washing-
ton Heights*), 158, 159
Santa Barbara (soap opera), 42
Saria, Katie (cast member, *Buckwild*), 142
Scahill, Andrew, 140
Schaefer, Eric, 199n7
Schlotterbeck, Jesse, 206n4
Schneider, Jack, 31
Schuller, Christina (cast member, *La-
guna Beach*), 95

Schulman, Nev (*Catfish* documentary),
175–176, 180–181, 183
Scopitone (film jukebox), 30
Sean (cast member, *The Real World*), 79
*Secret Life of the American Teenager,
The* (television series), 106
See It Now (television series), 63
Seibert, Fred, 32
self: care of, 50–51; "edited," 98, 108; elite
discourses of, 42; as salable commodity, 4, 7–8, 15
self-branding, 4, 6–10, 51, 85, 91–92, 112,
121, 127, 133, 170; as career strategy, 15;
culture of, 59; monetizable identity,
15, 69, 90, 92, 98, 105, 114, 146–149
"self-confidence, false," 14
self-governance, discourses of, 4–6
self-reflexivity, 1–2, 35, 40, 84–87, 105,
116
self-surveillance, 16, 42–43, 112, 122–123
semantics, 5
September 11, 2001, attacks, 12
serialized narrative, 21–22, 58, 94,
97–98, 114
Sesame Street (television show), 29
"seven strangers" model, 42, 57, 69–70,
74, 80, 82, 90, 153, 203–204n8
7 Up! (documentary), 60
Sex and the City (television show), 99
sexual predators, 177
sexual revolution, 27–28
Shales, Tom, 74
Shapiro, Ron, 44
"She Won't Dance with Me" (Stewart),
35
Shirley, Gary (cast member), 109–110,
116
Sigma Alpha Epsilon Pi (sorority), 54–55
Simple Life, The (reality show), 48–49
Sissonville, West Virginia, 22, 141,
143–144, 147
Situation, The (cast member, *Jersey
Shore*), 132, 133–134
16 and Pregnant (MTV reality show), 6,
19, 21, 88, 106–109, 112, 114, 171, 184,
185, 208n23, 208n27; opening sequence, 108–109

Skeggs, Beverley, 100, 140
soap operas, 27, 42, 68, 95
sobriety, discourse of, 65, 67–68
social capital, 96
"social hygiene films" (1920s), 28, 199n7
social media, 15–16, 56, 58; alt-right, 16,
150–151; "Facebook eye," 16, 69; fears
about, 177; instant rewards, 69; online
dating services, 179; online romance,
172; virtual relationships, 22–23. *See
also* Millennials (born 1981–1996)
social sciences, 61
Sokol Savage, Dia, 10, 19, 22, 107–109,
171, 198n10, 207–208n23; on extradiegetic narrative, 114–115
Sorority Life (MTV reality show), 20,
54–55, 206n12
"soundies," 30
Spears, Britney, 93
spectacularization, 22, 91, 127, 140, 162
Spencer, Richard, 150
Squires, Catherine, 8
Stanford prison experiment, 61
Staten Island, New York, 128
Stein, Louisa, 27
Steinberg, Sue, 34, 35
Stephanie (cast member, *The Real
World*), 79
Stewart, Rod, 35
Stiller, Ben, 41
Strauss, William, 12, 13
"stripping," 41
subcultural identity, 39, 52, 129–131,
133–134, 209n6
subjectivities, 3, 7, 15–16; feminine, 98,
206n7
Sup Dogs (hot-dog restaurant), 124,
208n1
Super Bowl XXXVIII, 92
surveillance, 67–68, 89; on *Candid
Camera*, 61; mythical rendered trans-
parent by, 164; self-surveillance, 16,
42–43, 112, 122–123; technologies of in
Real World, 68; as therapeutic, 72–73
Survivor (reality show), 15, 89
Swan, The (reality show), 5, 51
Sykes, John, 201nn16–17

tabloid celebrity, 47–49, 103–104, 207n15
tabloid series, 42
"Take On Me" (A-ha), 35
Tan, Cheryl Lu-Lien, 46
Tannenbaum, Rob, 29, 41
taste, defending, 46–47
technology, 5–6, 60–63; democratizing,
63; documentary camera, 60; 16-mm
cameras and portable sound equipment, 62–63; smaller apparatus, 67
Teen Mom (MTV reality show), 8, 19, 21,
48, 87, 88, 90–91, 100, 106–107, 110,
184; emotional labor in, 116–121; extradiegetic narrative in, 114–118; *Teen
Mom 4*, 10
Teen Mom identity, 6, 106–107; move toward Can-Do Girl status, 110–113. *See
also* At-Risk Girl identity
Teen Vogue, 99, 100
Teklits, Hannah, 181
telephoto lenses, 94, 102, 103, 127, 159
Telesonics, 30
television: afterschool specials, 28; big
three networks (NBC, ABC, and CBS),
25; classic era (1950s to 1980s), 25–27;
coaxial cable, 27; commercial needs
of, 63; content-promotion hybrids, 27;
as extractive industry, 90; as "idiot
box," 29; made-for-TV movies, 28;
Millennials' lack of interest in, 3–4;
nationwide programming, 27; niche
audiences, 25, 28, 31; pop music programs, 30; prime time, 1960s, 27; programming blocks, 30; sitcoms, 1960s
and 1970s, 27; social knowledge produced by, 61; unscripted programming, 46, 67, 91; youth-targeted, 19.
See also reality television
televisual activism, 75–76
themes, 5
Thornton, Sarah, 23
Thriller (Jackson), 39
"Thriller" video (Jackson), 39, 201n16,
201nn19–20
Timberlake, Justin, 92
Times Square, 44
To Catch a Predator (television show), 177

white girls, 19, 21, 46, 88, 89–123; advocacy model focus on, 107; as consumer citizens, 90, 206n7. *See also* At-Risk Girl identity; Can-Do Girl identity; *City, The* (MTV reality show); *Hills, The* (MTV reality show); *Laguna Beach: The Real Orange County* (MTV reality show); *16 and Pregnant* (MTV reality show); *Teen Mom* (MTV reality show)

whiteness: as absence/invisible, 73, 77–79, 139, 149, 183–185; as aspirational, 97, 127, 137, 184–185; colorblind ideology, 9, 17, 149, 162, 183, 204n14; ethnic, choice and, 131; as identity, 4, 8–9, 22, 70, 77–80, 149–152, 183–184; as racial category, 139–140, 185; "right to be various," 139; visibility of to white people, 17, 139–140, 149–151. *See also* Guido identity; Redneck identity

white people: "economic anxiety" of, 140, 151; elite, 123; not representative of all whites, 54–55, 206n12; racial fears of, 140, 150–151, 185. *See also* working-class people, white

white privilege, 49, 97–98, 140, 152

white supremacy, 17, 150–151, 185

"white trash," 140, 141, 144

Whitt, Ashley (cast member, *Buckwild*), 146–147

Who, the, 35

Williams, Linda, 59

Williams, Marlon (cast member, *The Real World*), 58

Wilson, Julie, 48, 50

Winick, Judd (cast member, *The Real World*), 78

Wiseley, Jordan (cast member, *The Real World*), 58

Wood, Helen, 140

working-class people, nonwhite, 52, 133, 155, 162; Italian Americans coded as, 123, 130–131, 137. *See also Jersey Shore* (MTV reality show); *Washington Heights* (MTV reality show)

working-class people, white, 21–22, 123, 124–152, 159–160, 185; employment, 114–116, 146–147, 160–161; humiliation of, in exchange for a living, 140. *See also* whiteness

World War II, hidden-camera programs after, 61–62

Writers' Guild strike, 60, 67

Yabroff, Jennie, 12

Yale obedience experiments, 61

Yetnikoff, Walter, 38, 201n19

Yiannopoulos, Milo, 150

Yo! MTV Raps, 38–39, *39*, 184, 201n23

"You Better Run" (Benatar), 33–34, 200n13

"You Better You Bet" (the Who), 35

"You Might Think" (Cars), 36

Young + Pregnant (MTV reality show), 185–186, *186*

Young Lawyer, 13

youth and identity, dominant discourse about, 6–7, 9, 11–13, 186

youth culture, 59, 130; Black and Latinx, 22, 33, 40; hip hop, 39–40; as white, 11, 24–25, 32–33, 77. *See also* Dominican American youth; marginalized communities/youth

Zamora, Pedro (cast member, *The Real World*), 43, 74–76, *77*, 79–80, 83, 87

Zimbardo, Philip, 61

Zimmer, Ben, 180

CPSIA information can be obtained
at www.ICGtesting.com
Printed in the USA
LVHW080142280221
680114LV00001B/90